Praise f[

D1120337

Living Authen.
Daoist Contributions to Modern Psychology

Western psychology has increasingly been embracing techniques and methods from ancient Eastern traditions. Mindfulness meditation is one of the strongest "new" developments in clinical psychology, and the efficacy of stimulating acupuncture points in treating post-traumatic conditions is causing the field to reexamine conventional protocols. *Living Authentically* invites Western therapists to enter into the world-view of Eastern philosophers and healers in ways that will expand their understanding and enhance their practices.
    —David Feinstein and Donna Eden, co-authors of *Energy Medicine* and *The Promise of Energy Psychology*

This book is essential reading for all Westerners seeking to integrate qigong, taiji, Daoist meditation, energy healing, and therapy practices with deep psychological insights from their own culture. It gives sharp focus to fuzzy issues: Reichian orgasm theory vs. Dao sex energy cultivation; psychological adjustment vs. *wuwei* and liberation; heady analytical thinking vs. whole-body process and correlative thinking; Jungian symbolic alchemy within ego vs. substantial alchemical distillation of an immortal soul; the Western "unconscious" vs. primordial-*qi* model. The work presents a breath-taking, cutting-edge Daoist dialectic with an amazing array of therapies—kinesiology, energy psychology, positive psychology, psychosomanautics, cognitive therapy, and more. It is a true milestone.
    —Michael Winn, founder of HealingTaoUSA.com, co-author with Mantak Chia

For the first time in history we have all the world's psychologies available to us and *Living Authentically* begins to make one of these psychologies, Daoism, available to us.
    —Roger Walsh MD, Ph.D., University of California, author of *Essential Spirituality: The Seven Central Practices*

The serious study and practice of Daoism as a totalizing system of bio-spiritual transformation is on the rise on three continents. The tradition is no longer being studied merely as an interesting, quaint, but impractical artifact of ancient Chinese spiritual and philosophical history. If you have been looking for a sophisticated overview of Daoism that is informed by the best of Western medicine and psychology as well, then look no further. This collection of essays should be included in every university library where Daoism is taught and a part of any comprehensive course on the tradition. The essays are authored by scholar-practitioners, and the whole is edited by perhaps the preeminent living Western scholar of Daoism, Livia Kohn.

—Ronnie Littlejohn, Belmont University, author of *Daoism: An Introduction*, co-editor of *Riding the Wind with Liezi*

Living Authentically: Daoist Contributions to Modern Psychology is just what the doctor ordered for practitioners of Chinese medicine in the modern world who have been trying to re-incorporate the spirit/mind into the secularized, "materialized," TCM we have been given from first Communist and now capitalist China. This new book returns us to our Daoist roots and provides deep consideration of how Daoism really understood the relationship of the body, mind and spirit and how this relationship could be influenced to create what we now call "psychological health." This book would make an excellent textbook in Chinese medicine schools where it could provide sophistication to exploration of just what the body mind spirit is/are and how to heal them.

—Mary Kay Ryan, Pacific College of Oriental Medicine, Chicago

Living Authentically

Daoist Contributions to Modern Psychology

edited by

Livia Kohn

Three Pines Press
P. O. Box 609
Dunedin, FL 34697
www.threepinespress.com

9   8 7 6 5 4 3 2 1

First Edition, 2011
Printed in the United States of America
⊗ This edition is printed on acid-free paper that meets
the American National Standard Institute Z39.48 Standard.
Distributed in the United States by Three Pines Press.

Cover art: Original photograph "Wismar, 1996," by Sharon Smith. Used by
permission.

Library of Congress Cataloging-in-Publication Data

Living authentically: Daoist contributions to modern psychology/ edited by
Livia Kohn. -- 1st ed.
    p. cm.
Includes index.
ISBN 978-1-931483-20-9 (alk. paper)
1. Taoism--Psychology. 2. Taoism--Study and teaching. I. Kohn, Livia, 1956-
BF175.4.R44L58 2011
150.88'299514--dc23
    2011022822

978-1-931483-20-9

Contents

Introduction

Mental Health in Daoism and Modern Science

LIVIA KOHN

There are many conceptual and practical overlaps between Daoism and modern science. The world of Dao and its material energy qi closely matches that of quantum physics. Body and mind are increasingly seen in terms of energetic networks and flowing patterns of interaction, matching the organ and meridian system of traditional China. Specifically Daoist body centers and activation methods, moreover, find their scientific matches in behavioral kinesiology and modern ways of working with the universal energy that pervades the body and all life.

Mental health in Daoism means the complete alignment of mind and spirit with the flow of Dao 道, the underlying, creative power of the universe that—if left to its own devices—manages everything to perfection. Part of the greater universe, mental health within the individual is a dimension of bodymind energetics, attained through the perfect balancing of the dynamic vibrations of a vital energy known as *qi. Qi* 氣 is the material aspect of Dao, the subtle matter-cum-energy that makes beings appear in physical form and come to life. Working with a model of dynamic processes—expressed in terms of yin-yang and the five phases—rather than of solid, stable entities, the Daoist understanding of mental health goes far beyond its Western counterpart, which tends to see it primarily as the ability to function consciously and competently in the world. In this respect, it is much like "health" in Chinese medicine: the integrated balance of physical well-being, personal happiness, good fortune, and harmony, it is much more than the mere absence of physical symptoms.

Daoists see body and mind along the same continuum of *qi* and tend to work with one through the other, yet they make a clear distinction between them. In addition, they also distinguish body and mind on the cosmic and personal levels—the pure body-form and spirit human beings receive from Dao versus the personalized body-self and mind they create through reactions to sensory stimuli and social adaptation. Much of Daoist practice, then, leads to a recovery of the original connection to Dao in the purer dimensions of the bodymind. It is an unlearning of personality structures, a reprogramming of interaction patterns into modes of greater harmony and enhanced purity. The practice, moreover, works closely with energy centers and pathways within the bodymind—the inner organs and meridians at the core of Chinese medicine as well as specific locations of cosmic power and divinity. Also, it does not stop with rectifying obvious dysfunctions, but goes beyond the attainment of mental balance toward a sense of at-oneness with creation and the transcendence of immortality.

However alien the Daoist vision may seem, in recent years many of its aspects have begun to play a role in modern science and psychotherapy—usually without any direct influence from the Chinese tradition. Thus, the world of quantum physics replicates much of the vibrational understanding of the universe described in terms of Dao and *qi*; energy medicine sees the body as a tensegrity system of multiple yet completely integrated energetic forces and finds repeated validation for things like prayer and the laying-on of hands; energy psychology makes use of internal energy systems from various cultures, including Chinese organs and meridians, and reports great success with tapping and subtle suggestion techniques; behavioral kinesiology makes use of energetic forces and networks as well as bodymind techniques that closely reflect Daoist models; and, last but not least, the integrated personality restructuring system of Core Health uses visualizations and suggestions along the lines of the Inner Smile meditation together with a vision of living life in complete harmony and inner peace.

In all these respects, as well as in many others outlined in this book, Daoism can contribute deeper dimensions of understanding mind, body, and universe while providing enhanced methods and systems of practice based on thousands of years of experience and experiment.

The World of Dao

Daoists see human beings as an integral part of nature and the greater universe, which functions in perfect harmony and is fundamentally good. Created in a series of transformations without a radical break from the pure, formless Dao, the universe manifests itself in a wondrous combination of manifold forces that ideally work together to constitute a cosmos of perfect goodness.

The goodness of the cosmos is all-pervasive and part of the inherent make-up of human beings. However, it is not necessarily a moral goodness that can be expressed in sets of rules and enforced by laws and other restraints. The goodness of the cosmos goes beyond human morality because it is cosmic and natural, and both cosmos and nature are cruel and unjust at times; they do not have a set of values that can be defined or to which they can be held. As the

Daode jing 道德經 (Book of the Dao and Its Potency) says: "Heaven and Earth are ruthless; they treat the myriad things like straw dogs"—the universe is not ethically good and treats all things as though they were without inherent value. The cosmos thus functions naturally in its own way, without guidelines, standards, and values, to the highest possible good of all (Kohn 2004, 13).

The natural goodness of the cosmos, which is present everywhere all the time, is intuited by human beings as a sense of well-being and inner harmony which they feel deep within and activate spontaneously, without thinking. To reach it with their limited sensory and intellectual faculties, they resort to conscious patterns, organizational models, rules and regulations. Mental and social structures thus form a secondary part of the cosmic harmony which Daoists embody; they ideally increase the overall potency of life. Nevertheless, perfected Daoists try to see and go beyond these structures, transcending the patterns of organized society in a spontaneous sense of cosmic oneness.

Both these aspects of Daoist living are authentic—perfect (*zhen* 真) in the sense of matching cosmic flow: they are true to the organizational manifestation of Dao in the world as well as to its inherent suchness as creative power. They reflect the dual nature of Dao, as already the *Daode jing* says: "The Dao that can be told is not the eternal Dao" (ch. 1). This distinguishes an eternal aspect of Dao that is ineffable and beyond sensory perception from visible and tangible patterns that manifest in the rhythmic changes and natural processes of the world.

The first, the eternal Dao at the center of creation, forms the ground and inherent power of human beings and the world, yet it is entirely beyond ordinary perception. Vague and obscure, it is beyond all knowing and analysis; we cannot grasp it however hard we try. The human body, senses, and intellect are not equipped to deal with it. The only way a person can ever get in touch with it is by forgetting and transcending ordinary human faculties, by becoming subtler, finer, and more potent, more like the Dao itself.

Dao at the periphery, on the other hand, is characterized as the give and take of various pairs of complementary opposites, as the natural ebb and flow of things as they rise and fall, come and go, grow and decline, emerge and die. Things always move in one direction or the other: up or down, toward lightness or heaviness, brightness or darkness. Nature is a continuous flow, described in terms of yin and yang as the alternation of complementary characteristics and directions that cannot exist without each other. This becoming can be rhythmic and circular, or it can move back toward the source of life in the ineffable Dao, which at the same time is a forward movement toward a new level of cosmic oneness (Kohn 2005, 9-10).

The connection of Dao to world, moreover, is expressed in terms of a vital energy known as *qi*. *Qi* is bioenergetic potency that causes things to live, grow, develop, and decline. People as much as the planet are originally equipped with prenatal or primordial *qi* that connects them to the greater universe (Dao at the center), but they also work with postnatal or interactive *qi*—through breath and food as well as sexual and emotional exchanges—which can enhance or diminish their primordial energy (Dao at the periphery).

Qi is a dynamic, vacillating energy that flows constantly, either properly (*zheng* 正) or in a wayward manner (*xie* 邪), usually described in terms of excess or deficiency. The quality of flow, rather than the quantity of energy, determines health and happiness, thus leading to a definition of mental health in terms of energetic smoothness, inner harmony, and an intuitive connection to Dao.

Modern Physics

In terms of science, the Daoist vision has much in common with modern physics whose chaos theory describes the world in terms of unceasing processes of movement, change, and transformation that yet come together in a well-functioning natural control system, marked by a fair degree of unpredictability and offering a constant chance of new possibilities and discoveries. The inherent processes of the world, moreover, are described in terms of quantum fields that, unlike gravity or magnetism, carry neither matter nor energy.

Quantum physics states that the subatomic world is in no way like the world we inhabit. Energy is not continuous, but instead comes in small units: quanta, the energy that electrons absorb or emit when changing energy levels; and gluons, the forces that hold atoms together. The most basic subatomic particles behave like both particles and waves, and many of these particles form pairs like yin and yang, where one cannot exist without the other. The movement, moreover, of these particles is inherently random. It is impossible to know both the exact momentum and location of a particle at the same time—in fact, there is an inverse relationship in that the more information one has about the former, the less is known about the latter, and vice versa (see http://phys.educ. ksu.edu).

Quantum physics has shown that matter is made up of vibrating energy and fields which change rapidly—trillions of times in one second. Atoms are largely empty and consist of a tiny nucleus that is ten thousand times smaller than the rest of the particle—99,999 parts being emptiness. Body and mind consist of the same vibrating atoms that are constantly oscillating, arising and dissolving: all empty, no solidity, no firmness. As a result, reality consists less of the combination of solid entities than of an interlocking web of fields that each pulsate at their own rate. These interlocking fields of vibration—described in Daoism as patterns of *qi*-flow—can come into harmony with each other and mutually support and increase their amplitude. But they can also interfere with each other and create disturbance. Since all fields are ultimately interlocked, even a small disturbance in any one of them carries into all the others. This holds true not only for the body, but also integrates the mind into a vibrational bodymind totality. Just as bodily transformations are of unlimited possibilities, so the mind is ultimately non-local: it can be anywhere and exchange information with anything instantaneously (see www.newscientist.com/hottopics /quantum).

Another way to understand this vibrational pattern of energy fields is through sound. Sound can appear as random acoustic disturbances, such as voices, body, hand, or air movements, or again in rhythmic patterns as a note, a single acoustic frequency (Bentov 1977, 23). An experiment known both to the ancient Chinese and modern physicists is the harmony created among two string instruments. If you pluck the string of one lute, the matching string on a lute sitting next to it will begin to vibrate. Similarly, if you apply the violin bow to sheet metal with sand, you get a distinctive pattern of standing waves or nodal points that form both active and quiescent areas. These show the pattern of *qi* in the universe, the alteration between up and down, activity and rest.

Smooth *qi*-flow is thus essentially entrainment or vibrational harmony among different objects or parts of the same entity. Various modes are possible. Superimpose two sounds of identical wave pattern: hill matches hill, valley matches valley, and the amplitude of the original wave pattern doubles. This is constructive interference or the productive pattern of *qi*-interaction, leading to proper flow. Superimpose two sounds of opposite wave pattern: the exact opposite happens, they cancel each other out and the wave vanishes into a straight line. This is disruptive interference, the creation of disharmony and a destructive or wayward form of *qi*- interaction.

In the case of varying wavelengths, moreover, some phases match each other while others do not. This results in a curve that goes up and down, is far apart at one point, then meets again and parts again. A rhythmic pattern of interaction emerges, typical for the natural and human world. This, in turn, matches not only the classical view of the movements of Dao and *qi* in the Chinese universe, but also modern physics. As described by David Bohm in *Quantum Theory* (1951), living organisms are intrinsically dynamic. Their visible forms are nothing but apparently stable manifestations of underlying processes that change continuously in rhythmic patterns—fluctuations, oscillations, vibrations, waves.

The ideal of harmonious *qi*-flow and entrained vibrations, then, is a completely resonant system. The waves of one entity impinge on another so that it moves in the same frequency. This, in essence, is the Daoist definition of mental and physical health: the *qi*-vibrations of each aspect of the bodymind resonate smoothly with all others. Individuals resonate harmoniously with the people and things around them; society and nature resonate perfectly with each other. The perfection and total harmony of Dao is reached when all beings and things hum on the same wavelength and frequency, in a state of optimum transfer and total resonance.

In terms of psychology, this means that the bodymind is a conglomeration of various vibratory fields. Never can there be just one single cause for a given symptom or mental state, but the interconnection of the whole needs to be examined. Nor can the mind be viewed in isolation, but should be seen in relation to many fields that go far beyond the individual: planets, earth, society, family, and so on. Disease and disorder may be related to the out-of-tune behavior of one or the other sector in the flow of vibration, but they affect the whole and can be approached from many different angles. Corrections come accordingly in various forms—mental and physical—and should have an effect on the entire system, applying a strong harmonizing rhythm to any given part of the vibration pattern. Eventually the flow moves back into its harmonious rhythm and health results.

Body and Mind

The Chinese generally do not radically distinguish between body and mind, seeing them both essentially as *qi*, with the *caveat* that the mind vibrates at a subtler and faster level. Still, it is a gross simplification to assume that they see body and mind as simply one entity: they make a clear a distinction between the two in idea as well as language. As Maxime Kaltenmark points out:

> Chinese terminology reflects subtle differences between states of a more or less ethereal quality, but of one and the same principle lying at the foundation of all the complex functions of man. The gross conditions of the body are as much included as are its finer essences and the higher mental states, which make up holiness.
>
> This, then, is the reason why one can say that the Chinese do not make a clear-cut distinction between what we call body and mind. Their outlook is in general much more oriented towards life as an organic whole and ongoing process. (1965, 655)

The main distinction is accordingly less between body and mind in the Western sense than between states that enhance primordial *qi* and favor ultimate realization of Dao versus those that do not.

There are accordingly two sets of terms for body and mind: the body-form (*xing* 形) and the body-self (*shén* 身) plus the spirit (*shén* 神) and the mind (*xin* 心). Both body-form and spirit are part of original Dao, pure and potent, connected to cosmic flow, ultimately impersonal, and essentially without end. Body-form is a replica of the universe, the material appearance of things, their being as entities quite distinct from other objects yet wholly integrated into the greater universe. Cosmologically, the body as form marks the beginning of the created world. "Before body-form, there is the One," says the *Huainanzi* 淮南子 (Book of the Prince of Huainan; 1.9b) of the Han dynasty. In later philosophical discourse, *xing erxia* 形而下, literally "below the forms," designates the created physical world, while *xing ershang* 形而上, "above the forms," stands for the realm of metaphysics and abstract speculation. In the Daoist vision, it moreover incorporates all kinds of cosmic forces: various souls, the five phases, the seven stars of the Dipper, as well as numerous celestial palaces, networks, and deities (see Kohn 1991; see also Huang 2010).

The spirit, on the other hand, is like Dao. The seventh-century philosopher Li Rong 李榮 says in his commentary to the *Xisheng jing* 西昇經 (Scripture of Western Ascension): "Spirit serves to give life to embodied beings. Without this, there would be no life. . . . It is only upon borrowing spirit that embodied beings can come to life. Spirit uses them as a habitation in order to attain completion. Without the joining of the spirit and embodied beings, there would be no life or completion" (4.14b; Kohn 2007, 96; see also Assandri 2009). Matching this, the eighth-century *Tianyinzi* 天隱子 (Book of the Master of Heavenly Seclusion) says: "Spirit arrives without moving and is swift without hurrying; it transforms along with yin and yang and is as old as Heaven and Earth" (sect. 8). The *Neiguan jing* 內觀經 (Scripture of Inner Observation), also from the mid-Tang dynasty, provides more detail:

> Spirit is neither black nor white, neither red nor yellow, neither big nor small, neither short nor long, neither crooked nor straight, neither soft nor hard, neither thick nor thin, neither round nor square. It goes on changing and transforming without measure, merges with yin and yang, greatly encompasses Heaven and Earth, subtly enters the tiniest blade of grass. Controlled it is straightforward, let loose it goes mad.
>
> Clarity and purity make it live, turbidity and defilements cause it to perish. Fully bright, it radiates to the eight ends of the universe. Darkened, it confuses even a single direction. Keep it empty and serene, and life and Dao will spontaneously be present. (2b; Kohn 2010, 101)

Oneness with spirit, then, means its liberation (*shenjie* 神解) and the attainment of spirit pervasion (*shentong* 神通), which manifests in the emitting of a bright radiance and the attainment of supernatural powers. Perceiving fully with spirit instead of the senses, Daoist immortals (as much as enlightened Buddhists) are omniscient and can penetrate all phenomena with equal ease.

In contrast to these pure dimensions of the human bodymind, body-self and mind are conscious constructs, largely defined in terms of afflictions. Already the *Daode jing* says: "The body-self is the reason why I have terrible vexations. If I didn't have a body-self, what trouble would I have?" (ch. 13). Li Rong cites it in his commentary and explains:

> Having a body-self means having vexations and adversities. Frustrated by sight and hearing, tortured by taste and smell, one is subject to pain, irritation, heat, and cold.

> As soon as there is a body-self the hundred worries compete to arise and the five desires (of the senses) hurry to make their claims. (Kohn 2007, 100)

This defines the body-self as an artificial creation, a conglomerate of the senses. It encompasses the various human sensations and feelings together with the judgments and evaluations attached to them and their resulting passions and emotions. Understood as the personal body or extended self, it is both a physical and a psychological entity inasmuch as people identify with their body image, their sensory impressions and desires. It is not part of the original human make-up: at birth, there are just body-form and spirit. Only when a sense of personal identity forms through the senses and social positioning, it becomes a body-self. The Daoist quest, then, in essence means to diminish the power of the body-self in order to retrieve and enhance the original purity of the body-form. Realizing Dao, therefore, means a "depersonalization," a change of body identity from person to body as form.

The same relationship also holds true for spirit and mind. The mind is the ruler of the emotions and close to the idea of the heart, which is also the physical organ it resides in. It is judgmental and evaluative, given to flights of fancy, and subject to sensory impressions and desires: for cosmic purposes, this kind of mind is entirely useless. On the other hand, the mind can become the vehicle of spirit, a psychological force that allows the purity of the cosmos to flow through it. This is often called "no-mind," a state when the perception of oneself as a limited entity is replaced by an almost mystical sense of oneness with all, openness to cosmic flow, a detached yet positive relationship to the world.

The Daoist path to full mental health thus consists of two major stages. First, there is a de-personalization, de-emotionalization of the individual: make your body-self no-self and your mind no-mind (*Xisheng jing* 5.1a). After this, the purified bodymind merges with the cosmic forces of body-form and spirit, leading to oneness with Dao and cosmic consciousness. Doing so, adepts recover their birthright as integral parts of the natural and supernatural world, foregoing all claims to be anything in and of themselves and never limiting pure spirit for mere emotional and egotistic purposes. "The world is me—I am the world." Far from being an expression of personal empowerment, this position heralds the complete abrogation of all active molding, of all outgoing force, of all purposeful deliberation and human thinking.

Energy Medicine and Psychology

Among Western science, the close integration of body and mind, combined with the vision of the human bodymind as interlocking energy fields that can function at different levels of purity, is most prominent in the emerging field of energy medicine. Recent research in biology, physiology, and physics has opened up many new venues of looking at the bodymind and begun to create a language that will eventually allow science to integrate Chinese concepts, demystify the phenomenon and experiences of *qi*, and make the Daoist perspective more widely accessible to the general public.

The most important new concepts emerging from this research are measurable biomagnetic fields and bioelectricity. Biomagnetic fields are human energy centers that vibrate at different frequencies, storing and giving off energies not unlike the bodymind in the Chinese system. Their energetic output or vibrations can be measured, and it has been shown that the heart and the brain continuously pulse at extremely low frequencies (ELF). It has also become clear through controlled measurements that biomagnetic fields are unbounded so that, for example, the field of the heart vibrates beyond the body and extends infinitely into space, verifying the Chinese conviction that people and the universe interact continuously on an energetic level (see Becker and Sheldon 1985; Gerber 1988; Seem 1989; Targ and Katra 1999).

Similarly, bioelectricity manifests in energy currents that crisscross the human body and are similar to the meridians of acupuncture. Separate from and, in evolutionary terms, more ancient than the nervous system, these currents work through the so-called cytoskeleton, a complex net of connective tissue that is a continuous and dynamic molecular webwork. Also known as the "living matrix," this webwork contains so-called integrins or trans-membrane linking molecules which have no boundaries but are intricately interconnected. When touching the skin or inserting an acupuncture needle, the integrins make contact with all parts of the bodymind through the matrix webwork. Based on this evidence, wholeness is becoming an accepted concept, which sees the bodymind "as an integrated, coordinated, successful system" and accepts that "no parts or properties are uncorrelated but all are demonstrably linked" (Oschman 2000, 49, citing E. F. Adolph).

The bodymind as a living matrix is simultaneously a mechanical, vibrational, energetic, electronic, photonic, and informational network. It consists of a complex, linked pattern of pathways and molecules that forms a tensegrity system. A term taken originally from architecture where it is used in the structural description of domes, tents, sailing vessels, and cranes, tensegrity indicates a continuous tensional network (tendons) connected by a set of discontinuous elements (struts), which can also be fruitfully applied to the description of the integrated system (Oschman 2000, 153).

The vision of the body as an energetic network and of the mind as a key factor in human energetics is thus becoming more familiar in Western culture. Without specifically speaking of yin and yang, the five phases, inner organs and meridians, energy medicine yet adapts an understanding of body and self that has been at the root of Daoist ideas and practices for millennia.

Energy psychology, on the other hand, takes the extra step and works with traditional models, seeing the body as consisting of "various interrelated energy systems (such as the aura, chakras, and meridians), which each serve specific functions" (Feinstein et al. 2005, 197). According to this understanding, the visible and measurable material body is supported by an underlying network or skeleton of living energy that forms the foundation of all bodily systems (see also Pert 1997; Gach and Henning 2004; Gallo 2004.).

Supported increasingly by electromagnetic measurements, followers of this new method distinguish seven major aspects of this energy network:

the meridian system defined as the energy bloodstream, which "brings vitality, removes blockages, adjusts metabolism, and even determines the speed and form of cellular change" (Feinstein et al. 2005, 198);

the chakras, energetic vortexes adapted from Indian body geography, which are concentrated centers of energy that supply power to specific organs and resonate with universal principles, such as creativity, love, survival, and transcendence;

the aura, a fundamental energy shield surrounding people that was studied extensively in the seventies (e.g., Krippner and Rubin1974), that is now seen as a protective energetic atmosphere that surrounds the person "like a space suit" and serves to filter outside energies (Feinstein et al. 2005, 200);

the basic grid, a sturdy fundamental energy net that can be compared to the chassis of a car;

the Celtic weave, a spinning, spiraling, twisting, and curving pattern of energies that creates a "kaleidoscope of colors and shapes" and functions as an "invisible thread that keeps all the energy systems functioning as a single unit" (Feinstein et al. 2005, 201);

the five rhythms, matching the five phases and their related organs, senses, muscles, and so on, which establish a person's primary rhythm and provide the basic blueprint of personal and interactive functioning;

the triple warmer, adapted from Chinese medicine and reinterpreted as an energy line that "networks the energies of the immune system to attack an invader and mobilizes the body's energies in emergencies" (Feinstein et al. 2005, 202), which is the key factor in the stress response according to this energetic vision;

and finally, the radiant circuits, an adaptation of the eight extraordinary vessels, now described as primary to the body's system in terms of evolution, "operating like fluid fields and embodying a distinct spontaneous intelligence" (Feinstein et al. 2005, 203).

Applying this vision of the human body, practitioners of energy psychology propose that people should enhance their "energy aptitude," perform daily exercises to harmonize the energies, and use specific tapping techniques to release tensions and emotional trauma (Kohn 2008, 26-27).

Energy aptitude means the ability to work effectively with one's internal energies. It has four components: a careful awareness of one's energetic patterns, the ability to influence these patterns in a beneficial way, the faculty to perceive energies in other people and outside objects, and to join or transform these outside energies in a beneficial way (Feinstein et al. 2005, 204-5).

Daily exercises include many moves familiar from Daoist practice: they involve pressing key acupuncture points while breathing deeply and visualizing energies flowing through the body. Like traditional Chinese and Indian exercises, they make use of various bodily postures and involve self-massages of key areas, such as the face, the scalp, and the abdomen. In some cases, meridian lines are opened through placing the hands at either end and allowing the energies to flow, in others simple bends stretches in conjunction with conscious breathing and mental release serve the purpose. While these are all similar to practices already advocated in Daoism, the closest exercise is the Auric Weave, a passing of the hands over the energy lines of the body, known as Dry Wash in traditional China and as Marrow Washing in modern qigong (Feinstein et al. 2005, 233-35).

The third and most important clinical application of energy psychology lies in tapping techniques that ease stress, release trauma, and heal ailments. Also practiced under the name Emotional Freedom Technique (EFT), the method has patients measure a problem on a scale from 1 to 10, then imagine the feeling associated with the issue, create a positive affirmation ("Even though I have . . ., I deeply and completely accept myself."), and repeat the affirmation while tapping a set of eight acupuncture points. The points range from the center of the forehead through the face, neck, and upper torso to the sides of the hands. After completion, patients re-measure the feeling, then repeat the technique—often with a slightly modified affirmation ("Even though I still have a remnant of . . .")—until it goes down to zero. Not only are urgent issues immediately relieved with this method, but even long-standing issues resolve with persistent tapping (Craig 2007).

The technique in this precise form is not found in traditional documents, but there is a Daoist method practiced today that involves tapping the three energy centers in head, chest, and abdomen as well as the third eye while chanting an incantation to the powers of chaos underlying all creation. There are also multiple qigong tapping routines that help recover health and stabilize energy (Johnson 2000, 703-7). Daoist materials, moreover, frequently require practitioners to "drum" certain areas of the body, most commonly the chest or abdomen, while holding the breath, thereby releasing stale or wayward *qi*, the traditional way of referring to past trauma, unwanted emotional baggage, and physical obstructions. Self-massages that involve tapping energy channels on arms and legs as well as around eyes and ears, moreover, are common and considered essential to establishing physical and mental health (Kohn 2008, 79-80).

The Daoist Bodymind

The Daoist bodymind closely connects to the greater universe. Like the body in Chinese medicine, it centers around the five inner (yin) organs of liver, heart, spleen, lungs, and kidneys, which form part of an intricate inner-body network encompassing transformative (yang) organs, the senses, extremities, fluids, tissues, and so on. Cosmologically, moreover, the organs and their correlates match the directions in space, the seasons in time, as well as all sorts of natural and celestial phenomena—including planets, sacred mountains, musical tones, colors, and many more.

Beyond this, the five inner organs are the energetic centers of an expansive network of *qi* conduits, meridians that connect them to the extremities on both sides of the body. They are also the seat of various physical aspects of the person (body fluids, tissues, senses, tastes, and so on) as well as of his or her mental dimension (psychological factors, emotions, virtues, etc.). The Daoist vision of the bodymind works with all these and in addition proposes three major energy centers and four essential energy lines. These form a vertical-horizontal network at the very root of the human being, created when Heaven and Earth first provide the person with primordial *qi*.

The three energy centers are called cinnabar or elixir fields (*dantian* 丹田). Located in the head, heart area, and lower abdomen., they each house the Three Treasures: spirit, *qi*, and essence (*jing* 精)—the latter signifying a denser energetic potency that makes up bones, brain, teeth, and nails and, in its fluid form, transmits the very power of life in male semen and female menstrual blood. Matching the three cosmic levels of Heaven, Humanity, and Earth, the three elixir fields are also known as the Heaven Palace, the Scarlet Palace, and the Earth Palace; as the residence of body gods, they have the more mythological names Niwan Palace, Purple Palace, and Yellow Court (Neswald 2009, 37-38).

The upper elixir field in the head is the place from where celestial energies are accessed or through which, at the stage of immortality, the spirit embryo passes to ascend to the otherworld. The central field is placed in the heart area, between the nipples and also called the Cavity of *Qi*. Holding *qi* for dispersal in the body either through ordinary activity or for immortality cultivation, it plays a key role especially in women's practice, strengthening and enhancing life energy. The lower field is commonly placed about 1.3 inches beneath the navel, in the center of the abdomen. Also called Ocean of *Qi*, it is the point where adepts find their center of gravity, their reproductive power, and their stability in the world (Kohn 2005, 59).

Connecting these three energy centers are four major energy conduits or extraordinary vessels. Most important is the Penetrating Vessel (*chongmai* 沖脈) which runs right through the center of the body. It begins at the perineum, a small cluster of muscles located between the anus and the genital organs, passes through the three elixir fields, and ends at the crown of the head, a point known as Hundred Meeting in medicine and as Heavenly Pass in Daoism. Connecting the kidneys and stomach, as well as the main energy centers, it is considered the main conduit of primordial *qi*. Adepts use it to send healing and spiritual intention into the depth of the elixir fields, thus opening their centers and connecting to the primordiality of the cosmos.

The second major energy line is the Belt Vessel (*daimai* 帶脈). It runs around the abdomen a few inches below the navel, connecting the Ocean of *Qi* in front with the Gate of Destiny in the kidney area in the back and linking the vertical meridians and the major storehouses of *qi*. Next are the Conception Vessel (*renmai* 任脈, yin) and the Governing Vessel (*dumai* 督脈, yang), which run along the front and back of the torso respectively, reaching from the pelvic floor to the head. They are of great importance both in all levels of Daoist practice, serving to mix *qi* and blood and to guide the *qi* along the major centers of the body.

The Conception Vessel begins at Meeting of Yin at the perineum, passes through the front of the body along its central line, and ends at the mouth. A carrier and major supporter of yin-*qi*, it supports uro-genital, digestive, and thoracic aspects of the body and, together with the spleen meridian, controls pregnancy and menstruation. The Ocean of *Qi* in the lower abdomen is actually one of its points, as is the navel, known as the Tower of Spirit, and the center of the chest, here known as the Ocean of Tranquility. Two further points on this energy line are the Central Court, which matches the heart area and thus the middle elixir field, and the Purple Palace, which here refers to the heart.

The Governing Vessel also begins at the pelvic floor, then passes along the back of the body, moves across the top of the head, and ends inside the mouth at the upper gums. It transports and aids yang-*qi* and has many points connecting to channels and inner organs. Its twenty-eight points include also the more spiritual points Gate of Destiny at the second and third lumbar vertebrae, Numinous Terrace at the sixth thoracic vertebra, as well as the Jade Pillow at the back of the skull (see Kaptchuk 1983; Larre and de la Vallée 1996).

The two meridians connect in the mouth as well as internally, descending back to the pelvic floor and forming a continuous, intricate inner loop. Rather than using this path, however, adepts tend to activate them as one straight circle of *qi*-flow. They place the tongue at the roof of the mouth as a bridge between the meridians, then inhale deeply into the abdomen to enhance their Ocean of *Qi* or lower elixir field. From there, they breathe out, envisioning their *qi* flowing downward to the pelvic floor and reaching the perineum.

Focusing on the coccyx, they inhale the *qi* up along the spine, passing through all the various points along the Governing Vessel. Reaching a point below the neck, they begin to exhale, carrying the *qi* further up along the back of the skull, across Hundred Meeting at the top, along the forehead and to the nostrils. From here they inhale again, envisioning the *qi* flowing down along the

Conception Vessel and through the Ocean of *Qi* into the pelvic floor, thus establishing a cycle of *qi* throughout the torso, which is known in Daoist practice as the "microcosmic orbit" (*xiao zhoutian* 小周天) (Neswald 2009, 35-37).

Daoists activate these three energy centers and four lines to reach a state of energetic perfection where primordial *qi* flows freely through the body and energizes every aspect of life. They are exceedingly conscious of personal energy management, both within the self and the environment. They exert strong control over housing, sleep gear, clothing, food, and social contacts and make sure to be active in self-management, working with physical movement, healing exercises, breathing, meditation, emotional modification, and the pursuit of classic virtues, such as honesty, wisdom, and benevolence. Their efforts overall reduce stress and strengthen the adrenal glands, which in Chinese and Daoist medicine are part of the kidney complex and thus the seat of vital essence. As a result, they prevent stress and disease and do not suffer from the common signs of aging. They create a happier and more wholesome life for themselves while contributing to a saner and more harmonious society.

Behavioral Kinesiology

The closest modern match to the complex energy centers and lines of traditional Daoism is found in behavioral kinesiology. In theory and practice, it supports everything Daoists have been saying for millennia about the nature of bodymind, self, and society. It also emphasizes the very same measures—social, physical, and psychological—people should take to enhance their well-being and find perfection within this world.

Kinesiology is the science of movement: how to move the body and use its joints, tendons, and muscles to create maximum efficiency and best performance. It is best known from sports culture and studied widely in departments of physical education at Western universities (Luttgens and Wells 1989). Behavioral kinesiology adds the dimension of personal perfection into the mix: the attainment of health, the extension of life expectancy, and the realization of virtues and inherent goodness in self and society. In other words, it is the study of how we can realize ideal health and harmony by living and moving most efficiently in our bodymind.

The key factor in behavioral kinesiology is the thymus gland. Located in the solar plexus and heart area, it was acknowledged by the ancient Greeks as the central seat of vitality. "Thymus is the stuff of life, vaporous breath, active, energetic feeling and thinking, material very much related to blood" (Spencer 1993, 47). The gland, although known to exist, was ignored in Western medicine for the longest time as not having a specific function, since it—like essence in Chinese medicine—grows during puberty, is reduced in adulthood, shrinks to a miniscule size during sickness, and shrivels up completely after death (Diamond 1978, 10). Recent studies have shown that the thymus gland, like the middle elixir field, is the center of immunological surveyance and works to produce lymphocytes, i.e., the white blood cells responsible for the immunological reaction in the body. Connected energetically to all the different organs and extremities of the body (1978, 28-29), it prevents disease and cancer if kept strong.

Not only the middle, but also the upper and lower elixir fields have a match in the West. The upper field is obviously the brain with its major center of mental and emotional processing. Reactions in the brain divide into two types: good and bad, pleasant and unpleasant. Usually the bad, unpleasant emotions are afflictive, negative, and destructive; they tend to cause people to withdraw or move away from the object or circumstance that caused them. Good, pleasant emotions are beneficial, positive, and engaging; they make people approach and seek out the object or circumstance that caused them (Goleman 1997, 34).

In terms of brain chemistry, withdrawal reactions are located in the right frontal cortex, while approach reactions are activated in the left frontal cortex. People are born with a tendency toward one or the other dominant activation: those with more right frontal cortex activity are more emotionally volatile, get sick more easily, have a harder time recovering, suffer from numerous ailments, find much difficulty in their communities, and die earlier. People with dominantly left frontal cortex activity are more positive, do not submit to stress, will not catch colds even if exposed to germs, and live longer and happier lives. The dominant mode of reaction can be changed through learning and systematic training, notably through detached awareness and mindfulness practice, such as advocated by traditional Buddhists and Daoists alike (1997, 68-69; Begley 2007, 226-33; see also Kabat-Zinn 2005).

The lower elixir field, the center of transformation in Daoist practice, in Western physiology matches the abdominal brain, the seat of inherent, spontaneous intelligence, in the vernacular described as gut feelings or intuition. A popular medical idea in the late nineteenth century (see Bedell 1885), it has reemerged in recent research as the seat of an active enteric nervous system that governs the well-being of the person (McMillin et al. 1999). Its activation is best known from Zen Buddhist practice, which requires a tightly held upright posture as well as conscious breathing and control over the diaphragm (Sekida 1975, 84).

Behavioral kinesiology claims that all illness starts at the energy level (Diamond 1978, 25). This matches the traditional Chinese contention that an imbalance in the bodymind system manifests on three levels. First, there are the initial "signs" of an illness, which may be very subtle and perceived merely as a slight irregularity by the patient. Second, these signs grow into specific "symptoms," detected by the physician in a thorough examination. If left unchecked, these may further develop into a full-fledged "syndrome," which creates invasive disharmony in both, the patient's body and social life (Kohn 2005, 63).

It also claims that the musculature of the body is immediately in contact with, and responsive to, any energy changes in the entire system and that, therefore, health and well-being—and, by extension, the benefits or harm of certain substances and the truth or falseness of a given statement—can be verified in a so-called kinesiological muscle test. In essence, this consists of the subject standing with one arm held out straight and a partner or tester trying to push it down. If the thymus gland, and thus the immunological system, is working well, if health is strong, if the examined substance is beneficial, or if the statement thought about is true, there will be a bounce or spring in the arm and it will not budge. In the opposite case, the muscles weaken and the arm is pushed down easily (Diamond 1978, 14-21; see also Levy and Lehr 1996). Just as a weak muscle signals energetic imbalance in this system, so the Daoist understanding claims that strong, vibrant muscles mean the presence of proper *qi*-flow and health. Acupuncture, meridian-based massages, and tapping as well as Daoist visualizations and meditative energy-guiding accordingly enhance energy flow and immunological strengthening as well as increase harmonious living in self and society.

Another Daoist practice that finds a match in behavioral kinesiology is placing the tongue at the roof of the mouth. Modern kinesiologists call this the "centering button," a place that opens the body's central power lines and releases stress (Diamond 1978, 31). In addition, matching traditional Daoist exercises, kinesiologists have found that when there is too much synchronous activity on either side of the body, it will suffer a cerebral-hemisphere imbalance and weakened muscles, a state they describe as "switching" (1978, 40). In other words, the subtle energy lines of the body need to be activated by using the opposite arm and leg as much as possible, creating a sense of good body coordination. The lines are also impacted by any kind of metal that may be placed in the body's center and prevent proper energetic integration (1978, 43). Positive energy is further enhanced by wide, open gestures, such as the spreading of arms in a blessing or the welcoming of loved ones at a reunion (1978, 49)—movements often seen in Chinese exercises where the *qi* is gathered or spread by opening the arms wide.

In other words, the muscles of the body provide a clear indication of physical and mental health and serve as a major way of enhancing overall well-being, which in turn has a direct impact on social and political harmony in the world.

Specific practices to stimulate the thymus gland and thus increase the vitality of the individual as outlined in behavioral kinesiology, moreover, closely match the repertoire of traditional Daoists. They include

—deep abdominal breathing and control of the diaphragm;

—self-massages of the chest and front line of the body (Conception Vessel);

—tapping of major energy centers, especially the center of the chest (middle elixir field);

—upright posture that allows for an equal flow of energy all over the body;

—conscious and careful movement that alternates the body's two sides, ideally to melodious music;

—careful selection of food, avoiding processed, preserved, or chemically altered items;

—wearing of loose and pure clothes, using natural fibers;

—environmental care, providing good air, light, housing, and natural settings (Fengshui);

—emotional refinement toward feelings of love and caring, and the pursuit of virtues;

—support for peace in the world and the creation of a harmonious society, since energy flows between people and is enhanced or reduced depending on each person's management (Diamond 1978).

Within this overall framework, John Diamond has a few specific recommendations. Most generally, he suggests that one should find a "homing" thought, a mental vision of oneself in a pleasant and stress-free situation, such as in nature, on a beach, or with loved ones, and practice smiling both inwardly and to others, to create an internal harmony and relax the facial muscles (1978, 47, 49). He also emphasizes the energetic benefits of beauty, as found in poetry, music, painting, art, and natural landscapes and suggests that one should regularly take so-called energy breaks by reciting poetry, looking at nature, viewing a painting, or walk about with the arms swinging (1978, 39). All these are practices Daoists have embraced for centuries, living in beautiful natural settings, pursuing arts and music, and practicing calming meditations (1978, 124).

In addition to widely recognized pollutants, such as denatured food, neon lights, smoking, and various irritating chemicals, Diamond also advises against contact with ugly sights and shrill or intensely pulsing sounds since they lead to "therapeutic weakening" (1978, 62). This, too, matches traditional Daoist rules against energetic pollution through encounters with dirt, death, or violence. Diamond especially singles out the weakening agents of aggressive art work and advertising as well as noise pollution through traffic, television, and rock music (1978, 65-66). In terms of practical objects, he suggests avoiding the use of sunglasses, wrist watches, nylon hats, wigs, and high heels as well as of metal chairs and seat cushions, mattresses, sheets, and clothing made from synthetic fabrics (1978, 74-77). While many of these guidelines involve physical objects and bodily practices, they all connect to the realm of the mind and have a powerful psychological impact. Working through the body on the mind, and through the mind on the body, thus forms a fundamental pattern in the Daoist way to mental health.

The Daoist Way

The Daoist way, then, proceeds on three levels that can be described as healing, longevity, and immortality. They signify three stages of perfection and empowerment along the same continuum of *qi*. They begin with what Daoists call the "normal mind," a state of internal stress and tension that comes when people, through interaction with the world on the basis of physical needs and sensory exchanges, develop passions and desires, intellectual distinctions and judgments and thus establish an identity in terms of body-self and mind. Having overshadowed their inherent purity of body-form and spirit, their primordial *qi* is no longer complete, so that, over time, they decline energetically and are subject to mental and physical ailments.

Healing, then, is the basic recovery of smooth *qi*-flow with medical means such as acupuncture, massage, herbal formulas, food cures, rest, and so on, from a level of severe imbalance to a more harmonious state, closer to matching the flow of Dao on the periphery. Psychologically it involves the reduction of toxic emotions, associated physically with the five inner organs, to appropriate reactions. As a result, for example, aggression—associated with the liver and the season of spring—is replaced by courage while fear, linked with the kidneys and winter, gives way to caution.

Longevity, next, comes in as and when people have become aware of their situation, and decide to take the healing process into their own hands. Having attained a basic state of good health with the help of medical means, they proceed to increase their primordial *qi* to and even above the level they had at birth. To do so, they live an overall relaxed and natural lifestyle, follow health-enhancing diets, supplement their food with herbs and minerals, and undertake breath control, healing exercises, self-massages, sexual hygiene, as well as various forms of meditations and visualizations. At this level, a key practice is the Inner Smile, which brings divine light into the five organs and transforms emotional reactions into altruistic patterns and goodwill, expressed in terms of the five Confucian virtues, so that courage evolves into benevolence and caution into wisdom—joined further by social responsibility, propriety, and honesty with self and others.

Sitting upright with eyes closed, practitioners place the tongue on the roof of the mouth to connect the energy lines as in the microcosmic orbit. They begin by first relaxing the forehead and envisioning a smiling energy as it flows between the eyebrows to the nose and cheeks, warming the whole face. Taking the smiling feeling lower, they smile into the neck and throat where stress tends to accumulate and allow this area to open. Next, they smile into the throat area to the thyroid and parathyroid glands, which frees the ability to speak and communicate. From here, they let the *qi* flow down to the thymus gland, the seat of love and enlightenment, and allow it to moisten and grow bigger. From here, practitioners allow the smiling *qi* to flow to the five inner organs in turn, envisioning them with their respective colors, appreciating them for their work, and allowing toxic tendencies emotions to leave and positive attitudes to enter. The practice concludes with the collection of smiling energy in the elixir field, where it is centered by being spiraled thirty-six times in an outward direction (women counter-clockwise, men clockwise), then twenty-four times the other way.

This matches other practices, such as visualizations of oneself in a larger, cosmic environment and—classically—placing of deities in the body and ecstatic excursions to the stars. They ensure not only that people attain their natural life expectancy and maintain mental harmony, but also lead to greater longevity as well as to an enhanced subtlety of perception. They fully match people with Dao at the periphery and bring them closer to its potency at the center of creation.

Immortality, third, raises the practices to a yet higher level. To attain it, people have to transform all their *qi* into primordial *qi* and proceed to refine it further to even subtler levels. This finer *qi* will eventually turn into pure spirit, with which practitioners increasingly identify to become transcendent spirit-people or immortals. The practice that leads there involves intensive meditation and trance training as well as more radical forms of diet, healing exercises, and mental *qi*-guiding. In contrast to health and long life, where the bodymind system is harmonized and made gentler yet remains fundamentally unchanged, perfected toward its original nature and matching the flow of Dao in the world, immortality means the overcoming of the natural tendencies of the bodymind and its transformation into a different kind of energetic constellation. The result is mystical union with Dao as creative force and the attainment of cosmic consciousness, apparent in telepathic and shamanic powers. It eventually leads to a bypassing of death and the taking-up of residence in heavenly paradises.

While the ultimate goal of Daoist practice is this transformation to transcendence or immortality, practitioners have always embraced all the different levels and increased their mental acuity and spiritual subtlety to find a closer connection to Dao and enhance quality of life. Mental health relevant to living in the world appears dominantly on the middle level, where the individual is still fully part of the world but his or her toxic emotions are transformed into virtues and self and mind are lessened to again let body-form and spirit shine forth in their original purity.

Core Health

Among psychological practices today, this structure and its related methods appear most clearly in a system called comprehensive kinesiology or "Core Health," developed by Edwin Carlson in an expanded application of behavioral kinesiology. He follows in the footsteps of David R. Hawkins (b. 1927), a psychiatrist who studied with John Diamond and first developed large-scale experiments with kinesiological testing. Examining thousands of subjects in many different cultures, Hawkins verified that the body reveals facts beyond conscious awareness and control and established a universal scale for the moral and spiritual potential of the world at large. This scale places people's responses in a range from 20 to 1000, with a watershed—the realm of courage—at 200. Anything below means people work entirely toward survival and generate wide ranges of negative emotions, such as fear, worry, anger, hatred, greed, and pride—feelings that pull the person away from their inner truth and what Daoists would call their authentic spirit. Above 200, more intellectual and spiritual values dominate, including trust, goodwill, forgiveness, love, and reverence to the point of sagely qualities such as serenity and bliss—attitudes that support the spiritual unfolding of higher values (see Hawkins 2002).

Hawkins himself experienced the ultimate realization of the human self and mind in a state of complete clarity and stillness. He describes it as follows:

> That which is the Self is total and complete. It is equally present everywhere. There are no needs, no desires, or lack. . . . A glance at the body reveals it to be the same as everything else—unowned, unpossessed by an individual, equal to the furniture or other objects and merely part of all that is. There is nothing personal about the body and no identification with it. It moves about spontaneously, correctly executes itsbodily functions, and effortlessly walks and breathes. It is self-propelled and its actions are determined and activated by the Presence. (2002, 4)

Ed Carlson, in turn, developed specific methods to release toxic patterns and reach this cosmic state, closely resembling Daoist ways. He begins by encouraging people to remember a "perfect moment," a time when they were fully at one with themselves and the world was good. Mentally reliving their perfect moment, people experience a first glimpse of wholeness. He then encourages them to release toxic emotions, focusing first or all on anger—at others, self, and God—in a process he calls "Heart Forgiveness" (Carlson 2007). Practitioners begin with a basic relaxation, then visualize the subject of their anger. They see their heart as having lips and being able to communicate, so that it can tell the subject of their anger just how hurt they were. Next, they see their heart as having arms while visualizing the original purity in the other's heart and move forward to let the two hearts embrace. From here, in a practice closely reminiscent of the Inner Smile, they see a spark of original purity light up inside their heart and spread divine, cosmic radiance through their organs, body, and auras. Kinesiological testing before and after the practice shows just to what degree this process releases toxicity and negative internal patterns.

Moving on from there, Carlson further guides practitioners to expand energetically into the greater universe, rising in an almost ecstatic excursion beyond their home, city, country, and even the planet into the vastness and stillness of the galaxy. Coming back from this extraterrestrial journey, they compress back into their bodies but maintain that sense of cosmic vastness and ultimate oneness with forces far greater than themselves. An overall sense of peace and inner stability results, leading to a life filled entirely with perfect moments, to full authenticity of living, and the "seven fruits of the spirit," which closely resemble Daoist virtues: love, joy, peace, patience, kindness, gentleness, and in-powered self-control. Like advanced Daoists, the people shaped by this modern system are free from toxic emotions and neurotic patterns and rest peacefully in their destiny which forms part of the larger cosmos. By just being who they are, they make the world a better place.

Bibliography

Assandri, Friederike. 2009. *Beyond the Daode jing: Twofold Mystery in Tang Daoism.* Magdalena, NM: Three Pines Press.

Becker, Robert O., and Gary Sheldon. 1985. *The Body Electric: Electromagnitism and the Foundation of Life.* New York: William Morrow and Co.

Bedell, Leila G. 1885. *The Abdominal Brain.* Chicago: Grass and Delbridge.

Begley, Sharon, ed. 2007. *Train Your Mind to Change Your Brain.* New York: Ballentine.

Bentov, Itchak. 1977. *Stalking the Wild Pendulum: On the Mechanics of Consciousness.* New York: E. P. Dutton.

Bohm, David. 1951. *Quantum Theory.* New York: Prentice-Hall.

Capra, Fritjof. 1975. *The Tao of Physics: An Exploration of the Parallels Between Modern Physics and Eastern Mysticism.* Boulder: Shambhala.

Carlson, Ed. 2007. *Heart Forgiveness: Creating Freedom.* www.CoreHealth.us.

Craig, Gary. 2007. "The EFT Manual: Emotional Freedom Techniques." http://www.emofree.com

Diamond, John. 1979. *Behavioral Kinesiology.* New York: Harper & Row.

Feinstein, David, Donna Eden, and Gary Craig. 2005. *The Promise of Energy Psychology.* New York: Penguin.

Gach, Michael Reed, and Beth Ann Henning. 2004. *Acupressure for Emotional Healing.* New York: Bantam.

Gallo, Fred, ed. 2004. *Energy Psychology in Psychotherapy.* New York: Norton.

Gerber, Richard. 1988. *Vibrational Medicine: New Choices for Healing Ourselves*. Santa Fe: Bear and Company.

Goleman, Daniel, ed. 1997. *Healing Emotions: Conversations with the Dalai Lama on Mindfulness, Emotions, and Health*. Boston: Shambhala.

Hawkins, David R. 2002a. *Power Vs. Force: The Hidden Dimensions of Human Behavior*. Carlsbad, Calif: HayHouse.

Huang, Shih-Shan Susan. 2010. "Daoist Imagery of Body and Cosmos, Part 1: Body Gods and Starry Travel." *Journal of Daoist Studies* 2:57-90.

Johnson, Jerry Alan. 2000. *Chinese Medical Qigong Therapy: A Comprehensive Clinical Text*. Pacific Grove: International Institute of Medical Qigong.

Kabat-Zinn, Jon. 2005. *Coming to Our Senses: Healing Ourselves and the World through Mindfulness*. New York: Hyperion.

Kaltenmark, Max. 1965. "La mystique taoïste." In *La mystique et le mystiques*, edited by A. Ravier, 649-69. Paris.

Kaptchuk, Ted J. 1983. *The Web that Has No Weaver: Understanding Chinese Medicine*. New York: Congdon & Weed.

Kohn, Livia. 1991. "Taoist Visions of the Body." *Journal of Chinese Philosophy* 18: 227-52.

_____. 2004. *Cosmos and Community: The Ethical Dimension of Daoism*. Cambridge, Mass.: Three Pines Press.

_____. 2005. *Health and Long Life: The Chinese Way*. Cambridge, Mass.: Three Pines Press.

_____. 2007 [1991]. *Daoist Mystical Philosophy: The Scripture of Western Ascension*. Magdalena, NM: Three Pines Press.

_____. 2008. *Chinese Healing Exercises: The Tradition of Daoyin*. Honolulu: University of Hawai'i Press.

_____. 2010. *Sitting in Oblivion: The Heart of Daoist Meditation*. Dunedin, Fla.: Three Pines Press.

Larre, Claude, and Elisabeth Rochat de la Vallee. 1996. *Eight Extraordinary Vessels*. Cambridge: Monkey Press.

Levy, S. L., and C. Lehr, C. 1996. *Your Body Can Talk: The Art and Application of Clinical Kinesiology*. Prescott: Hohm Press.

Luttgens, Kathryn, and Katherine F. Wells. 1989. *Kinesiology: Scientific Basis of Human Motion*. Dubuque, IA: Wm. C. Brown Publishers.

McMillin, David L., Douglas G. Richards, Eric A. Mein, and Carl D. Nelson. 1999. "The Abdominal Brain and the Enteric Nervous System." *Journal of Alternative and Complementary Medicine* 5.6. www.meridianinstitute. com.

Neswald, Sara Elaine. 2009. "Internal Landscapes." In *Internal Alchemy: Self, Society, and the Quest for Immortality*, edited by Livia Kohn and Robin R. Wang, 27-53. Magdalena, NM: Three Pines Press.

Nichols. T. L. 1853. *Esoteric Anthropology*. New York: Stringer & Townsend.

Oschman, James. 2000. *Energy Medicine: The Scientific Basis*. New York: Churchill Livingstone.

Pert, Candace. 1997. *Molecules of Emotion: Why You Feel the Way You Feel*. New York: Scribner.

Seem, Mark D. 1989. *BodyMind Energetics: Toward a Dynamic Model of Health*. Rochester, VT: Healing Arts Press.

Sekida, Katsuki. 1975. *Zen Training*. New York: Weatherhill.

Spencer, Colin. 1993. *Vegetarianism: A History*. New York: Four Walls Eight Windows.

Targ, Russell, and Jane Katra. 1999. *Miracles of Mind: Exploring Nonlocal Consciousness and Spiritual Healing*. Novato, Cal.: New World Library.

Ancient Daoist Philosophy and Authentic Living

XICHEN LU

There are many ideas related to psychological treatment in ancient Daoism. Thus, "recover the simple and return to nature" can prevent self-aggrandizement and self-centeredness, promote true self-development, and display the unique personality. "Live for and care about people" can relieve the extreme focus from one's symptoms and passive emotions to find spiritual happiness and a meaningful life. "Push far toward emptiness, hold fast to quietude" can comfort negative moods of fickleness and anxiety and inspire creative thoughts. The dialectical thinking, moreover, of "good fortune rests on bad fortune" can help people to face success and failure leisurely and get on with life.

The earliest and best known representative of ancient Daoist thought is the *Daode jing* (Book of the Way and Its Virtue), found in various ancient manuscripts and translated innumerable times into other languages. The work is associated with the philosopher Laozi, allegedly a contemporary of Confucius (550-479 BCE), who later grew into the Highest Lord Lao, a major deity of the religion still worshiped widely today. The text also establishes major fundamental tenets of Daoist worldview, such as Dao, yin-yang, simplicity, sage, and nonaction that give guidelines for authentic living and are highly relevant to modern psychology.

The *Daode jing* or—as it was known in early China—the *Laozi* is a short text of about five thousand characters, commonly divided into eighty-one chapters and two parts, one on Dao or the "way" (ch. 1-37), and one on De or "virtue" (ch. 38-81). It is written in verse—not a rhyming, steady, rhythmic kind of verse, but a stylized prose that has strong parallels and regular patterns—and contains sections of description contrasted with tight punch lines. Many of its lines are terse, almost aphoristic in nature; the text reads more like a collection of sayings than a comprehensive philosophical discourse (see LaFargue 1992; Kohn and LaFargue 1998).

Finds of early manuscripts, notably the silk texts at Mawangdui of 168 BCE and the bamboo slips recovered from Guodian of about 350 BCE, show that the transmitted version was complete by the second century BCE and in

25

large segments existed well before then (see Henricks 1989; 2000; Allan and Williams 2000). It can, therefore, be said that the *Daode jing* accurately represents early Daoist thought and visions of authentic living.

The text contains numerous ideas that directly relate to psychological treatment and self-improvement. For example, "recover simplicity and return to authenticity" can prevent self-aggrandizement and self-centeredness while promoting true self-development and the enhancement of one's unique personality. "Always helping the people and rejecting no one" can relieve an extreme focus on one's own misery and symptoms, eliminating the sense of vicitimization and passive emotions and opening the path to spiritual happiness and a meaningful life. "Attain utmost emptiness, maintain perfect stillness" can help reduce negative moods of fickleness and anxiety, inspiring creative urges and authentic thinking. The dialectic, moreover, of "good and bad fortune depend on one another"can help people face success and failure in a leisurely manner, allowing them to overcome disappointments and get on with life.

Recover Simplicity

In modern society, people often feel tired in body and mind. One important reason for this is that they have lost their connection with their true self and fail to live authentically. As Erich Fromm has pointed out:

> Our society is run by a managerial bureaucracy, by professional politicians; people are motivated by mass suggestion, their aim is producing more and consuming more, as purposes in themselves. All activities are subordinated to economic goals, means have become ends; man is an automaton—well fed, well clad, but without any ultimate concern for that which is his peculiarly human quality and function. (1956, ch. 2)

Often keen to catch current trends, always rushing and competitive, people consciously or unconsciously follow someone else's guidelines and values. Thus they suffer acutely from a lack of authentic being, blindly run after the masses—they have lost their self and live with split personalities and in fundamental insincerity. It is thus not surprising that that they should be deeply tired in body and mind. Clinical experience has clearly shown that it is impossible to maintain self-respect and one's own unique nature under these circumstances, that blind comparison with others and giving oneself over to outside goals leads to a sense of internal disassociation, a fraudulent presentation to the world, a façade of reputation. This in turn often produces anxiety, worry, helplessness, and other negative feelings which weaken the person further and may even lead to insanity.

As long as two thousand years ago, Laozi already saw a similar phenomenon and admonished people return to the basics, to recover simplicity and live authentically. He uses terms like "simplicity" (*pu*) and "authentic" or "true" (*zhen*) to indicate the state people occupied as infants, how they started out without any molding or influence by outside visions and requirements. He also speaks of the natural so-being of things in themselves (*ziran*) and focuses on people's inherent nature (*xing*). Only by recovering their true inherent nature and returning to inherent simplicity can people realize their uniqueness in true authentic living. The *Daode jing* says:

> Know glory and keep to humility, be the ground of the world.
> As the ground of the world, universal virtue will suffuse you:
> You return to being perfectly simple! (ch. 28)[1]

> Let the people always follow these rules:
> Manifest plainness! Embrace simplicity!
> Reduce selfishness! Have few desires! (ch. 19)

The word for "simple" and "simplicity" used here is *pu*, which literally means "uncarved wood," the natural tree or rough timber before any processing, chopping, or carving. Laozi uses the term as a metaphor for the true self, telling people that life does not in fact consist of social status, material wealth, or other external things. Position, rank, and fame as much as plenty of goods and even wealth alone cannot make anyone happy, and there are numerous patients who are depressed despite their extreme wealth and superior status. Anyone who relies heavily on these in his or her life will have an overblown mask covering their true personality—a factor Carl Jung found true for many of his patients in the social elite.

For Laozi, only one who lives authentically in his or her inherent simplicity is a true human being, a fully upright man. As the text says, "He dwells in substance, not dilution; in reality, not glory—accepts one, rejects the other" (Addiss and Lombardo 1993, 38). The same passage, rendered slightly more literally, is: "He dwells in the fruit (reality), and does not rest with the flower (appearance); therefore, he rejects the one and accepts the other" (Chan 1963, 158). In other words, only by sticking with actual reality and recovering one's inner truth—through reverting to simplicity in all things and a returning to the basics—can one come to put down the mask and learn who one really is. This, in turn, will make it possible to live out one's original nature to the best of one's ability and find true authenticity. It is an excellent way out of the predicament of modern society and brings enormous relief.

This inner authenticity, moreover, leads to the ability to truly value others and support all people and all beings in their own quest for living truly. It re-

---

[1] Editor's note: Unless a specific translation is noted in parentheses, I provide my own. For a discussion of the numerous different, and different kinds of, translations of the *Daode jing*, see LaFargue and Pas 1998.

sults in an overall respect for people's different abilities and characteristics. As the text states:

> The sage
> is always there to help the people; he rejects no person.
> He is always there to help all beings; he rejects no creature.
> Thus it is said:
> he is at one with universal light. (ch. 27)

One who has realized authenticity is "at one with universal light," that is, with Dao. He is a sage (*shengren*)—what the *Zhuangzi* calls the perfected (*zhenren*): socially responsible, unassuming and nondescript in his person, yet entirely benevolent and helpful in all situations. He does not speak or preach but acts appropriately at all times. He may have a high position in society—and ideally is even the ruler (and thus, in ancient China, usually male)—but he will not think of himself as "possessing" anything, nor will he insist on his position, his way, or his personal wishes. On the contrary, his mind will be full of Dao, seeing the inherent patterns of nature and the world and thinking of the greater good of all. He is a representative of universal virtue, embracing all people and creatures and developing peace within and goodness without.

This also implies a great respect for the needs and abilities of others. Thus the *Zhuangzi* emphasizes that each being and species has its unique properties and specific tendencies: "Fish live in water, but people die in water." Applied to humanity, this means that each individual has his or her own strengths and limitations, through which he adapts to the nature of things. Everyone has some flaws when seen from a certain perspective, but everyone also has unique talents, abilities, and strengths. Focusing on one's shortcomings, trying to achieve things that one is not inherently able to accomplish, trying to get ahead in all sorts of social and professional arenas not only leads to extreme competitiveness, but also sets goals that are inherently impossible to achieve. Putting forth ever increasing efforts toward such goals can only lead to an ever intensifying fear of failure, to self-blame and self-anger, and eventually to utter mental and physical exhaustion,

It is, therefore, much better to put one's efforts into returning to the basics and delve deeply into oneself to recognize where one's strengths and talents really lie. For continued mental, physical, and social health it is essential that people in modern societies learn to see beyond the glorious image of the false and develop the courage to be true to themselves beyond all worldly bias and apparent rewards. They have to come to a correct understanding of the self, to fully accept this self, and live for and within their specific capabilities. In addition, from this position of inner security and empowerment, they must also come to respect other people's personalities, letting them live out their particular truth and giving everyone—especially those who depend on them, such as children, relatives, and employees—the space to develop freely and uniquely.

Between Heaven and Earth, each of us is unique and irreplaceable! Our uniqueness is a gift of Dao and nature which allows us to live out our true selves while taking excellent care of all the people and beings we come in contact with. We can indeed be truly ourselves and, by doing so, fully accomplish the mission given to us in the form of our unique talents and abilities—thereby to let the "universal light" of Dao shine ever more brilliantly!

Let Go of the Little Self

Living out one's destiny in true authenticity does not mean that one becomes self-centered, egotistic, and selfish. On the contrary, realizing our true inherent nature means that we can go beyond our limited little self and discover just to what degree we all complement each other, can be better people, improve ourselves, and greatly increase our pleasure in living. The little self, our acquired personality and social persona, with which we identify all too often, really is a just a great source of trouble. As the *Daode jing* says:

> The body-self is why I have terrible vexations.
> Without a body-self, what trouble would I have? (ch. 13)

What Laozi means here is that the reason why people have all sorts of worries, troubles, and concerns is that they pay much too much attention to themselves in their "body-self" (*shen*), which is a social construct different from their mere body as form and also from their inherent nature and destiny. The more they manage to lessen and loosen their attachment to this body-self, the more they reduce the intensity and quantity of personal grief, frustration, and inner tension. "Without a body-self, what trouble would I have?" Some schools of contemporary psychology agree with this general concept and offer treatments that lead people to find identity beyond the self-centered ego. The more this fades, moreover, the easier it is for them to shift their attention from themselves to others. This in turn will effectively remove all worry and anxiety. A classical example is found in people who have lost a loved one turning their grief into altruistic action, such as the woman who has lost her husband and now take care of orphans or other people in need.

The *Daode jing* formulates the dialectical relationship between self-distancing and social involvement as follows:

> The sage places his body-self last,
> but finds himself in the front of things;
> He puts his body-self outside,
> yet finds himself always involved.
> In fact,
> because he completely lacks any self-interest,
> he can always realize what is best for him. (ch. 7)

Superior leadership lies in placing one's own personal self-interests second to those of the people. This alone makes it possible for everyone to realize what is best for them. But, first of all, one must let go of one's body-self, forget all egoistic concerns, and open completely to thinking of and caring for others. This in turn will assure that everybody can realize his or her interests and create greater personal freedom, greater living space, and better survival for all. As the *Daode jing* says:

> The sage does not accumulate,
> The more he does for others, the more he gains himself
> The more he gives to others, the more he has himself.
> The way of heaven is to always benefit, never harm!
> The way of the sage is to always work, never compete! (ch. 81)

That is to say, doing things for others and thinking of others first not only helps the people, but also allows the individual to see his or her own personal value from the perspective of the greater good. This in turn brings inner joy and spiritual enrichment, greatly adding to the overall meaning of life.

Maintain Stillness

Recovering simplicity and returning to inner authenticity beyond the social construct of the body-self is first level of an inner transformation that allows us to find great meaning in self and life. It is means developing great respect and support for each individuals's personality and inherent nature, recognizing how we are all unique and different from others. We all have our particular personality style and inherent tendencies, such as being fundamenally extroverted or introverted, our specific way of managing self, life, and world.

On another, deeper level, this transformation means recognizing and activating our deepest inborn nature, which comes from and directly relates us to Dao. Dao as the underlying pattern of existence is common to all people, shared by the myriad beings, the fundamental unity of the world that creates harmony beneath all multiplicity. All people and creatures have the same structure as myself; all beings and things share the same root with me; the world and I spring from the same source. How, then, can I reach and live a level of authenticity that takes this ultimate unity into account?

The *Daode jing* says:

> Attain utmost emptiness, maintain perfect stillness.
> The myriad things arise together,
> and, I see, return to the same place.
> All things flourish, but each returns to its root.

> Return to the root means stillness.
> In stillness, we recover destiny.
> Recovering destiny, we find inner constancy,
> Having constancy, we shine forth.
> Not knowing constancy,
> we go astray and end in disaster. (ch. 16)

This indicates a method of meditation, not unlike the "sitting in oblivion" advocated in the *Zhuangzi*. The passage encourages us to become empty and open, quiet and still, to rest the numinous spirit of our hearts in a state of complete relaxation and inner peace. For a short period, we give ourselves permission to let go of conscious awareness, rational thinking, and sensory involvement with the outside world. We turn our attention inward and go back to the quiet contentment of our heart, finding the core of inner stillness, the true home of our spirit, our connection to Dao. Diligently attaining emptiness and maintaining stillness, we learn to bring the subtle powers of Dao into our life in all its different dimensions, to let the light of spirit shine forth brightly. This in turn allows us to make things grow without limit, come and go without stopping, and—most importantly—nurture, enhance, and preserve our unique destiny in the world. As the Japanese Zen master Daisetz Suzuki says,

> No great work has ever been accomplished . . . without breaking through the ordinary level of consciousness and letting loose the hidden powers lying further below. These powers may be devilish sometimes, but there is no doubt that they are superhuman and work wonders. When the unconscious is tapped, it rises above individual limitations. (1959, ch. 3)

Not only that, the power freed by connection to Dao and our inherent nature also effectively eliminates all tendencies toward fear and insecurity, providing a sense of inner stability that makes it impossible for other people's feelings and actions to disrupt or annoy us. "One learns to experience the world without anxiety or fear" (Suzuki 1933, 25). Mental stability increases, stress is released, and life improves.

A more detailed outline of early Daoist meditation appears in the "Neiye" 內業 (Inward Training) chapter of the *Guanzi* 管子 (Works of Master Guan). According to this, adepts sit in meditation to withdraw from sensory stimulation. They pursue the fourfold alignment of body, limbs, breath, and mind. First they take a proper upright posture and align their limbs, then they breathe deeply and consciously, regulating the breath and creating a sense of stillness within. From there they practice single-minded focus for the attainment of a tranquil mind, also described as the "cultivated," "stable," "excellent", and "well-ordered" mind. This well-ordered mind then creates an open space within, a lodging place for vital energy and spirit.

Once filled with their potency, adepts achieve complete balance in body and mind. They reach a level of simplicity that allows them to let go of things and be free from sensory overloads. Finding a state of serenity and repose in detachment from emotions, they walk through life in harmony with all, free from danger and harm. At peace within and in alignment with the world outside, they attain a level of physical and mental health that keeps them fit and active well into old age. Reaching beyond ordinary life, they gain a sense of cosmic freedom that allows them to "hold up the Great Circle [of the heavens] and tread firmly over the Great Square [of the earth]" (Roth 1999, 112-13).

In other words, the more we let go of the knowledge and skills, calculations and schemes habituated during socialization, the more our authentic self and true inherent nature begin to shine forth. Our perception and consciousness, now dominated by concepts of worldly organization and thoughts on how best to manage the activities of daily living, gradually return to an inner harmony and mental stability that allow decisions to arise from our heart while joining the internal rhythm that all human beings share with the universe. Unifying with Dao, we gain a sense of connection to and oneness with all beings, and our spirit—in conjunction with the greater universe—recovers its authentic being and maintains harmony in all situations.

Maintaining stillness forms the foundation: it allows the development of unlimited potential, stimulates creative thinking, and brings about the most effective functioning of the body. There is by now plenty of clinical evidence to show just how peaceful the mind can become, how healthy the body, and how much inherent well-being and goodness people can in fact attain. Scientific research has shown that the human brain brings forth wave signals at different frequencies: in a state of quietude and serenity, it has alpha waves that vacillate at 8-14 Hz per minute. This means that the brain consumes very little physical and mental energy, yet it operates at a rapid and smooth pace. Full of inspiration and intuition, lively and active, it is open to learning and thinking.

In a state of emptiness and deep meditation, people reach an even deeper level of relaxation that moves them further into the subconscious. The brain here oscillates in theta waves, at a frequency of the 4-8 Hz per minute. It is in a state that greatly supports creativity and allows inspiration to burst forth. People fully connect to their intuition and have great access to deep learning and clear memory. Maintaining stillness thus means to place the brain into a state of either alpha or theta waves. Allowing the person to experience themselves in their own small universe, completely at one with their deepest self and in harmony of the universe, it lets the mind rest and soothes the spirit, letting Dao flow freely and in deep peace. To "attain utmost emptiness and maintain perfect stillness" while letting go of all excessive pursuits of material goods and social status in society—Laozi's admonition "Reduce selfishness! Have few desires!" provides great inspiration.

Have Few Desires

A major topic in modern psychology is the great attachment people have to things outside, their intense involvement with outer goals, which causes an increasing alienation from their inner self and the spiritual life. In this context Avner Offer, the Chichile Professor of Economic History at Oxford University, notes that our enemy is not unemployment, poverty, terrorism, or the avian flu, but the overwhelming wealth that came with economic success:

> North America and Europe are about three times as wealthy as they were in 1950. I call that affluence. However, abundance and novelty cause harm as well. They displace the stock of pre-existing possessions, virtues, relations, and values. . . . Disorders abound—family breakdown, addiction, stress, road and landscape congestion, obesity, poverty, denial of health care, mental disorder, violence, economic fraud, and insecurity. Social critics warn that communities are unraveling and 'social capital' dissipating, interpersonal trust is declining, and subjective well-being is stagnant. (2006, 1-2).

People run after the fruits of success, but they rarely take the time and leisure to enjoy them; all they have is the idea of a happy, fulfilled life in their minds. Constantly buffered by the maelstrom, forever involved in the rat race of the strife for success, they have lost the ability to enjoy a simple life that alone offers the path to happiness.

In contrast, the Daoist sage is "free from desires and does not value rare goods" (ch. 77), developing an attitude that helps his own and the lives of others to move toward lasting happiness. As Laozi advocates having few desires, he insists, "To rule the people and serve Heaven, there is nothing better than to be frugal." This also means that the individual's "roots are deep and stalks are firm, leading to long life and eternal vision" (ch. 59; Chan 1963, 167-68). To him, there is "no calamity greater than not knowing when it is enough" (ch. 46), while "true wealth is to know" just that (ch. 33). It provides an inner sense of security. To wake people up, Laozi vigorously questions modern values:

> Which means more to you—
> you or your renown?
> Which brings more to you—
> you or what you own?
> And which would cost you more
> if it were gone? (ch. 44; Bynner 1944, 73)

Forever running after wealth, power, and sensory pleasures, giving in to insatiable desires, people today have lost all perspective and become materialistic and unscrupulous. Overwhelmed by material goods and outside involvement, they are disconnected from their original purpose and have lost their basic mental stability. The unbounded pursuit of material comfort causes endless

trouble and an overwhelming tiredness in body and mind. The only way out is
to change our internal values and cognitive patterns. Laozi says:

> Knowing when it is enough, there is no shame;
> knowing when to stop, there is no peril. (ch. 44).

He strongly advocates that people give up the pursuit of material goods and
fancy living conditions, instead selecting an approach to life that helps them to
reduce stress. As he notes:

> The more taboos and prohibitions there are in the world,
> The poorer the people will be.
> The more sharp weapons the people have,
> The more troubled the state will be.
> The more cunning and skill people possess,
> The more vicious things will appear.
> The more laws and orders are made prominent,
> The more thieves and robbers there will be.
>
> Therefore, the sage says:
> I take no action, and the people are naturally transformed.
> I rest in stillness, and the people become naturally upright.
> I engage in no activity, and the people become naturally prosperous.
> I have no desires, the people of become naturally simple. (ch. 57; see
> Liu 1998, 219)

Here he links "having few desires" with "maintaining stillness," allowing people
to find peace within and get away from the pursuit of outside goals and the
manifold distractions of their heart. Providing relief of psychological problems
caused by intense involvement with material goods, they gain great freedom of
mind. This, in turn, results in an attitude to the world described as nonaction.

Practice Nonaction

Modern society is characterized by fierce competition. The challenges people
face, their failure to accomplish set goals, the frustration of daily living they
have to contend with cause endless anxiety and worry. Nonaction (wuwei 無爲)
is one way to resolve this. It does not mean doing nothing, becoming like a
vegetable, or being utterly spontaneous without any planning whatsoever.
Rather, it means letting go of egotistic concerns and materialistic desires on the
personal level, finding a sense of where life, nature, and the world are headed
on the social level, and abstaining from forceful and interfering measures in the
political realm. As the text says:

> Act on things and you will ruin them.
> Grasp for things and you will lose them.
> Therefore, the sage acts with nonaction and has no ruin,
> Lets go of grasping and has no loss.
> (ch. 64; Henricks 2000, A:6)

In traditional China this idea was mainly applied in politics, but over the years people have also found it helpful in ordinary life. Liu Xiaogan, in one of several discussions of naturalness and nonaction as understood today (1991; 1998; 2001), presents the case of a farmer who is about to modernize his farm. If the farmer looks around and finds many modern methods being applied, understands the rationale behind them and their advantages for everyone concerned, and if he has both the time to investigate the new methods and the money to make the investment, then the time is right and things in all likelihood will proceed smoothly.

If, on the other hand, he works only for egotistic profit to the detriment of everyone else, or if a government or corporation forces him to change his basic methods at a time when he has neither time for exploration nor money to invest, then he is likely headed for trouble and disaster. "The principle of naturalness," Liu says, "always prefers inner dynamism to external force" (1998, 223). Nonaction accordingly means that things grow and develop in their own way and to the benefit of all, and that human beings have to find alignment with the natural patterns to fulfill themselves and avoid harming others and the world at large.

Flow with Life

Another dimension of nonaction is the understanding of life as a flow, as part of Dao as continuous movement in various phases of up and down. In terms of personal application, in modern societies full of intense strife and ruthless competition, this means realizing how circumstances and opportunities change, learning about good and bad fortune in their mutually dialectic interchange. It means developing the true wisdom of living authentically.

Dao is the source of all things, the underlying force, the overarching law that pervades all beings. It is also the law inherent in the unfolding and development of things. Dao has its own dynamic pattern, its particular rules of change and transformation. What, then, are these rules? The *Daode jing* says:

> Reversion is the action of Dao;
> weakness is the function of Dao.
> All things in the world come from being;
> and all being comes from nonbeing.
> (ch. 40; Chan 1963, 160)

This means that all things and all creatures, although present and existing in the world, ultimately come from and return to the underlying ground of the cosmos—Dao, nonbeing, the ultimate. Also, under the eternal, all pervasive guidance of Dao each of these beings moves forward and reverts to its root in an ongoing cycle of transformation, a transformation that is soft and weak and flowing. Therefore, everything in the world is impermanent, changeable, in continuous flux: it is neither good nor bad. As the text has:

> Bad fortune rests upon good fortune;
> good luck hides within bad luck.
> Who knows their limit?
> There is nothing proper or wayward at all times:
> proper reverts to being slanted,
> good turns into disastrous. (ch. 58)

In other words, all things are interdependent and subject to complex transformations: a near disaster often contains the seeds of blessings while a spate of good luck eventually ends and may turn into ill. All good and bad fortune, gain and loss, success and failure are just aspects of the ongoing transformation of things, the ever-changing pattern of Dao. The only true way of being in the world is by holding on to one's inner authenticity while flowing along with change in all aspects of life.

The various immediate difficulties we face in life are thus part of larger, ongoing process; they do not represent life's ultimate purpose or outcome. They show us that the world is never absolutely good or bad, that energy constantly changes from proper to wayward and back again. This in turn means that when we look at our current experiences of negative events from a different, wider, Dao-based perspective, we find positive elements in them and gain new values. A run of bad fortune, a period of ill health, a series of frustrations are certainly painful and seem cruel, but life means personal growth and the exploration of new dimensions. Seeing things from this angle, our experience can temper the will, build character, and enhance wisdom. It allows us to gain a more accurate grasp of who we are and where our true authenticity lies. It provides a more careful understanding of the environment and promotes our becoming stronger and more mature.

For this reason, pain and difficulties—what Laozi calls "bad fortune"—are great assets to life. Understanding this at a deep level, we can turn the tables on misfortune. Seeing how being and nonbeing constantly produce and succeed each other, flowing with life through all good and bad fortune allows people to live the wisdom of continuous transformation. It opens us to see failures as opportunities for recovery and weaknesses as the starting point of self-realization, thus leading to a positive attitude toward life rather than feelings of frustration or depression. It also makes us realize that success and advantages are temporary fruits of our labors and the right circumstances, so that we do not get carried away. Thus, we can be like the perfected in the *Zhuangzi*: without resentment when in a lowly situation, free from pride in success, never plotting our affairs; we can be without regret if things go wrong and remain free from self-congratulations when they go well (ch. 6). Or, as the *Daode jing* says:

> The most fruitful outcome does not depend on force,
> but succeeds without arrogance:
> without hostility, without pride,
> without resistance, without violence.
> (ch. 30; Addiss and Lombardo 1993, 30)

Flowing with life is the key vision of ancient Daoist thought, combining a strong sense of inner authenticity with the appreciation of the vagaries of life. It can be applied in modern life along the lines of cognitive therapy. As described by Albert Ellis (1975) and Aaron Beck (1975), cognitive or rational emotive behavior therapy seeks to help the patient overcome difficulties by identifying and changing dysfunctional thinking, behavior, and emotional responses. It works, just as ancient Daoist thought, by modifying beliefs, identifying distorted thinking, relating to others in different ways, and changing behaviors. The goal in both cases is a greater sense of inner authenticity reached through the appreciation of how one's thoughts and perceptions color emotions and lead to certain kinds of behavior, how certain ways of being in the world are unhelpful and dysfunctional and can be replaced by more appropriate and life-enhancing attitudes. The main difference is that ancient Daoists worked with an elaborate cosmology and were secure in their trust in Dao as the ubiquitous and ever-supportive ground of being. Just connecting to the root of all existence lies at the core of the Daoist path to authentic living—all other methods, conceptions, and guidelines serving as support systems, different routes to the same all-embracing thoroughfare.

Bibliography

Addiss, Stephen, and Stanley Lombardo. 1993. *Tao Te Ching*. Indianapolis: Hackett Publishing Company.

Allan, Sarah, and Crispin Williams, eds. 2000. *The Guodian Laozi*. Berkeley: Institute of East Asian Studies.

Beck, Aaron T. 1975. *Cognitive Therapy and the Emotional Disorders*. New York: International Universities Press.

Bynner, Witter. 1944. *The Way of Life According to Lao tsu*. New York: Perigree.

Chan, Wing-tsit. 1963. *A Source Book in Chinese Philosophy*. Princeton: Princeton University Press.

Ellis, Albert. 1975. *A New Guide to Rational Living*. New York: Prentice Hall.

Fromm, Erich. 1956. *The Art of Loving*. New York: Harper.

Henricks, Robert. 1989. *Lao-Tzu: Te-Tao ching*. New York: Ballantine.

_____. 2000. *Lau Tzu's Tao Te Ching: A Translation of the Startling New Documents Found at Guodian*. New York: Columbia University Press.

Kohn, Livia, and Michael LaFargue, eds. 1998. *Lao-tzu and the Tao-te-ching*. Albany: State University of New York Press.

LaFargue, Michael. 1992. *The Tao of the Tao-te-ching*. Albany: State University of New York Press.

_____, and Julian Pas. 1998. "On Translating the *Tao-te-ching*. In *Lao-tzu and the Tao-te-ching*, edited by Livia Kohn and Michael LaFargue, 277-302. Albany: State University of New York Press.

Liu, Xiaogan. 1991. "*Wuwei* (Non-Action): From *Laozi* to *Huainanzi*." *Taoist Resources* 3.1: 41-56.

_____. 1998. "Naturalness (*Tzu-jan*), the Core Value in Taoism: Its Ancient Meaning and Its Significance Today." In *Lao-tzu and the Tao-te-ching*, edited by Livia Kohn and Michael LaFargue, 211-28. Albany: State University of New York Press.

_____. 2001. "Nonaction and the Environment Today: A Conceptual and Applied Study of Laozi's Philosophy." In *Daoism and Ecology: Ways Within a Cosmic Landscape*, edited by Norman Girardot, James Miller, and Liu Xiaogan, 315-40. Cambridge, Mass.: Harvard University Press, Center for the Study of World Religions.

Offer, Avner. 2006. *The Challenge of Affluence: Self-control and Well-being in the United States and Britain since 1950*. Oxford: Oxford University Press.

Roth, Harold D. 1999. *Original Tao: Inward Training and the Foundations of Taoist Mysticism*. New York: Columbia University Press.

Suzuki, Daisetz T. 1933. *Essays in Zen Buddhism: Second Series*. London: Rider & Co.

_____. 1959. *Zen and Japanese Culture*. New York: Pantheon Books.

The Zhuangzi

A Holistic Approach to Healthcare and Well-being

The ancient classic Zhuangzi offers various methods to deal with the adaptive problem of chronic stress, related to 60 to 90 percent of all office visits to medical doctors. It comes with specific physical and psychological symptoms, connected to acute (allostasis) and chronic (allostatic load) activation of the fight-or-flight response. The Zhuangzi has much to offer to stress management, clearly addressing the adaptive problem of chronic stress while offering an adaptive solution, focused on chronic primal thinking, which results in health and well-being. It proposes a psycho-educational, holistic (mind, body, and environment) approach that incorporates personal responsibility, simplification of life style, cognitive re-structuring, and various self-cultivation and self-refinement techniques that still and empty the mind-and-heart. All these result in the elimination of chronic stress and the physical and psychological disorders associated with it.

The border guard of Changwu said to Zilao, "As a ruler do not be unrefined and uncultivated. When governing the people, do not be reckless and careless. In the past, when I planted grain, my plowing was not deep. Because I plowed in this manner, my crop was shabby. My weeding was inadequate. Because I weeded in this manner, my crop was inadequate. The next year, I changed my methods and was extremely attentive. I plowed deeply and skillfully weeded. The crop was bountiful. I had more than I could eat for an entire year."

Upon hearing this, Zhuangzi said, "People today treat their body and regulate their mind much in the same manner that the border guard described. They retreat from the natural world (*tian* 天), are separate from their own nature (*xing* 性), extinguish their natural feelings (*qing* 情), and have lost their spirit (*shen* 神) in order to be part of the affairs of the multitude. For those whose nature is unrefined and uncultivated, the seeds of likes and dislikes will grow like reeds in their nature. In the beginning, as they sprout, they are taken to be helpful to the body. At the end they have pulled the individual out of his or her nature. Merging, they fester and then burst out spreading throughout the body. Ulcerations, pus, internal fever and congealed urine are what occur.[1] (ch. 25; Guo 1974, 452-53)

This passage from the ancient Daoist text *Zhuangzi* provides a graphic description of what may occur if individuals allow socially contrived absolute thoughts, concepts, judgments, and values to interfere with or stress their own nature. It also suggests a solution for physical and psychological healthcare, which is focused on individual responsibility for health and well-being through a process of attentiveness, concentration, commitment, cognitive restructuring, self-cultivation, and self-refinement.

Healthcare and Stress

Utilizing research-based evidence, the medical doctor Herbert Benson noted, in his 1998 testimony before the United States Senate, that symptoms reported in 60 to 90 percent of all office visits to medical doctors in the United States are associated, primarily, with chronic stress (Kroenke and Manglesdorff 1989, 265; Soebel 1995, 234-239; Benson 1998; Santee 2008). He also stated that it was not possible to explain these symptoms or treat these stress-related illnesses from a disease-based or medical-model perspective that relies on surgery and drugs (Benson 1998). In 2010, the American Institute of Stress has estimated that 75 to 90 percent of all primary care office visits to medical doctors are stress-related (2010a; 2010b).

A high percentage, according to the evidence, of chronic illnesses, both physical and psychological, are associated with chronic stress (NIH 2004; 2010; NIMH 2009a; 2009b; American Academy of Family Physicians 2010; Mayo Clinic 2010a; 2010b). Cardiovascular disease, cancer, high blood pressure, asthma, gastro-intestinal disorders, suppression of the immune system, as well as immunological diseases, neurodegenerative diseases, anxiety, and depression are all linked with chronic stress (Esch et al. 2002a, RA99; Esch et al. 2003; Benson and Casey 2008, 35-39; Santee 2010). Chronic stress not only exacerbates anxiety and depression but also, according to the research, may cause them (Esch et al. 2002b, 206; Benson and Casey 2008, 6).

Stress is normal. The stress response, also known as the fight-or-flight response has both physical consequences (rapid or shallow breathing and in-

---

[1] All translations or interpretations of the *Zhuangzi* and its commentaries are my own, based on Guo 1974. The text *Zhuangzi*, consisting of 33 chapters, is attributed to, at least in part (chs. 1-7 and possibly 16-27), to a man named Zhuang Zhou or as he is commonly referred to as Zhuangzi (4th-3rd c. B.C.E.). He is the second major thinker in early Daoism only behind the legendary Laozi (5th c. B.C.E.) the purported author of the *Daode jing*. A brief discussion of the text can be found in Kohn 2000.

creased heart rate) and psychological changes (increased anxiety). These effects were selected, through the process of evolution, because they allowed our distant ancestors to become aware of, respond to, and resolve acute adaptive problems or threats, such as survival and reproduction, in various environmental contexts (Benson 1975, 24; Santee 2007a, 2008; Buss 2008; Confer et al. 2010; Santee 2010). It worked.

However, the fight-or-flight response and all of its subsequent physical and psychological changes did not evolve to address chronic threats (Stefano et al. 2001, 7). Its chronic activation (i.e., chronic stress) is harmful both physically and psychologically to the individual (Stefano et al. 2001, 7; Kemeny 2003, 126). That chronic stress is prevalent is made quite clear by the 2009 *Stress in America Survey* by the American Psychological Association. It indicates that 75 percent of the sample (N = 1,568 adults) reported moderate (51 percent) to high levels (24 percent) of stress (APA 2009).

While the fight-or-flight response evolved to address real physical threats, the brain does not make a distinction between a real physical and a psychosocial threat generated by our misperception, imagination, and/or thinking. In either case, the fight-or-flight response will be activated. In fact, the majority of the threats we perceive today are psychosocial in nature, chronic, self-generated through our thinking; they activate the fight-or-flight response inappropriately (Deckro et al. 2000, 282; Sapolsky 2001, 7-8; Stefano et al. 2001, 7; Casey et al. 2009, 231).

Normal stress (allostasis) is beneficial as the activation of the fight-or-flight response assists us in solving acute, real, physical, adaptive problems or threats. Once this has been resolved, the stress response turns off and the body returns to its natural, relaxed state. The chronic activation, due primarily to dysfunctional thinking, of the fight-or-flight response or chronic stress (allostatic load), on the other hand, is not beneficial: the physical and psychological changes it generates provide no assistance in addressing the perceived problem or threat (McEwen 2002, 5-10). In addition, it does not turn off until the individual stops thinking about the self-generated threat

When the flight-or-fight response is activated, in addition to the physical changes that occur, there are psychological changes: hyper-vigilance, hyper-arousal, and increased levels of anxiety. They occur for keeping the individual aware of the perceived acute threat and thus enhance his or her chances of survival. A specific type of thinking, also part of our evolutionary survival tool-kit, occurs to keep the individual free from distractions and focused upon the perceived threat for the purpose of resolving it either by fleeing, freezing, or fighting. This type of thinking is self-centered, absolute, biased, black and white, dichotomous (win or lose; die or survive; right or wrong; good or bad; etc.), inflexible, mechanical, and automatic. It occurs within milliseconds and is not consciously chosen as is reflective or contemplative thinking: it is called primal thinking (Beck and Weishaar 2005, 239, 245, 248).

Primal thinking is quite problematic, however, when it is inappropriately activated by a self-generated threat, which is psychosocial, imagined, unrealistic, and/or insoluble (Beck and Weishaar 2005, 239, 248). It is then dysfunctional as it compromises normal reasoning, keeps the mind agitated by maintaining the self-generated threat, and will not turn off until the individual stops thinking about the self-generated threat.[2] Its inappropriate activation is the cause of the continual or chronic rumination about irresolvable events in the past and the continual or chronic worrying about events in the future. Primal thinking generates the absolute, black-and-white musts, shoulds, and oughts within the context of how you must think and behave, how others must think and behave, and how the environment or world must behave (Ellis 2003, 32-34; Santee 2008).

It is this primal thinking, although it is not called as such, that the *Zhuangzi* addresses through what is essentially a psycho-educational, holistic (mind, body, and environment) approach. This incorporates personal responsibility, life-style simplification, cognitive restructuring, and self-cultivation or self-refinement techniques that still the mind and lead to the elimination of chronic stress and the physical and psychological disorders associated with it.

The Zhuangzi

To utilize the teachings of the *Zhuangzi* to address healthcare issues it is necessary to determine if there is a commonality between the text and the research linking thinking, perceived threats, chronic stress, and physical and psychological disorders. That life is perceived as stressful and threatening is clearly indicated in the following passage:

> Once a person receives his or her body, it is not forgotten until it is used up. Interaction with things is that of destruction and waste. This goes on until exhaustion like a galloping horse unable to stop. Is this not sad? All one's life is one of labor and toil, not seeing the results of your work. So tired, exhausted, and weary, not knowing to where you will return. How can this not be tragic? People say they are not dead. Of what benefit is this? Your form changes and your heart-mind goes along with it. Is it possible not to call this a great tragedy? (ch. 2; Guo 1974, 35)

---

[2] Cognitive therapists Beck and Weischaar (2005, 247) refer to this dysfunctional thinking as cognitive distortions. For an extensive list of cognitive distortions, see Emotional Competency (2010). Cognitive therapists Ellis and MacLaren (2003) refer to this dysfunctional thinking as irrational thoughts. For a brief discussion of the cognitive therapy of Ellis and Beck, see Santee (2008, 98-100).

This suggests chronic physical and psychological stress. The uncertainty or threat of not knowing what occurs after you die, of not knowing the meaning or purpose of life is certainly indicative of continual anxiety and worry and thus chronic psychological stress. The portrayal of ongoing labor and toil, and the descriptors of tired, exhausted and weary, moreover, are indicative of chronic physical stress.

The link between dysfunctional thinking, chronic stress, and physical and psychological harm is described as follows:

> That which is respected in the world is wealth, status, longevity and approval. That which a person enjoys is a comfortable life, tasty food, beautiful clothes, pleasant sights and sweet sounds. That which is not respected is poverty, dishonor, dying young and disapproval. That which is viewed as suffering is a person that is not comfortable, a mouth that does not have tasty food, a body that does not have beautiful clothes, eyes that do not have pleasant sights and ears that do not have sweet sounds. Because of the fear of not attaining these, there is overwhelming stress (*dayou* 大憂). Those who treat the body in this way are indeed foolish.
>
> Now for those who are rich, the person suffers and is made ill as they accumulate more wealth then they can possibly use. Those who treat the body in this manner are fragmented. Now, those who hold a position of high status are troubled, day and night, about good and bad. Those who treat their body in this manner are out of touch. People are born and all of life is a participation in stress (*you* 憂).[3] Those who seek a long life are of a confused mind. They are chronically stressed (*jiuyou* 久憂) about death. Why suffer? To treat the body in this manner is to be far away from it. (ch. 18; Guo 1974, 317)

The commentaries by Guo Xiang 郭象 (252-312) and Cheng Xuanying 成玄英 (fl. 631-652) to this passage reinforce the link between dysfunctional thinking, chronic stress, and physical and psychological harm to the individual.[4] Guo Xiang states: "If all of these are let go, the body is not affected. Yet if you attain them your very nature is harmed. Nowadays everything is reversed. If you do

---

[3] The character *you* 憂 is translated and interpreted as "stress." The components of or definitions of this character suggest a compromised heart-mind. This stress clearly interferes with the functioning of both body and mind. That it is chronic is made clear in this passage where the author notes that stress pervades one's entire life (*all of life is a participation in stress*). That stress is overwhelming, physically and psychologically, is clearly expressed in this passage through the use of the concept *dayou* or "great," "extended," or "large stress." That the author was aware of the relationship between dysfunctional thinking, chronic stress, and suffering is evident in this passage, where thinking about avoiding death, which is the primal fear or threat, is associated with "long lasting stress" (*jiuyou*) and physical and psychological "suffering" (*ku*).

[4] For a discussion of the philosophy of Guo Xiang, see Kohn (1992, 69-80). For an inquiry into understanding the *Zhuangzi* during the Tang dynasty through the commentary of Cheng Xuanying, see Yu 2000.

not attain them you become stressed (*you*). This is foolish" (Guo 1974, 317). Cheng says similarly:

> All of these things are not beneficial to people. Yet the prevalent fashion is that if you do not attain them you are suffering. . . Now, those who have positions of high status are deeply stressed (*you*) as they worry about their future good fortune. Thus day and night their ruminations about doing good and avoiding evil fatigue their bodies and frighten their heart-minds. Is it not careless to treat the body constantly in this manner? (Guo 1974, 317)

The physical and psychological symptoms associated with chronic stress and primal thinking are further made clear in the following passage regarding people in general. It links together threat-based, compromised, agitated, opinionated thinking, absolute judgments, disturbed sleep, distractibility, and emotional disturbance:

> When a person is asleep, the mind is entangled. When the person is conscious, the body is tense. Interacting in the world creates entanglements. Daily their heart-minds battle: plodding, concealing, and tentative. Their small fears result in apprehensiveness. Their large fears result in being overwhelmed or depressed. In judging right and wrong, their words shoot out as if an arrow was released from a bow. They hold onto their judgments as if they were sacred oaths. Guarding what they call their victory, they are executed like autumn moving into winter. (ch. 2; Guo 1974, 31)

Cheng's commentary to the first two lines is revealing psychologically, as it links a stressed mind to disturbed sleep and physical illness:

> When a person is awake, the mind races about, is agitated, covets and is restrictive. As a result, the person dreams when asleep. Because the mind is agitated, the understanding is entangled. Consequently the body is vulnerable or tense and gets infected with illness and disease (*ran* 染). (Guo 1974, 31)

The Authentic Person

Zhuangzi not only links dreaming with chronic stress, but also firmly establishes that chronic stress is a fundamental adaptive problem for all human beings. He emphasizes this in a discussion comparing the stress-free breathing of the authentic person, a Daoist role model, with the chronically stressed breathing of everyone else. He says:

> What is meant by an authentic person? The authentic person of ancient times was not opposed to being without, did not brag about his accomplishments, and did not meddle in the affairs of others. This being so, he did not regret when he

was wrong and was not conceited when correct. He did not tremble when ascending heights, did not get wet when entering water, and did not get hot when entering fire. Such is his knowledge of being able to ascend and draw near to Dao.

The authentic person of ancient times slept without dreaming, was not chronically stressed (*you*) when awake, and ate without indulging. The authentic person breathes from the heels. All other people breathe from their throats. Being restricted, the words in their throats are like retching, their desires longstanding and deep, and their inherent nature shallow.

The authentic person of ancient times did not know life to be ecstatic or death to be dreaded. Emerging he was not joyful. Returning he was not resistant. He was carefree in his going and coming. He did not forget the place of his beginning nor seek the place of his end. Accepting life, he was happy. Forgetting life, he returned. This is called not using the heart-mind to abandon Dao. Not using people to assist nature. This is called the authentic person. (ch. 6; Guo 1074, 123-24)

Thus, the authentic person does not dream. This is because his mind is not agitated with expectations, desires, worries, wishes, hopes, and fears. Not engaging in continual threat-based, primal thinking, he is not chronically stressed. Guo's commentary further indicates that the reason for this lack of dreaming is that "he does not have expectations" (Guo 1974, 124). The authentic person essentially has a stress-free, restful sleep. Since there is nothing on his mind when he goes to sleep, he does not dream. Cheng's sub-commentary further supports this insight:

> Those who dream have vain hopes and unsatisfied wishes. The authentic person is without emotions and has cut off all deliberation. Therefore, when he sleeps he is anchored in a quiet place and does not dream. (ch. 6; Guo 1974, 124)

In other words, the authentic person is not chronically stressed when asleep, is not chronically stressed when awake, and is not chronically stressed when he eats or during other activities of life. The strongest indicator of this state is his breathing, which is deep unlike that of the multitude who breathe rapidly and shallowly. Ongoing rapid, uneven, disturbed, coarse, and shallow breathing is indicative of chronic stress. Guo's commentary notes that the breathing of the multitude of people is "uneven and coarse" (Guo 1974, 124).

Guo also comments on not being chronically stressed while awake: "Accepting whatever is encountered, he is at peace." Cheng adds: "To the extent that you realize that everything is what it is, you will be without stress" (*you*) (Guo 1974, 124). The authentic person essentially accepts what life has to offer. He does not try to create an artificial, absolute, dichotomous, value laden, egocentric edifice that hides the continually changing process of existence. He is not engaged in continual, threat-based, primal thinking. By realizing and accepting existence for what it is, not trying to coerce or interfere, and thus identifying with it, he is at peace and without chronic stress. This is evident in the fact that when he eats, "he simply eats." He is not distracted by anything and he does not savor or relish what he ingests (Guo 1974, 124).

While the authentic person is not chronically stressed and thus does not suffer from the various associated physical and psychological disorders, unfortunately everyone else, at least from Zhuangzi's perspective, is and does. This being the case, the multitude of people when the text was written and the people of today are essentially the same insofar as they are all chronically stressed. What, then, is the solution the *Zhuangzi* offers to address this situation? How is it implemented?

The text is very clear: simply be empty! That is all! Empty of artificial, contrived absolute, abstract values and desires such as fame and status; empty of entanglements with society; empty of artificial, contrived, abstract, absolute thoughts, concepts, dichotomies, thinking, and knowledge. Essentially, be empty of all threat-based, chronic primal thinking and the contrived desires associated with it. It says:

> Do not be a corpse of fame. Do not be a residence of schemes. Do not be controlled by interactions. Do not be ruled by knowledge. Live your life in the endless and roam in the boundless. Use up that which you received from nature, and do not see any attainment. Be empty (*xu* 虛), that is all! The actualized person (*zhiren* 至人) uses the heart-mind like a mirror.[5] Neither leading nor welcoming. Responding and not storing. Thus, they are able to succeed without being harmed. (ch. 7; Guo 1974, 165)

The individual who is free from chronic stress, therefore, accepts existence for what it is: a continual process of change. As such there is nothing to hold on to or possess, because everything changes anyway. Like a mirror, when engaging existence there is interaction and reflection or response. There are, however, no absolute value judgments about or dwelling upon the interaction. Once the engagement has concluded, there is nothing left to hold on to or possess. Nothing has been stored to ruminate upon or worry about. Thus there is no foundation for chronic stress.

The solution being to become empty, how does one do so? What is the process leading to emptiness? In this regard, the *Zhuangzi* offers several integrated and interrelated methods of cognitive restructuring, attitude change, behavioral change, and meditation.

---

[5] The *zhiren* is another name for the *zhenren*; see Robinet 2008, 879-81.

Cognitive Restructuring

The focus of the cognitive restructuring that is used in the *Zhuangzi* is quite different from that used by cognitive therapists today, such as Ellis and Beck. They tend to focus on the specific problem (emotional, behavioral, or interpersonal) that brought the client into therapy and the irrational thoughts (Ellis) or cognitive distortions (Beck) that maintain it. Once the problem has been resolved by changing the dysfunctional thinking, the client returns to his or her social environment to reengage with life in a more functional manner (Ellis 2005; Beck and Weishaar 2005).

The focus in the *Zhuangzi* is comparatively much more global in nature. It restructures how the individual thinks about existence while clearly noting that society with its absolute, abstract, contrived dichotomies, standards, values, theories, norms, desires, expectations, rituals, and rules is the primary source of the dysfunctional thinking. Not only does it empty out the individual of these obstructions, but it also focuses on changing the individual's attitude about engaging existence and thus his or her behavior. From the perspective of the *Zhuangzi*, the approach of the cognitive therapists would be woefully inadequate in addressing the problem of chronic stress: only partial in nature, it does not address the root of the problem, which is society itself.

Probably the most fundamental fear or threat, and thus the primary source of chronic stress, to human beings is knowing that they will die while not knowing what happens after. In order to address this fear or threat, societies have created various absolute concepts, standards, values, ritualistic procedures, and organizations that, in theory, resolve the issue of uncertainty and allow the individual to deny change and live forever in some eternal realm.

The issue of death is a fundamental concern. The *Zhuangzi* contains numerous stories and tales about how to change our thinking or attitude about death and thus remove the chronic stress associated with it.[6] For example:

> Zhuangzi's wife died. Huizi came to condole and found Zhuangzi sitting on the floor, with his legs spread apart, beating on a basin and singing. Huizi said, "You have lived together, raised children, and grown old. That you do not weep is one thing. But beating a basin and singing, isn't that going too far?"
>   Zhuangzi replied, "Not so! When she first died, how could I alone not be like others? Examining her beginnings, she originally was without life. Not moving, without life, originally without form. Not moving, without form, originally without *qi* 氣. Undifferentiated! Suddenly, within the obscurity a change and

---

[6] Stories, tales and discussions of death as inevitable, the acceptance of it, and simply being another change, as is life, in an ongoing process can be found in numerous chapters such as 2-6, 18, and 22. Graham (1981, 84), Ames (1998, 13), and Coyle (1998, 204-205) argue that the central focus of ch. 6 is on resolving the issue of death.

there is *qi*. *Qi* changes and there is form. Form changes and there is life. Now, another change and there is death.

"This is the movement of the four seasons. Spring, autumn, winter and summer waiting on each other. She is presently lying down at rest in a gigantic room. Yet if I followed those who shouted and wept, I would consider myself as not understanding my destiny. Thus, I stopped!" (ch. 18; Guo 1974, 319-20)

Huizi sees Zhuangzi's behavior as socially inappropriate. It is bad enough that Zhuangzi is not weeping, but to sit with his legs spread apart—like a lunatic or a demon--beating on a basin, and singing at the death of an individual, especially his wife, violates societal norms, expectations, and rituals. Huizi's expectations are: 1) Zhuangzi must behave according to the norms of society; 2) Zhuangzi must behave according to the expectations of Huizi; and 3) Huizi himself, must behave according to the norms of society.[7] This rigid, inflexible primal thinking of Huizi is generated by the perceived threat and thus the fear of his own death. He must maintain these absolute standards, norms, and rituals regarding death to protect himself psychologically from the inevitability of, and the uncertainty associated with, his own death. This is why he became so stressed when Zhuangzi did not behave as expected.

Zhuangzi, on the other hand, felt sad about the death of his wife, which is a normal reaction. Yet, he still accepted her death as being part of the natural process of change. Thus he was not confined or controlled by the absolute unchanging norms, standards, and rituals of society. His thinking, attitude, and behavior, unlike that of Huizi, were consistent with the continually changing behavior of existence. Thus, the cognitive restructuring of the *Zhuangzi* removes or empties out the mind of society's absolute, abstract, threat-based, rigid, and dichotomous thinking regarding death and thus changes our attitude and behavior toward death—and, by extension, toward life and society itself. Zhuangzi was not agitated in his mind by thoughts of death: he was not chronically stressed.

The *Zhuangzi* in this context points out variously that, although language is functional, it has limitations (see ch. 2). It points out that holding on to absolute, abstract, artificial concepts, theories, desires (such as fame and fortune), and dichotomies (right or wrong, good or bad) is harmful physically and psychologically. This is made clear in another dialogue with Huizi:

Huizi said to Zhuangzi, "Is man originally without feelings?"
"It is so."
"If man is without feelings, how can you call him a man?"

---

[7] The must-based expectations of Huizi are a prime example of the must-based irrational thinking addressed by the cognitive therapist Ellis. See Ellis and MacLaren 2003, 32-34; Santee 2008, 99-100.

"Dao allows appearance, nature allows form, how can this attainment not be called a man?"

"Since he is already called a man, how can he be without feelings?"

"Right and wrong is that which evokes feelings. That which I call being without feelings is man not using the words good and bad to internally injure himself, always being natural, and not adding on to his life."

Huizi said, "Not adding on to his life, how can his body exist?"

Zhuangzi replied, "Dao allows appearance, nature allows form, and not using good and bad to internally injure his body. Now you forget your spirit, strain your essence, lean on a tree, sing, hold your lute and shut your eyes. Nature chose your form, yet you use it to cry out about hard and white." (Guo 1974, 119-21)

For Zhuangzi, there are natural feelings and artificial feelings. The authentic person has natural feelings and is free from artificial ones. Artificial feelings are excessive and evoked by absolute, abstract concepts and dichotomies such as right/wrong and good/bad. Cheng's commentary notes:

That which evokes feelings is right and wrong, yours and mine, good and bad, abhorrence and adoration, etc. If he is without right and wrong, etc., although he has form and appearance, he truly is a person whose feelings will not be evoked. (Guo 1974, 120)

Attitude and Behavioral Change

The *Zhuangzi* restructures thinking, attitude, and behavior and changes one's perceptions of the landscape of life by focusing on individuals that society marginalizes, ostracizes, and often simply ignores. It has many tales (esp. in chs. 4-7, 29) where the deformed, the disabled, the impaired, the crippled, the mentally deranged, and the criminal are portrayed as enlightened. In contrast, those supposedly enlightened (such as Confucius) appear as inferior to them. The goal, then, is to restructure the individual's attitude and perceptions by removing society-imposed absolute, restrictive, and limiting biases, judgments, values, and assumptions. When this occurs, obstructions are removed, the heart-mind flows freely, and chronic stress ends:

In the state of Lu, there was a man called Wangtai who, because of punishment for a crime, had one foot cut off. His followers were equal in numbers to those of Confucius. . . . Changji, a disciple of Confucius, said, "If this criminal who has had a foot cut off is superior to my Master (Confucius), how far superior he must be to the common person. This being so, in what unique way does he use his heart-mind?" Confucius said, "Life and death are great concerns, yet he does not allow these changes to bother him. If Heaven and Earth were to collapse, he would not regret it. He examines things without being artificial and does not alter them. As it is the destiny of things to change on their own he guards his root." (ch. 5)

The *Zhuangzi* also challenges the thinking, attitude, and behavior of individuals by restructuring their perception of what society regards as being useless. The usefulness of the useless is explored in chapters 1, 4, 20, and 26. For example:

> Huizi said to Zhuangzi, "Your words are useless."
> Zhuangzi said, "You need to understand useless before you can even begin to understand useful. The earth is wide and large, yet that which a person uses is only what supports his feet. This being so, if you dig away this dirt until you reach the Yellow Springs [netherworld], would the person still be able to use it?"
> "It would be useless."
> "That being so, it is quite clear that the useless can be useful. (ch. 26; Guo 1974, 470-471).

The *Zhuangzi* makes is quite clear that there are: 1) events or occurrences in life beyond the control of the individual; and 2) interactions and necessities that cannot be avoided. By emptying your heart-mind of that which you cannot resolve and by accepting that which you cannot avoid, the heart-mind will flow without any obstructions. This, then, is the attitude and behavior the *Zhuangzi* is trying to establish. The following three passages make this clear:

> Take responsibility for your own heart-mind so that sorrow and joy do not easily affect you. Knowing what you cannot resolve, and being at peace with it by adapting to destiny, is the perfection of power. As a subject and a son, there is that which you cannot avoid. Forget about your ego and deal with the situation. (ch. 4; Guo 1974, 86)
> Reside in the world by letting your heart-mind flow without any obstructions. Accepting what you cannot avoid as well as nourishing what is within is perfection. What more can be said? (ch. 4; Guo 1974, 89)
> To know what you cannot resolve and to be at peace with it by adapting to destiny, only the person of power is able to do this. (ch. 5; Guo 1974, 108)

The behavior that is prescribed by *the Zhuangzi* for interacting in the world is known as non-interference, often also called "nonaction" (*wuwei* 無爲). The practice of *wuwei* is applicable to both that which you cannot control and that which you cannot avoid. Understanding that there are occurrences, events, or people over which you have no control and refraining from trying to interfere with them is *wuwei*. By not attempting to force, coerce, control, manipulate, or seek self-gain from those occurrences, events, or people is *wuwei*. As the text says: "If the sage is unable to avoid attending to the world, it is best if he practices non-interference. If he does not interfere, then he will be at peace with his nature and destiny" (ch. 11; Guo 1974, 201).

Guo's commentary explains: "Non-interference does not mean to be reticent. Just allow each thing to accomplish what it does. Then one's nature and destiny will be at peace" (Guo 1974, 201). It leads to true happiness: "I take *wuwei* to be true happiness" (ch. 18; Guo 1974, 318). Guo's commentary clarifies, "The happiness of non-interference means to simply be without chronic stress (*you*), and that is all" (Guo 1974, 318).

While one can, in the beginning, certainly attempt to practice non-interference with others or oneself consciously and rationally, the actual behavior of *wuwei* occurs naturally because of emptying the heart-mind of obstructions and artificiality. According to *Daode jing* 48, *wuwei* is activated through a gradual process of diminishing. The Heshang gong version, commonly dated to the second century B.C.E. calls it "forgetting knowledge" (*wangzhi* 忘知). It explains "diminishing" as the gradual decreasing of inclinations and desires for cultural ornamentation, rhetorical devices, and artificiality.

> Those who engage learning, gain day by day.
>> Learning means the study of politics, teaching, rituals and music. One who gains daily means the inclination and desire for cultural ornamentation, rhetorical devices, and artificiality increases more and more each day.
> Those who engage Dao, lose daily.
>> Dao means the way of naturalness [*ziran* 自然]. One who loses daily means the inclination and desire for cultural ornamentation, rhetorical devices, and artificiality decreases day by day.
> Losing and continually losing.
>> Losing is the continual loss of inclinations and desires. As a result they gradually disappear.
> By which non-interference [*wuwei*] is reached.
>> Just like an infant, indifferent to and without care for fame and gain. Without any artificiality.
> Not interfering, there is nothing that is not accomplished. [8]
> (Wang 1993, 186-88)

Naturally refraining from interfering and removing obstructions and artificiality from the heart-mind is ultimately rooted in the body and direct experience. It is not a rational process. It is based in meditation.

---

[8] The translation of this section of this chapter and the commentaries to it are my own. The Heshang gong version appears in Wang (1993).

Meditation

While Zhuangzi's cognitive restructuring is certainly necessary and beneficial in guiding and changing how the individual perceives, thinks, feels, and behaves regarding society and the various environmental contexts that make up the world, it is in and of itself incomplete. It is incomplete because it is purely rational and ignores the body. The insight of the *Zhuangzi* is that the ultimate removal or emptying out of obstructions from the heart-mind require 1) moving beyond the purely rational into the body, and 2) eliminating any sense of an absolute separate self or world. This emptying out of the obstructions is experiential in nature and is the foundation of harmonization with Dao, happiness, and removing chronic stress. It is to realize, not rationally, but experientially that there is simply is one continual process of change.

The *Zhuangzi* presents two fundamental experiential processes or techniques for the emptying out of socially and self-imposed restrictions and boundaries: sitting in oblivion (*zuowang* 坐忘) and heart-mind fasting (*xinzhai* 心齋).

About oblivion, the *Zhuangzi* has a discussion between Yan Hui, a disciple of Confucius, and Confucius—the latter being, for the purpose of restructuring the reader's attitude, in the inferior role:

> Yan Hui said, "I succeeded."
> Confucius said, "What do you mean?"
> "I forgot self-less love [*ren*] and appropriate choice [*yi*]."
> "Fine. Yet you are still not there."
> Another day, they saw each other again. Hui said, "I succeeded."
> "What do you mean?"
> "I forgot appropriate behavior [*li*] and music [*yue*]."
> "Fine. Yet you are still not there."
> Another day, they saw each other once again. Hui said, "I succeeded."
> "What do you mean?"
> "I sit in oblivion."
> Confucius, somewhat startled, said, "What do you mean sit in oblivion?"
> "I let my body fall away. I dismissed my senses. I separated from form and got rid of knowledge. I am the same as the great passageway [*datong* 大通]. This is the meaning of sitting in oblivion."
> "Being the same, thus you are without partiality. Transformed, thus without absolutes. The results are quite worthy." Confucius then requested to become his disciple. (ch. 6; Guo 1974, 152-153)

Cheng Xuanying links the practice to an empty heart-mind ("Be empty, and that is all!") and thus relates it to the solution provided by the *Zhuangzi* to the adaptive problem of chronic stress.

Because he is able to sit straight and in the proper manner (*duanzuo* 端坐) and forget, his heart-mind is empty and unaffected. This is the meaning of sitting in oblivion... The great passageway is the great Dao. All things are able to emerge in the passageway of Dao. Therefore, it is said that Dao is the great passageway..... Being the same as the great Dao, there is no right and wrong or good and bad. Every thing is dissolved by the process of continual change. There are no absolutes to hold on to, grasp or maintain. (Guo 1974, 153-54)

Unremitting primal thinking is eliminated and the individual is no longer chronically stressed. Based on the text and the commentary, the practice of *zuowang* appears to consist of 1) sitting straight and in the proper manner,[9] 2) not attending to or dwelling upon sensory perception, and 3) not attending to or dwelling upon thoughts. As a result, the heart-mind is empty and unaffected (not agitated), the attention is cleared of obstructions, and the practitioner is gradually absorbed into or identified with the continually changing present.

The other major form of meditation is mind–heart fasting:

Confucius said: "Unify your will. Do not listen with the ears, listen with the heart-mind. Do not listen with the heart-mind, listen with vital energy [breath, *qi*]. Listening is stopped by the ear. The heart-mind is stopped by symbols. *Qi* is empty [*xu* 虚] and waits for things. Dao is a gathering of emptiness. Emptiness is heart-mind fasting."

Yan Hui asked, "Having not yet reached a point of applying this to myself, my self was real. Having applied it, I do not begin to have a self. Is it possible to call this emptiness?"

"That's it!" (ch. 4; Guo 1974, 80-81)

This practice recognizes the artificiality, limitations, restrictions, biases, distractibility, and imposition of boundaries by both the senses and rationality. It focuses on eliminating these by unifying the will and listening with *qi*. For Guo, a unified will means to "dismiss differences and allow a single focus" (Guo 1974, 80). Cheng, providing more depth about the notion of a unified will and the art of heart-mind fasting notes: "Your heart-mind is without differences, is very

---

[9] The character *duan* 端 consists of the radical *li* 立 (established, fixed, upright, erect, vertical, stand) and the character *duan* 耑 which Karlgren describes as a sprout or plant (*che* 屮) growing upwards with its roots in the earth below (1975, 320). The combination *duanzuo* 端坐 is suggestive of sitting with the head being softly pulled upward (much like a puppet's head being pulled up by a string) thus gently and naturally straightening the back, with the lower half of the body contacting (probably in some type of cross-legged position) and being rooted downward into the ground. This being the case the body is naturally (*ziran*) aligned along the *baihui* and *huiyin* points. The combination *duanzuo* is found as well in the *shuyi* 樞翼 section of the Tang text *Zuowang lun* where it is also used to describe how to sit. For a definitive analysis of the history and practice of *zuowang*, see Kohn (1987; 2010). Also see Kohn (2008, 103-7).

still, is empty, forgets and dissolves to be in accord with the single process of transformation" (Guo 1974, 80). He says:

> The heart-mind has knowledge and sensations that cause it to be agitated and entangled. Qi is without feelings and rumination. Empty and flexible, allowing things to be. Thus, eliminate the knowledge and sensations and replace then with emptiness and flexibility. Dissipating them again and again gradually ascending into the profound mystery. (Guo 1974, 80)

This practice is a step-by-step process that eventually leads to complete emptiness. The environment is engaged with qi. As qi is empty, it is unaffected by knowledge and sensations. By listening with qi, the heart-mind is not entangled or agitated. It does not interfere with things, but is simply empty. This emptiness is the very solution that the *Zhuangzi* proposes for the elimination of what we today call chronic stress: "Be empty--that is all!"

The practice of sitting in oblivion appears to require that the practitioner temporarily disengage from society and the surrounding environment, turn inwards, forget or empty out, and become absorbed into the continually changing present. The practice of heart-mind fasting seems to require that the practitioner engage with society and the surrounding environments, empty out or forget, be guided by qi, and dissolve into the continually changing present.

Both techniques are experiential in nature and rooted in the body. Both gradually eliminate contrived, self-imposed, and society-imposed absolute thoughts, differences, distinctions, values, desires, and restrictions. Both eliminate any sense of a separate, independent self; and both empty out the heart-mind, thus eliminating chronic stress. Chronic stress being eliminated, there is the direct experience of the here and now, the present, and the identification with the continual process of change.

Conclusion

> The nameless man said, "If you let your heart-mind be without artificiality, are in accordance with emptiness of qi, adapt to the naturalness (*ziran*) of the world, and be without selfishness and bias, then the world will be healed or governed. (ch. 7; Guo 1974, 159)

This succinctly describes the personal responsibility, self-refinement, and self-cultivation advocated in the *Zhuangzi*—not only for healing oneself or governing the world, but also for removing chronic stress, becoming physically and psychologically whole, and enhancing overall well-being. To be without artificiality, to be in accordance with vital energy and breath, to adapt to the naturalness of the world, and to be without selfishness and bias requires, according to the *Zhuangzi*, cognitive restructuring, attitude and behavioral adjustment or simplification, and meditation.[10]

The *Zhuangzi* clearly links dysfunctional thinking (chronic primal thinking) with self-generated and society-generated threats and fears. These perceived threats and fears give rise to chronic stress and the subsequent physical and psychological problems associated with it. Thus, to improve health and overall well-being requires changing how the individual thinks about existence and all that is entailed with it. This being the case, there is a focus on cognitive restructuring which aims at emptying the heart-mind of artificiality, absolute thoughts, dichotomies, standards, values, theories, norms, desires, expectations, rituals, and rules. Not only does it aim to empty out the individual of these obstructions, but it also focuses on changing the individual's attitude, feelings, and behavior about engaging existence.

For the *Zhuangzi* the fundamental purpose of cognitive restructuring is to point out the problems or obstructions and serve as a beginning point for their elimination. The problem with cognitive restructuring is that it is one-sided as it is purely rational in nature. For a more holistic approach, the body is required for the ultimate elimination of the problems or obstructions. The actual elimination of these problems or obstructions occurs through the process of meditation, which incorporates the body.

The process of meditation, as advocated by the *Zhuangzi*, is a gradual process that eliminates chronic primal thinking and any sense of an absolute, separate, individual sense of self. This being the case how one perceives, feels about and behaves in the world is changed. Being empty there is no artificiality, selfishness, or bias. The individual listens with *qi*, does not interfere with herself or others (*wuwei*), and is naturally (*ziran*) in harmony with all things.

The *Zhuangzi* clearly offers a holistic solution to the problem of chronic stress and the physical and psychological problems associated with it. It offers a way to happiness and spirituality.

---

[10] Regarding the physical and psychological benefits of meditation, see Kohn 2008 and Santee 2007; 2010.

Bibliography

American Academy of Family Physicians. 2010. http://familydoctor.org/online/famdocen or home/common/mental health /stress/ 167.printerview. html. Accessed 4/7/10

American Institute of Stress. 2010a. *Stress.* http:/or www.stress.org/Stress.htm. Accessed 3/27/10

American Institute of Stress. 2010b. *Stress Reduction.* http:/or www.stress.org/Stress_ reduction.htm Accessed 3/27/10

Ames, Roger, ed. 1998. *Wandering at Ease in the Zhuangzi.* Albany: State University of New York Press.

APA. 2009. *Stress in America 2009.*http:/or www.apa.org/news/press/releases/stress-exec-summary.pdf Accessed 3/25/10.

Beck, Aaron T. and Marjorie E. Weishaar. 2005. "Cognitive Therapy." In *Current Psychotherapies*, edited by Raymond J. Corsini and Danny Wedding, 238-68. Belmont: Brooks/Cole.

Benson, Herbert with Klipper, Miriam Z. 1975. *The Relaxation Response.* New York: Avon Books.

———— 1998. Testimony of Herbert Benson regarding Mind/Body Interventions, Healthcare, and Mind/Body Medical Centers before the United States Senate Appropriations Subcommittee on Labor/HHS & Education.

———— and Casey, Aggie. 2008. *A Harvard Medical School Special Health Report: Stress Management.* Boston: Harvard Medical School.

Buss, David M. 2008. *Evolutionary Psychology: The New Science of the Mind.* Boston: Pearson.

Casey, Aggie, Bei-Hung Chang, James Huddleston, Narmin Virani, Herbert Benson, and Jeffery A. Dusek. 2009. "A Model for Integrating a Mind/body Approach to Cardiac Rehabilitation: Outcomes and Correlators." *Journal of Cardiopulmonary Rehabilitation and Prevention* 29.4:230-8.

Confer, Jaime C., Judith A. Easton, Diane S. Fleischman, Cari D. Goetz, David M. G. Lewis, P. E. Perilloux, and David M. Buss. 2010. "Evolutionary Psychology: Controversies, Questions, Prospects, and Limitations." *American Psychologist* 65.2:110-126.

Coyle, Daniel. 1998. "On the *Zhenren.*" In *Wandering at Ease in the Zhuangzi*, edited by Roger Ames, 197-210. Albany: State University of New York Press.

Deckro, Gloria R., Keli M. Ballinger, Michael Hoyt, Marilyn Wilcher, Jeffrey Dusek, Patricia Myers, Beth Greenberg, David S. Rosenthal, and Herbert Benson. 2002. "The evaluation of a mind/body intervention to reduce psychological distress and perceived stress in college students." *Journal of American College Health* 50.6:281-87.

Ellis, Albert. 2005. "Rational Emotive Behavioral Therapy.: In *Current Psychotherapies*, edited by Raymond J. Corsini and Danny Wedding, 166-201. Belmont: Brooks/Cole.

————, and Catharine MacLaren. 2003. *Rational Emotive Behavioral Therapy.* Atascadero: Impact Publishers.

Esch, Tobias, George B. Stefano, Gregory L. Fricchione, and Herbert Benson. 2002a. "Stress in Cardiovascular Diseases." *Medical Science Monitor* 8.5:RA93-RA101.

_____, George B. Stefano, Gregory L. Fricchione, and Herbert Benson. 2002b. "The role of stress in neurodegenerative diseases and mental disorders." *Neuro Endocrinology Letters* 23.3:199-208.

_____, Gregory L. Fricchione, and George B. Stefano. 2003. "The therapeutic use of the relaxation response in stress-related diseases." *Medical Science Monitor* 9.2: RA23-34.

Graham, Angus C. 1981. *Chuang-Tzu: The Inner Chapters.* London: George Allen & Unwin.

Guo, Qingfan. 1974. *Zhuangzi jishi* 莊子集釋. 2 vols. Taipei: Chung Hwa.

Karlgren, Bernhard. 1975. *Analytical Dictionary of Chinese and Sino-Japanese.* Taipei: Ch'eng-Wen Publishing Company

Kemeny, Margaret E. 2003. "The psychobiology of stress." *Current Directions in Psychological Science* 12:124-29.

Kohn, Livia. 1987. *Seven Steps to the Tao: Sima Chengzhen's Zuowanglun.* St.Augustin/Nettetal: Monumenta Serica Monograph XX.

_____. 1992. *Early Chinese Mysticism: Philosophy and Soteriology in the Taoist Tradition.* Princeton: Princeton University Press.

_____. 2000. "*Zhuangzi*: Book of Master Zhuang." In *The Encyclopedia of Taoism*, edited by Fabrizio xfadio, 1297-1300. London: Routledge.

_____. 2008. *Meditation Works: In the Hindu, Buddhist and Daoist Traditions.* Magdalena, NM: Three Pines Press.

_____. 2010. *Sitting in Oblivion: The Heart of Daoist Meditation.* Dunedin, Fla.: Three Pines Press.

Kroenke, Kurt, and David Manglesdorff. 1989. "Common symptoms in ambulatory care: Incidence, evaluation, therapy, and outcome. *The American Journal of Medicine* 86:262-66.

Mayo Clinic. 2010a. *Stress: Win Control over the Stress in Your Life.* http:/or www.mayoclinic.com/print/stress/SR00001/METHOD=print. Accessed 4/7/10.

_____. 2010b. *Simplify your Life to Reduce Stress.* http:/or www.mayoclinic.com/health/ simplify-your-life/MY01230/METHOD=print; http://www.nlm.nih.gov/ medlineplus/stress.html. Accessed 4/7/10

McGrady, Angele. 2007. "Psychophysiological mechanisms of stress: A foundation for the stress management therapies." In *Principles and Practices of Stress Management*, edited by Paul M. Lehrer, Robert L. Woolfolk, and Wesley E. Sime, 16-37. New York: Guilford Press.

McEwen, B., with Elizabeth Norton Lasley. 2002. *The End of Stress As We Know It.* Washington, D. C.: Joseph Henry Press.

NIH. 2004. *Setting Priorities for Basic Brain & Behavioral Science at NIMH Final Report of the National Advisory Mental Health Council's Workgroup on Basic Sciences – May 2004.*

http://www.nimh.nih.gov/about/advisory-boards-and-groups/namhc/reports/ bbbs-research.pdf

NIMH. 2009a. *New Look at Data Confirms Strong Association between Depression and Stressful Life Events.* http://www.nimh.nih.gov/science-news/2009/much-touted-depres-sion-risk-gene-may-not-add-to-risk-afterall.shtml

———. 2009b. *Research Shows How Chronic Stress May be Linked to Physical and Mental Ailments.* http://www.nimh.nih.gov/science-news/2009/research-shows-how-chro-nic-stress-may-be-linked-tophysical-and-mental-ailments.shtml

———. 2010. *Stress.* http://www.nlm.nih.gov/medlineplus/stress.html. Accessed 4/7/10.

Robinet, Isabelle. 2008. *"Shengren."* In *The Encyclopedia of Taoism,* edited by Fabrizio Pregadio, 879-81. London: Routledge.

Santee, Robert G. 2007a. *An Integrative Approach to Counseling: Bridging Chinese Thought, Evolutionary Theory and Stress Management.* Los Angeles: Sage Publications.

———. 2007b. "Potentials for Daoist healthcare in America." Paper presented at the Fourth International Conference on Daoist Studies: Daoism in Action. Hong Kong, November 21-25.

———. 2008. "Stress management and the *Zhuangzi." Journal of Daoist Studies* 1: 93-123.

———. 2010. "Sitting in oblivion and the relaxation response: An inquiry into managing the physical and psychological symptoms of chronic stress." Paper presented at the Sixth International Conference on Daoist Studies: Daoism Today: Science, Health and Ecology, Los Angeles, June 2-6.

Sapolsky, Robert. 2001. *Why Zebras Don't Get Ulcers.* New York: W. H. Freeman and Co.

Sobel, David S. 1995. "Rethinking medicine: Improving health outcomes with cost-effective psychosocial intervention. *Psychosomatic Medicine* 57:234-44.

Stefano, George B., Gregory L. Fricchione, Brian T. Slingsby, and Herbert Benson. 2001. "The placebo effect and relaxation response: Neural processes and their coupling to constitutive nitric oxide." *Brain Research Reviews* 35:1-19.

Wang, Ka 王卡. 1993. *Laozi Daodejing Heshanggong zhangju* 老子道德經河上公章句. Beijing: Zhonghua shuju.

Yu, Shiyi. 2000. *Reading the Chuang-tzu in the T'ang Dynasty: The Commentary of Ch'eng Hsuan-ying (fl. 631-652).* New York: Peter Lang Publishing.

The Somatic Mind

Daoism and East Asian Medicine

STEPHEN JACKOWICZ

East Asian medicine, at the root of Daoist worldview and cosmology, provides a framework for understanding consciousness as an integral part of the body's metabolism and supplies many normative interventions that help people to maintain psychological functions. Its fundamental concepts include the cosmic, vital energy of qi, its storage centers and flow channels described in terms of inner organs and meridians, the five spirits or psychological forces associated with them, as well as a set of seven emotions or personal energetic ways of interacting with the world. Medicine also provides a variety of practices that balance energetic flow and thus enhance the spiritual, emotional, and cognitive components of the mind. Both its vision and application form the ground from which much Daoist understanding and practice evolved.

In the Han, under the impact of yin-yang and five phases cosmology and in contrast to the *Zhuangzi*, both psychological theory and practice in Daoism became more somatic and body oriented. Daoists adopted the prevailing medical model and began using methods from the preventative and health-enhancing branch of East Asian medicine (*yangsheng* 養生, lit. "nourishing life"). On this basis, medieval religious practitioners developed a plethora of techniques to transform the mind toward greater spiritual subtlety, including ways of healing it and bringing it into a state of harmony: what we would call psychological health.

---

[1] The term "East Asian Medicine" is used throughout this article to refer to the traditions of medicine that grew out of the Sinitic-influenced cultures of East Asia. Each of the national variations of medicine and the historical developments have enough in common to be mutually intelligible, however, each also has a unique and native character that denies the use of the term Chinese medicine to encompass them all.

To understand how the mind works in this medico-religious system, we need to appreciate certain basic facts. First, East Asian medicine underwent varied stages of development, during each of which physicians variously organized, schematicized, and utilized the concept of mind. Second, it evolved into different cross-cultural expressions throughout East Asia, so that Chinese medicine differs from its Korean, Japanese, and Vietnamese counterparts not just in geography, but also in theory and technique. Third, its concept of mind is close but not identical to that developed in Buddhism, Daoism, and even Confucianism where morality and the spiritual growth of the individual are central. Fourth, the medical understanding of the bodymind has had a major impact on Daoist theory and practice.

What, then, is the mind?

The Mind

Although all kinds of living creatures have active consciousness of the environment, the idea of a "mind" generally applies to more abstract mental activities, including various basic functions such as sensory awareness and response as well as conscious navigation of the world. Communication is a slightly higher mental function, while memory, learning, concentration, feelings, and abstract thought are more developed. Beyond these, aberrant behavior, neurosis, psychosis, depression, and so on are diseased aspects of the more developed faculties of mind.

Generally, the mind is an elusive concept. Unlike the brain, which has identifiable physical structures, the mind is a construct to appreciate the integrated operations of consciousness. The West has psychological and philosophical models of the mind, as well as those put forth by popular writers. In East Asia, each religion has its own variant model. However, all cultures and models share certain generalities.

For one, the mind has several parts. There is a realm of conscious activity, an unconscious, and a zone between often called the subconscious. The conscious aspect of the mind is the realm of thought and choice; it is the most developed aspect of the mind and exists in its highest development in human beings more so than in other animals and primates. The conscious aspects of the mind are associated with the frontal lobe of the brain and especially with the left hemisphere as well as with the prefrontal cortex. It relates to language and communication, making choices, and engaging in complex intellectual behaviors.

However, the conscious mind only works in concert with the subconscious and unconscious. The subconscious aspect of the mind is associated with the right hemisphere of the brain, the hippocampus, and the anterior cingulate gyrus. It is the where memory, emotion, deep-seated beliefs, habits, and conditioned responses reside. The conscious and subconscious parts of the mind are in perpetual interplay, creating in the individual the experience of a clear zone of thought, which is conscious, and a zone of mental currents or processes, which are not clearly conscious or expressed in linear fashion but rather symbolic and unspoken, emotive currents behind the thought process. Behind the subconscious is the realm of mind that is unconscious. This level is deepest and most primitive, sometimes called the "reptilian mind." Here autonomic processes and limbic responses interrelate with the more developed aspects of abstract thought. The unconscious thus provides a link between body and mind and is the realm of instinct, violence, and satisfaction.

This general schema describes bio-physiological aspects of consciousness, it does not account for the complexities of human mental activity, nor does it provide a framework for cognitive or spiritual development. Much ethical and spiritual literature is devoted to an understanding of mind that is functional more than physiological. In that regard, there are amorphously described constructs such as character, personality, or ego. These constructs hope to represent the associations, beliefs, habits, and thought processes that collectively are the "self." Spiritual literature and practice speaks of the "ego" in this context, but not in the strictly Freudian sense. It understands the ego as a factor of bondage that keeps the seeker from developing potency and growing spiritually. Many spiritual practices accordingly serve to overcome these entrenched aspects of self-definition that handicap the aspirant.

The most obvious difference of the Asian way of looking at the mind is that it never loses touch with the body. Asian traditions have in fact been criticized for their tendency to somatize mental states. This feature of linking mental faculties and components of consciousness to the body dates back to the formative period of East Asian medicine. The *Huangdi neijing* 黃帝内經 (Yellow Emperor's Inner Classic) already has: "Human beings have five inner organs [energetic centers] which transform into five energies, thereby generating [the excessive emotions of] joy, anger, sorrow, worry, and fear." Emotions are thus rooted in the organs whose transformative relationships give rise to energetic patterns that then manifest as emotions.

While Westerners consider the mind as a singular integrative entity, composed of conscious and subconscious layers, traditional East Asian thinkers define it as a heterogeneous grouping of components. To them, the mind consists of various parts that work together like a committee rather than being a single entity. If the committee operates efficiently, there is proper mental functioning. If not, disharmonies develop and disease occurs, which may eventually lead to mental disease. Underlying these various agencies, moreover, is the universal vital energy known as *qi*, the core concept of both medicine and Daoism.

Vital Energy: Qi

No discussion of East Asian medicine can ignore the concept of *qi* 氣. *Qi* is an elusive concept often trivialized into a new-age genericism called "energy." However, the concept of *qi* is much deeper and pervasive. *Qi* is the material substrate of existence, the *materia mundi*, a phenomenal manifestation of Dao. Ancient sources associate *qi* with mist, fog, and moving clouds. Shang dynasty (1766-1122 B.C.E.) oracle bones record *qi* with two parts: a person eating and rice in a pot. This image relates to the fundamental qualities of *qi* to warm, rise, transform, and nourish. *Qi* is thus intrinsic in the substrate of the body and well as the processes of interaction between the metabolism and the outside world. It is matter and energy in a primordial dance of interaction, development and dissolution. The foundation of human metabolism and life, it is the core of the East Asian worldview.

Qi animates life and furnishes functional power of events. The root of the human body, its quality and movement determine human health and form the foundation of spiritual transformation. *Qi* can be discussed in terms of quantity, since having more means stronger metabolic function. This, however, does not mean that health is a byproduct of storing large quantities of *qi*. Rather, there is a normal or healthy amount of *qi* in every person, and health manifests in its balance and harmony, its moderation and smoothness of flow. This flow is envisioned in the texts as a complex system of waterways with the "Ocean of *Qi*" in the abdomen; rivers of *qi* flowing through the upper torso, arms, and legs; springs of *qi* reaching to the wrists and ankles; and wells of *qi* found in the fingers and toes. Even a small spot in this complex system can thus influence the whole, so that overall balance and smoothness are the general goal.

Human life, as already the *Zhuangzi* says, is the accumulation of *qi*; death is its dispersal. After receiving a core potential of primordial *qi* at birth, people throughout life need to sustain it. They do so by drawing postnatal *qi* into the body from air and food, as well as from other people through sexual, emotional, and social interaction. But they also lose *qi* through breathing bad air, overburdening their bodies with food and drink, and getting involved in negative emotions and excessive sexual or social interactions.

Although everything is made of *qi* and partakes of the myriad interactions intrinsic to the *qi*, the nature of the interactions is categorized as proper or improper. The proper and harmonious interaction of *qi* is termed *zhengqi* 正氣, translated as "proper *qi*," "correct *qi*," or "upright *qi*." The goal of East Asian health practices is an optimization of the proper *qi* in the metabolism. Daoist spiritual practices also seek the cultivation of proper *qi*, at first from an internal perspective in the body and the mind, but then to an extension into the world. Personal health will then yield to a harmonious and healthy family, society, and world, creating a state known as Great Peace (*taiping* 太平), venerated by Confucians and Daoists alike.

However, if the *qi* does not interact properly and instead refracts, schisms, or eddies, it may give rise to states of heat or cold, deficiency or excess, blockages or rushes. Improper *qi* is termed *xieqi* 邪氣, variously translated as "wayward *qi*," "heteropathic *qi*," "pathogenic *qi*," or even "evil *qi*." These variant renderings have implications in English, which dispose the reader to a specific interpretation that is more limited than the original term. Xie*qi* is not a disease. Rather, it is the precursory imbalance that may lead to disease in body and mind, by extension corrupting family, community, and the world.

The harmonious state of proper *qi* is a fragile interweave of interactions that must be safeguarded for health as well as for spiritual well-being and development. Internal causes including the emotions can upset the balance, as can external factors (heat, cold, bacteria, viruses) that challenge the metabolism's ability to change. Once imbalanced and driven into a wayward state, the metabolism will degrade and illness can occur. Therefore, the individual needs to safeguard the proper relationships of *qi* in the body- mind as well as in the world of man and nature. The goal of self-cultivation is the elevation and perfection of *qi*: the optimal functioning of the metabolic processes in the body. Control of *qi*, on the other hand, means the power to guide the metabolism. Both control and perfection relate directly to mental states and form the foundation of Daoist spiritual cultivation. What, then, are the bodymind components that Daoists transform in their quest?

Organs and Meridians

The core focus of East Asian medicine and beginning Daoist practice is on the five inner organs (*wuzang* 五藏), sometimes also called "orbs," which are yin in nature and serve to store and maintain *qi*. Associated with the five phases (markers of the changing patterns of yin and yang) and their cosmic correlates (directions, colors, seasons) as well as with five yang or transformative organs and with the five senses, they are as follows:

yin/yang	phase	direc	color	season	organ1	organ2	sense
minor yang	wood	east	green	spring	liver	gall bladder	vision
major yang	fire	south	red	summer	heart	sm. intestine	taste
yin-yang	earth	center	yellow		spleen	stomach	touch
minor yin	metal	west	white	fall	lungs	lg. intestine	smell
major yin	water	north	black	winter	kidneys	bladder	hearing

Each of these organs has an associated meridian that correlates it to the exterior of the body. There is a large body of literature regarding the meridian system. Known as the *jingluo* 經絡, the system is a complex network of interwoven conduits of variant sizes and directions. The "structures" of the system are translated as "meridians," "channels," or "vessels." Each of these terms is inaccurate to describe the nature of the system. The term *jing* means to weave. The *jing* are the major weavings of relationship that connect the interior to the surface of the body in predictable formats of interaction.

Loci on the path of the weaving can influence the relationship of the surface to the interior. These loci are termed *xue* 穴, "holes," which are more commonly termed points. The *luo* are collateral relationships. Some of the *luo* are constant relationships of *qi*, which connect the *jing* weavings, or provide a venue for toxins to exit the system and gather in the bladder for expulsion from the body. Other *luo* are fine network relationships between the inner structures of the body, which connect every aspect into a gossamer web of minute coherency.

When referring to the *jingluo* system, the common understanding is that there is a circuitous flow somewhat akin to the circulatory system. This, however, only developed in the Han dynasty. Earlier sources indicate a non-circuitous relationship of the *jingluo* system, which later became part of a codification system of "regular" channels that have both a circuitous relationship as well as a predictable frequency of *qi*-dynamic.

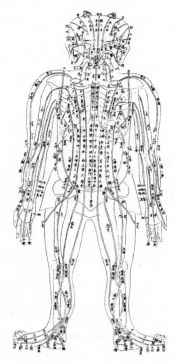

Some later sources, too, maintain that there are extraordinary channels, (*qimai* 奇 脈), which are not circuitous and do not have a mobile *qi*-dynamic. Various lineages and approaches to East Asian medicine emphasize the use of different parts of the meridian system. Daoist practices accept the meridian system as a construct of the body and a venue of coherency between body, mind, and world. As such, the meridian system becomes a component within the practices intended to rarify and perfect the self.

The Five Spirits

In addition to the meridians, the five yin organs are connected to five psychological agents known as the "five spirits" (*wushen* 五神). Thus the kidneys house the incarnate will (*zhi* 志); the liver, the spirit souls (*hun* 魂); the spleen, the intention (*yi* 意); the lungs, the material souls (*po* 魄); and the heart, the spirit (*shen* 神). While medicine aims to create harmony among these, Daoist practice goes further, aiming at the complete transformation of the person's *qi* into spirit, a subtler and more etheric form of being. Still, even Daoists begin with physical reorganization. Thus, they first control sexual energies (kidneys, will) and food intake (spleen, intention), then move on to work with breathing practices (lungs, material souls) and engage in visions of the divine (liver, spirit souls) to eventually reach oneness with Dao (heart, spirit). In all cases, they use the medical paradigm and medical methods to reach first to the mental, then to the spiritual levels of being.

More specifically, the incarnate will resides in the kidneys and is associated with the water phase. In East Asian medical theory, the kidneys form the base of the metabolism and serve as the storehouse of vital essence (*jing* 精). This means that weaknesses in the kidneys have correlative changes in the life force as well as in the will. Commensurately repetitive failure to assert one's will can deplete the functional strength of the kidneys. On a deeper, spiritual level, the incarnate will also connects the person to his or her life path or "destiny"— understood as an incarnate "destination," a direction of internal development that leads to the most harmonious and self-actualizing life one can possibly have. Here medicine and religion cross paths most closely, and some practitioners see the purpose of Chinese medicine in assisting people to understand and embrace their incarnate will to make their best life choices (e.g., Jarrett 2000; 2006)

In practice, a patient may show a deep and slow pulse, cold lower extremities, dark circles, under the eyes, and a "groaning" quality to the voice; he describes a listless drift and lack of meaning in his life. Such are clear signs of kidney deficiency, including the inability to manifest the will. Most simply, if the patient exhibits a weak willpower, one strengthens the kidneys to correct the deficiency. The potential intervention is varied. However, with acupuncture one can use "Seat of the Will" (*Zhishi* 志室, BL 52) in concert with other, kidney-supporting points. Another possibility is an herbal decoction which uses herbs to strengthen kidney-yang or reinforce essence, such as *Buguzhi* 補骨脂 (Fructus Psoralae), or *Suoyang* 鎖陽 (Cynomorium Stem). Breathing practices may also be prescribed such as rubbing the kidneys while making the sound *hai*, which is considered strengthening. Physical exercises, such as "standing on stake"— similar to Mountain Pose in yoga—may help as may postures and moves derived from the martial arts. The overall approach is to supplant the mental quality by venues of physical interaction.

Daoist practices in their turn would begin with reinforcing the will, enabling the practitioner to bear the demands of spiritual development. As the incarnate will relates to the kidneys and the core vitality of the body, Daoist methods need to fortify this foundation so that one can reach the heights of spiritual attainment. A strong foundation helps to avoid the distraction of nagging health concerns and allow the aspirant the greatest chance of prolonged practice and success.

Adepts first fortify the incarnate will, then focus on the control and restriction of intake, thereby addressing the spleen and the intention—both associated with the earth phase. Intention here is an organizing principle of consciousness, which allows the mind to "auto-pilot" itself through routine tasks. Just as the stomach digests foodstuffs and organizes the dissemination of their essences throughout the body, the intention organizes cognitive input and helps to digest the phenomenal world mentally, thus allowing the individual to recognize and navigate the material landscape. If the intention begins to break down, the individual is unable to maintain the categorizations that are considered normal, necessary to remain within the boundaries of sanity. In a mild form, an imbalance accounts for anaphasia; in severe cases it manifests as schizophrenia. The intention, moreover, is uniquely influenced by both diet and fluid metabolism—and even Western practitioners will prescribe a rotational diet for schizophrenics (see Philpott and Kalita 2000).

According to Chinese theory, if the diet is heavy in sweets and creamy or greasy food, the metabolism becomes "damp" (shi 濕). A damp metabolism is more viscous in its fluid base, which impedes the speed of metabolic reactions. The digestive tract slows in its secretion of the proper enzymes, and peristalsis slows down. The secretion of mucus thickens while neurokinesis slows with the viscosity of synaptic gap fluids. The overall burden on the metabolism is the hallmark of dampness—which is not the disease, but the precursor to disease: it provides the disease a platform of development. In terms of intention, dampness blocks the normal functioning and organizational capacity of the intention. Just as the damp condition impairs the physical metabolism, so it does the mind's ability to organize and stay on top of demands. Beyond a damp state, moreover, it is also possible that the patient develops a "phlegm" condition—more far-reaching and dangerous.

In practice, a patient with a slippery pulse, a thick coating on the tongue, heavy limbs, and lethargy, presents indications of a problem with the spleen. Further possible symptoms include disorganization, confusion, muddled thinking, and poor planning. In such a case acupuncture applied to points such as Earth Mechanism (Diji 地機, SP 8) can be utilized to bolster the spleen. Herbal decoctions such as Guipitang 歸脾湯 (Save Spleen Decoction) may help. Breathing practices such as open-glottis breathing can also benefit. In all modes, the physical interweave is again addressed to correct the mental issue.

Daoist practices that address the spleen are based on dietary regulation. Through dietetic practice, the aspirant first creates regularity within the metabolism that allows the intention to function at a normal state. Once this is established, the tendency to over-think or obsess is less and can be controlled. Further dietary control takes the aspirant away from rich foods and ultimately weans him entirely from grains (see Kohn 2010). Minimizing the sugars intrinsic to such foods, it becomes possible to obviate the insulin shocks and cycles, thus creating a calmer and more even-keeled mental state requisite for prolonged spiritual practice. This leads seamlessly to the next step, addressing the material souls in the lung via breath control.

The material or corporeal souls reside in the lungs and are associated with the metal phase. Seven in number, they are forever dissatisfied and insatiable spirits. Arising from the corpses in the area of conception, they enter the developing fetus from earth as soon as the body has the capacity to hold them. Misshapen and almost monstrous, embodying socially relevant wants and desires, they serve as a way for the medical system to account for the never ending dissatisfaction inherent in human life as well as for the community drives which, when unrequited, account for the unfinished and ungrounded feeling of human existence. They are beastly in shape and quite disastrous in their activities. The Daoist *Baosheng jing* 保生經 (Scripture on Preserving Life, DZ 871) of the ninth century describes them:

> The seven material souls consist of the energy of yin and of evil. They are basically demons. They can make a person commit deadly evils, be stingy and greedy, jealous and full of envy. They give people bad dreams and make them clench their teeth, incite them to say "yes" when they think "no."
>
> They cause people to lose their vital essence in sexual passion, dissipate it by hankering after luxury and ease. Through them, people waste their original purity and simplicity. (2a)

These souls, far from looking like human beings, are strangely formed devils, having birds' heads, only one leg, tails, abominable outgrowths, and the like. Their names are accordingly nasty: Corpse Dog, Arrow in Ambush, Bird Darkness, Devouring Robber, Flying Poison, Massive Pollution, and Stinky Lungs (3ab).

A patient with a sallow complexion, kyphotic posture, a floating or weak pulse, and a sorrowful voice may well have feelings of depression and sadness, attributed to the unsettled material souls. Acupuncture and moxibustion on points such as Door of the Material Souls (*Pohu* 魄戶, BL 42) are appropriate in this case. Herbs that bolster the *qi* and address an insufficiency in the lungs can also help, one example being "Constrained Metal" (*Yujin* 郁金, Radix Curcumae). Further, breathing practices that use the resonant sound "ah" are good for supplanting lung *qi*.

Daoist aspirants face the task of quelling the material souls so that they do not divert their attempts at spiritual development. Breath control and reinforcing of the lungs are the beginning of this work, as well as meditations for subjugation. Once in control of these basal aspects, Daoists can turn their attention to the inner vision of higher spiritual forces in the body. Among these, the spirit or ethereal souls are predominant. The character consists of the word for "cloud" in combination with that for "ghost." It reflects the understanding that these souls are related to cosmic ether, to primordial energy. The translation "ethereal soul" conveys this association.

The spirit souls represent the aspect of the human being that precedes the physical body and survives its demise, thus almost analogous to the Western concept of soul. Since they are, moreover, related to the wood phase and housed within the liver, problems related to them are treated through the liver.

The liver maintains the normal systemic metabolic responses among its other physiologic functions. If the body experiences a stagnation of metabolic energy or blood circulation, the liver may be affected which can also impact the spirit souls. Someone in such a state will feel dysphoric and depressed. Since the souls resemble the body, the entire complex of proprioception falls under this category. Liver and spirit soul disorders often come with dysmorphic states and dissociation, often in the aftermath of traumatic experiences.

Patience suffering from such conditions usually present with a wiry pulse, feel often angry and frustrated, and cannot appreciate the higher aspects of life. This means that the spirit souls are unable to roost within the liver. If diagnosed as a stagnation of liver *qi*, this condition is helped by acupuncture on points such as Soul Gate (*Hunmen* 魂門, BL 47) and with herbal formulas, such as *Xiaoyao san* 逍遙散 (Free and Easy Powder). However, if the issue is that there is not enough blood to contain the yang spiritual forces, the herbal formula *Suanzao rentang* 酸棗仁湯 (Sour Jujube Decoction) is better. Breathing techniques using a hissing sound to benefit the liver may also be prescribed.

Daoist theory of the spirit souls developed over time. Originally considered a single spiritual force, they were expanded into three figures envisioned as body gods. The *Baosheng jing* says:

The three spirit [yang] souls are located beneath the liver. They look like human beings and all wear green robes with yellow inner garments. Every month on the third, thirteenth, and twenty-third day, they leave the body in the evening to go wandering about.

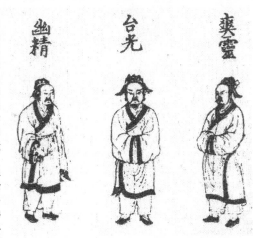

At this time, lie down with your feet up, your head supported by a pillow, and your legs stretched out straight. Fold your hands over your heart, close your eyes, and hold your breath. Click your teeth three times. (1b)

The names of these positive aspects of human existence are "Spiritual Guidance," "Inner Radiance," and "Dark Essence" (1a). As shown in the text, they look noble, appear human in shape, and are dressed in courtly garb. To support them in their beneficent activities, the text recommends physical exercises, breathing practices, as well as meditations and incantations. Treated in this manner, the three spirit souls will bring out the best in people and take care that "there is no disaster or affliction [to the person], and all evil demons are subdued. The body at peace, you attain Dao. Then there is no more suffering or pain" (2a; Ishida 1987, 86).

While the three spirit souls, the representatives of Heaven, therefore guide people toward greater goodness and spiritual transformation, the seven material souls, essential aspects necessary for physical survival, pull them toward worldliness, tension, and conflict. While following the latter leads to loss of vital energy, illness, and death, cultivating the former brings about a transformation toward purity, health, and long life.

Daoist aspirants finally turn their attention to attaining unity with the Dao. This brings them to address the heart and the spirit, both associated with the fire phase and housed in the heart. Spirit (*shen*) is the one aspect of the five wills that carries a broad physiologic meaning. First, it represents the overall functioning of the metabolism: if the individual is active, alert, and vibrant, then he is considered to "have *shen*." Second, it describes the diagnostic parameters of the body having an overall normal or normative *gestalt* upon inspection. The face, tongue, pulse, and abdomen may thus be evaluated for *shen* or its lack. Third, it represents the ability of the consciousness and sensory apparatus to integrate responsive awareness. If the body or mind is diseased, or if the mind is preoccupied with worry or concerns, the spirit is "disturbed." This may lead to a failure of the normal integration of consciousness and aberrant forms of behavior. Thus, the spirit in its cognitive and conscious aspects is a fragile interweave of the healthful functioning of the other four spirits, the emotions, the cognitive field, and the organic physiology.

In practice, a disorder of the spirit will show aberrant behavior and irritation and be visible in a rapid pulse, red tongue, and elevated body temperature. Acupuncture on points such as Spirit Gate (*Shenmen* 神門, H 7) may be indicated as well as herbs that ground the spirit can be used such as *Muli* 牡蠣 (Concha Ostreae, oyster shells). Breathing practices resonating the sound *he* also help. However, if the person is very agitated, cooperation in such methods may be hard to obtain, and extreme imbalance in the heart can present with psychosis-like symptoms. Such extreme states are most often associated with a specific pathology known as "phlegm misting the mind."

Daoist adepts, having developed a strong foundation though their practice concerning the other four organs, are less likely to exhibit spirit pathologies. Their goal is to expand consciousness so that their spirit embraces the nature of Dao and their vantage point shifts from internal to external. They cosmicize the sense of self, becoming a conscious aspect of the complex interweave of the universe.

The Emotions

In addition to the five spirits, East Asian Medicine recognizes that the emotions play a part in the consciousness. Today seven emotions (*qiqing* 七情) or deep emotional currents, also described as "affects," are recognized. They combine to a blended hue of feeling (*gan* 感), which is the constructed summation of the internal emotional state of a given moment. This internally generated response is conjoined with the sensory response (*jue* 覺) to denote the combined internal-external correlated response: how you feel at the moment.

Before the modern standard of seven emotions, texts worked in sets of five, speaking of the "five wills" (*wuzhi* 五志) corresponding to the five phases and the five spirits. The *Huangdi neijing* has them as anger (*nu* 怒), worry (*you* 憂), sadness (*bei* 悲), excessive joy (*xi* 喜), and fear (*kong* 恐), associated respectively with the liver, spleen, lungs, heart, and kidneys. However, the fifth chapter describes them in relation to the directions and as damaging certain organs while controlling each other. Within the framework of that discussion, the "emotion" of thought (*si* 思) is introduced as damaging the spleen: it is subject to anger and controls fear. Thought here seems a cognate of worry. However, the same passage also has worry damaging the lungs while being controlled by joy, thus almost replacing the role of sadness. Still, the text states that sadness controls anger. Doing so, it adds thought as a sixth emotion to the list, confounding the correspondence with the five phases. A seventh emotion, moreover, is fright, shock, or terror (*jing* 驚), a variant of fear. How these seven correlate to the dominant five-phases model has never been resolved; modern TCM texts include the various emotions without a universally accepted rationale.

The classic five emotions, moreover, in non-medical and Daoist texts, were connected to the so-called five constants (*wuchang* 五常), which are essentially Confucian virtues that refine and alleviate the impact of the emotions. Part of immortality practice is to transform their excessive self-focused energies into altruistic, outgoing patterns. The five constants include: 1. benevolence (*ren* 仁) matching the wood phase, liver, and anger; 2. propriety (*li* 禮) relating to the fire phase, heart, and excessive joy; 3. integrity, honesty, or trustworthiness (*xin* 信) connected to the earth phase, spleen, and worry; 4. righteousness or self-lessness (*yi* 義) linked to the metal phase, lungs, and sadness; and 5. wisdom (*zhi* 智) connected to the water phase, the kidneys, and fear (see Jarrett 1998). Later developments sought to elaborate and clarify them variously, and individual thinkers identified several schemata (see Fruehauf 2006).

The seven emotions as codified today are best understood as deep movements of emotional force, accounting for the range of emotional response by arising in various measures. They are, moreover, each interpreted differently depending on the context and the underlying health of the person's organs and meridians.

To begin, anger or aggression is associated with the liver. Proper liver organ and meridian function as well as joint health allow its appropriate generation and expression. The liver generates an upward flow of *qi* that results in physiological and behavioral changes, such as increased blood pressure, higher mental clarity, faster heart rate, etc. Behaviorally it can be expressed as motivation and determination, matching the physiological changes typical of a motivated "get up and go" attitude. However, if external circumstances do not allow the fruition of one's actions, then this same energy is expressed as frustration or anger. It is important to understand that aggression *per se* is not an intrinsically positive nor negative emotion, but a specific movement of the *qi* dynamic of emotion, which arises from the liver and finds expression as an identifiable emotional signature relevant to external circumstances shaping its release and expression.

The emotion associated with the heart is usually translated joy. It is an expansive movement of *qi* that spreads in every direction, thereby slowing the action of the heart. If able to expand without resistance, it often appears as happiness or joy. If the restricted or overabundant due to pathologies such as "effulgence of heart fire," it can result in frenzy or mania. Hyperventilate patterns, psychotic states, high anxiety, and the like are all signatures of its negative expression.

Worry is associated with the spleen or, at times, the lungs. It is a stagnation of the movement of *qi* and almost always appears in a negative frame. However, in Confucian texts, it can also mean concern for the sake of others and thus be more positive. Perhaps that is why thought or thoughtfulness is also considered an emotion. Fundamentally, worry is a form of "over-thinking." This binds the *qi*, which tends to express itself in digestive disorders. Yet thought also means organization and planning, parallel to the digestive features attributed to the spleen: the ability to separate, digest, and apportion materials into useable components. If one cannot organize or plan properly, thought is not sufficiently expressed; similarly, if one over-thinks things, one's behavior shifts toward being overly organized, obsessive and rigid. In its extreme expression, the person may experience Obsessive Compulsive Disorder. Any such disharmonies are addressed by treating the spleen not just with medical intervention but especially also with dietary means.

The lungs are the seat of sadness, grief, melancholy, or depression—this scatters or consumes the *qi*. On a more positive note, this emotive force can manifest as a calming and settling of the cognitive state, resulting in introspection and compassion. If the sense of sadness or grief is appropriate to the situation and persists for a limited duration without paralyzing the person, it is a normal and healthy expression of this emotion. However, if the person cannot function and grieves incessantly, lacks situational focus, or falls into a depressive state, sadness is pathological and needs to be treated through the association with the lung.

The kidneys manifest fear and anxiety, which sinks the *qi*. In its healthy expression, it appears as caution or reservation, a well-founded non-paralytic fear, which may counterbalance the expansive aspects of joy. But if it is improperly expressed or excessive, it manifest as relentless fear and unfocused panic that will impede or even paralyze normal activity.

These five emotive movements interact with each other according to the five-phases model. In a healthy state, they mutually generate and restrict each other so that the range of emotion remains within the overall harmonious flow and is appropriate to outside circumstances. Their interaction results in a blended hue of emotional responses, leading to complex and often-contradictory emotional states that manifest in people's daily lives. This integrated expression is called feeling (*gan*), which indicates an active function that correlates and emotive responses so that they can be brought into the cognitive field. The transmission of the various emotive states into cognition, moreover, is an expression of the relationship of the liver to the pericardium.

The last of the various emotions is fright, shock, or terror (*jing*), an extreme expression of fear, which descends the *qi* densely inward and causes it to lose its course. Its severity injures the cognitive emotional system, creating a response that resembles medical pathology of "internal cold," a restriction and retardation of the normal metabolic response. *Jing* then is best understood as the emotive response to trauma. In Western medical theory, trauma freezes emotive states and can even schism the consciousness (see Herman 1992). The same holds true for the Chinese emotion: it freezes the blood and can warp the emotive response into a fractured state. Understanding *jing* as an expression of cold in the body, its treatment involves the application of warming techniques. This emotion does not have a positive side; it is only the response to overwhelming external factors. Also, it is short lived and only its metabolically cold signature persists.

Blood and Phlegm, Repression and Possession

All these components of the individual's emotive makeup come into the conscious sphere through the pericardium (*xinbao* 心包). Seen as the structure that surrounds the heart, this organ serves as an emotional protector, to whom feeling—the complex combination of emotive states—is transmitted through the blood.

Blood in East Asian medicine is both the red fluid in the body's vessels and the "matrix of the mind" (Wang 1993). As a substrate of consciousness it is an indication of the relation of circulatory response to state of mind. Cephalic circulation varies with mood and thought, expressed in the blood-mind relationship. The protective role of the pericardium is an expression of the ability of the consciousness to divorce itself from the emotions and control its impulses. Feeling as emotional summation, however, is unchecked by any buffer, and thus tends to shape behavior in a vitriolic, capricious dance that follows the ever-shifting blend of emotions. The pericardium thus provides a buffer for the emotions that allows consciousness to remain unimpeded by their direct influx and limits the impulse-action response of the mind.

Another body fluid that plays an important role in understanding pathologies is phlegm (*tan* 痰). Phlegm is formed in a complex process involving digestive and cognitive components. If the underlying force of digestion, known as spleen yang, is weak, the food essence fails to be separated and raised to be metabolized. The non-separated food essence congeals into dampness. When damp fluids migrate to the torso, they are subject to the fire of the metabolism of the heart and may be transformed into phlegm. This in turn affects the body by forming nodules or by interfering with the heart, either physically or mentally.

If phlegm clogs the heart physically, it experiences aspects of congestive heart failure. If it "mists the mind," the patient exhibits aberrant behavior patterns, irregularity in the interpretation of sensory inputs, and increasing departures from reality. Pathology ranges from mild ticks or oddities to full psychosis. In treatment the "orifices" of the senses need to be opened, so that normal function is re-established. One way to look at phlegm is as a severe thickening of the interstitial fluid, leading to the denaturing of so that the protein structures and creating rubbery strands that are like true mucosal phlegm in the body's deep structures. Again, like dampness, phlegm itself is not a disease but rather the change in fluid substrate that predisposes body and mind to disease. Like physical phlegm that is hard to expectorate, the insubstantial phlegm that affects consciousness is recalcitrant to resolution.

A further condition related to the emotions is *yu* 郁, "constraint" or "repression." It is emotive force turned back on itself and can originate with any of the seven emotions, if it remains unexpressed. Once repressed to a high degree, it damages the liver, impeding the ability to assay the integration of emotional responses mentally. Patients experience a frozen emotional state that is not in keeping with the constantly adjusting and restructuring mélange of emotive movements. This leads them to be divorced from true emotive states and to feel detached and disaffected to the point where they require intervention to reestablish normal emotional integration and restore the ability to be in touch with underlying states. Repression is thus the somatic expression of the restricted emotive force, similar in many ways to Freudian neurosis.

In the traditional context of Confucian society, repression was a common emotive response to the authoritarian control that ranged from the imperial court through the descending levels of government and into the family structure. Thus all levels of social interaction and relationship had defined and restrictive roles to which individuals had to conform. Lack of conformity was met not only with reproach, but also with physically punitive measures. These social forces made the prevalence of repression in the cognitive emotive physiology of the population a common occurrence, so that East Asian medicine developed an understanding of repression centuries before Freud.

Beyond this, the Chinese medical tradition gives credence to demonic influence (*emo* 惡魔) as a potential cause of mental illness. Although better known as an aspect of Chinese religion, demons also play a role in Chinese medicine and diagnosis. Great physicians, such as Sun Simiao 孫思邈 (581–682)—highly influential in Tang-dynasty medicine as well as Daoism—tend to view disease as a process instead of divine retribution and argue that demons should be treated as if there is an extreme excess of yang-*qi*. He also compiled a list the so-called ghost points, a series of thirteen acupuncture points used to end demonic possession. Modern TCM has less discussion of demons as a cause of disease, however, J. R. Worsley (1923-2003) places some importance on them. He developed an approach based predominantly on five-phases theory called Traditional or Five Element Acupuncture and a major trend in Western practice (see Eckman 1996). It still maintains a "de-possession treatment," needling points to call forth the "internal and external dragons" which expel demonic influence.

The modern practice of East Asian medicine has interacted with New Age thought in the West. Since the alternative community was first to embrace it, East Asian medicine in the West has being connoted as intrinsically spiritual, as juxtaposed to Western pharmaceutical medicine. This social phenomenon has lead to hybrid avenues of understanding where demonic influence, negative karma, or evil *qi* are considered the cause of disease and described in semi-sentient vocabulary. Most East Asian practitioners today dismiss such understanding and consider demonic medical theory as an historical phase.

Daoist Centers and Channels

In addition to the spirits, and emotions, the East Asian medical tradition recognizes three elixir fields (*dantian* 丹田). Each elixir field is a locus of the metabolism of the three segments of the body (pelvis, abdomen, and thorax) and holds one of the three vital substances of essence, energy, and spirit. Their importance is limited in medicine and more prominent in Daoist alchemical theory. Daoists visualize them and enhance them energetically so that they grow stronger. To do so, they calm the emotions, balance the spirits, open the orifices of the heart-mind, and develop an awareness of the elixir fields. This allows them to transmute the self from the base metals of ordinary life to the gold of immortality. In pursuit of spiritual attainment, there are also impeding spirits which need to be addressed. The Daoist traditions posit three nefarious spirits, known as the Three Deathbringers, which eat away at the three elixir fields, arresting spiritual development. These need to be starved and eliminated by strict adherence to good behavior, the application of dietary and herbal remedies, as well as pertinent rituals. Slowly they can be replaced by upright divinities, the Three Ones, who will lead the adept to immortality.

Daoist adepts visualize the Three Ones as manifestations of three kinds of cosmic or primordial *qi* in the three elixir fields. They in turn govern the twenty-four fundamental powers of the human body, which correspond to the twenty-four energies of the year and the twenty-four constellations in the sky. The exact procedure of the meditation varies according to season, but if at all possible should be performed at the solstices and the equinoxes.

To prepare for the practice, adepts have to purify themselves by bathing and fasting. They enter the meditation chamber at midnight, the hour of rising yang. Then they light incense, and click their teeth thirty times. Facing east, they close their eyes and visualize the Northern Dipper slowly descending toward them until it rests right above their heads with the handle pointing straight east. This preliminary measure serves to protect adepts from evil influences during the practice.

Then they start with the Upper One. They visualize a ball of red energy in the Niwan Palace, the upper elixir field in the center of the head. Within this ball of energy, a red sun about nine inches in radius will appear. Its brilliance envelops practitioners to such a degree that they enter a state of utter oblivion. As soon as they have reached this state, the god Red Child becomes visible. The ruler of the Niwan Palace, he holds a talisman of the white tiger, the sacred animal of the west. He also has an attendant: the god of the subtle essences of the teeth, the tongue, and the skull, who holds a sacred scripture in his hands.

The Middle and Lower Ones are similarly imagined as residing in the other elixir fields, the Scarlet Palace of the heart and the Ocean of *Qi* in the abdomen and are accompanied by assistants who govern the five inner organs as well as the extremities, senses, and fluids of the body. Through visualization, adepts keep them securely in the body; over time, they learn to communicate with them, which leads to the attainment of yet higher stages. At this point, adepts transpose the visualized gods back to their true realm in the stars and paradises and themselves take flight to visit those extraterrestrial realms— dimensions that will be their true home once their limited existence on this earth has come to an end (see Robinet 1993).

Reorienting the body to be the container of heavenly palaces and deities, to be in fact a cosmos in itself, adepts attain oneness in body and spirit with the cosmic dimensions of the universe. As all parts of the body transform into divine entities and firmly guarded by their responsible gods, the adept's physicality turns into a cosmic network. His bodymind becomes the celestial realm in which the gods reside. Visualizing and feeling the gods within the bodily self, the Daoist becomes a more cosmic being, transforming but not relinquishing his physical, embodied nature.

Conclusion

Mind in East Asian medicine is a complex interweaving of spirits, emotions, emotive filters, sensory inputs, and internal spiritual loci. These structures are integrate with other components of the body—organs, tissues, meridians, and points—to provide a highly developed venue for treatment and adjustment in a holistic body-centered approach. Interestingly, although the tradition has a highly developed model of the mind, it never gave rise to talk therapy and in a sense developed psychiatry rather than psychotherapy. Treatment may be with acupuncture, herbs, massage, or energy healing. The variant methods used in China, Japan, Korea, Vietnam, and the West all approach the mental and emotional states through the body, however, they all differ in the venues by which they choose to treat. For example, modern TCM will access emotional issues by treating the liver directly, while Japanese acupuncturists may utilize the Fukaya theory to treat mental illness by moxibustion under the thoracic vertebra's spinous processes. Thus the specific format of intervention may change, however, the underlying axioms about how the mind and emotions relate in consistent throughout the traditions.

Daoism is based on personal transformation. Steeped in the East Asian worldview, Daoism rests axiomatically on the medical understanding of the interconnected nature of body and mind. However, Daoism seeks to remold the bodymind material into a spiritual organization. Beginning with physical substrate, the aspirant creates a foundation for the emotional cognitive exploration of his self to redefine the internal apportionment of being into a cosmic integration wherein the very soul of existence is parcel to his spirit. Thus the two aspects of East Asian culture, medicine and Daoism, utilize the same elements but with different end compounds in mind.

Bibliography

Birch, Stephen J., and Robert L. Felt. 1999. *Understanding Acupuncture*. New York: Churchill Livingstone.

Cheng, Xinnong ed. 1987. *Chinese Acupuncture and Moxibustion*. Beijing: Foreign Languages Press.

Dharmananda, Subhuti. 2004. What is Phlegm-Mist Affecting the Orifices of the Heart? http://www.itmonline.org/arts/phlegmmist.htm

Eckman, Peter M.D. 1996. *In the Footsteps of the Yellow Emperor*. San Francisco: Cypress Book Company.

Eskildsen, Stephen. 2004. *The Teachings and Practices of the Early Quanzhen Daoist Masters*. Albany: State University of New York.

Fruehauf, Heiner. 2006. "Il Disease Comes From the Heart: The Pivotal Role of the Emotions in Classical Chinese Medicine. http://www.scribd.com/ oc/17849966/Emotions-Fruehauf

Herman, Judith M.D. 1992. *Trauma and Recovery.* New York: Basic Books.

Jarrett, Lonny S. 2000. *Nourishing Destiny: The Inner Tradition of Chinese Medicine.* Stockbridge, Mass.: Spirit Path Press.

Kohn, Livia. 2008. *Chinese Healing Exercises: The Tradition of Daoyin.* Honolulu: University of Hawai'i Press.

_____. 2010. *Daoist Dietetics: Food for Immortality.* Dunedin, Fla.: Three Pines Press.

_____, with Stephen Jackowicz. 2005. *Health and Long Life: The Chinese Way.* Cambridge, Mass.: Three Pines Press.

Larre, Claude. 1996. *The Seven Emotions.* Cambridge: Monkey Press.

Philpott, William H., and Dwight K. Kalita. 2000. *Brain Allergies: The Psychonutrient and Magnetic Connections.* Los Angeles: Keats Publishing.Corte Madera: The Waite Group.

Wang, Daodan, ed. 1993. *Zhongyixue.* Beijing: Zhonguo yixue chubanshe.

Wu, Nelson and Andrew Wu. 1999. *The Yellow Emperor's Canon of Internal Medicine.* Beijing: China Science and Technology Press.

Zhang, Yanhua.2007. *Transforming Emotions with Chinese Medicine.* Albany: State University of New York Press.

"Turning the Light Around"

in The Secret of the Golden Flower

CHRISTOPHER COTT & ADAM ROCK

The Taiyi jinhua zongzhi, *known in the West as* The Secret of the Golden Flower, *is a key text of Daoist psychological transformation. Utilizing detailed qualitative techniques, the authors extract its primary elements and present a set of five themes of spiritual cultivation: 1) refining the material soul into the spirit soul and consciousness spirit into primordial spirit; 2) refining the illumination of consciousness into that of inherent nature; 3) harmonizing the breath; 4) combining water and fire; and 5) joining Heaven and Earth. The first two describe the process of "turning the light around," a meditation that reverts the outward flow of consciousness to develop the inherent potential that is obscured by ordinary cognitive processes. The other three describe a sequential process that occurs when "turning the light around" is put into practice.*

Daoism is an integrative religious and spiritual tradition that has had a pervasive influence on the development of Chinese and other East Asian cultures (Robinet 1997). Despite a growing interest in Eastern philosophical and religious traditions (e.g., Buddhist psychology and mindfulness meditation; see DeSilva 2000; Kabbat-Zinn 1991), Daoism has received little attention from Western psychologists. Daoists, like Buddhists, have produced a sophisticated set of practices aimed at opening the practitioner to an ostensibly elevated mental and spiritual level (see Kohn 1989; 2008a; 2008b; 2010). In addition, Daoism also includes methods designed to enhance physical health and wellbeing (see Engelhardt 2000). The scientific study of the physiological benefits of these practices is in its formative stages, but the field is expanding and results to date are promising (Chen 2004; Sancier 1996).

Daoism has a significantly different theoretical basis from Buddhism and other non-Western psychologies, such as Advaita Vedanta, Western psychologists have studied to date. It may offer valuable new perspectives regarding non-Western modes of thinking concerning psychology, spirituality, and the philosophy of mind. In addition, it is noteworthy that millions of Chinese, Koreans, and others consider themselves Daoist, at least in part, and that Daoism in many ways forms the fundamental background of the Chinese way of thought (Nisbett 2003). The psychological study of Daoism may therefore contribute to a greater understanding of East Asian culture in particular and cross-cultural psychology in general.

Daoist Psychological Insights

Psychological research on Daoism has tended to be mainly from the Jungian and humanistic traditions. Given that it has a strong association with ostensibly trans-ego experiences, it is surprising to find that there is almost no work by transpersonal psychologists. Cott and Rock (2009) suggest that the psychologists most suited to studying Daoism might be transpersonal, indicating that many forms of Daoist praxis and the experiences associated with them are likely to fit clearly within the domain of transpersonal research.

For example, Hartelius, Caplan, and Rardin (2007) conducted a thematic analysis of 160 definitions of transpersonal psychology from 1968 through 2002, producing three themes that broadly capture key definitional elements. They indicated that transpersonal psychology is a) beyond-ego, b) integrative or holistic, and c) transformative. Daoism clearly adheres to all three. An example of "beyond-ego" Daoism can be found in the *Wudao lu* 悟道錄 (Record of Awakening to Dao) by Liu Yiming 劉一明(1734-1821), which states: "When inward and outward are illumined, and all is clear, you are one with the light of the sun and moon. . . the subtle body of a unified spirit, pervading the whole universe" (Cleary 1988, 4).

Principles such as yin and yang pervading all aspects of reality indicate the holistic nature of Daoism, as exemplified in the Daoist version of the *Yijing* 易經 (Book of Changes) for example. The transformative nature of Daoist praxis may also be exemplified in the progressive sequence of stages as presented in the current analysis of the *Taiyi jinhua zongzhi* 太一金華宗旨 (Great Unity's Instructions on [Developing] Golden Florescence), best known in the West—and in the following referred to--under the title "The Secret of the Golden Flower" (trl. Cleary 1991; Wilhelm and Jung 1962).

There is potentially a great deal of information within Daoism that may be of interest to transpersonal psychologists, such as a variety of meditation states and methods for achieving them. There is, for example, the "oblivion" method outlined in the *Zuowang lun* 坐忘論 (Sitting in Oblivion; see Kohn 1987; 2010) and various subtle energetic phenomena associated with "nourishing life" (*yangsheng* 養生). There is also the accumulation and manipulation of *qi* 氣 (see Despeux 2008a), as well as the out-of-body experiences and methods for inducing them, such as travels to heavenly realms as described in some Highest Clarity (Shangqing 上清) texts. Materials here are specifically the *Jiuzhen zhongjing* 九真中經 (Central Scripture of the Nine Perfections; see Miller 2008) and the *Sanyi tujue* 三一圖訣 (Illustrated Formulas of the Three Ones; see Wong 1997).

Cott and Rock (2009) also discuss two primary sources of Daoist information that may be amenable to psychological study: living and textual. The living Daoist tradition is today comprised of the Celestial Masters (Tianshi 天師) and Complete Perfection (Quanzhen 全真) schools. The other two major schools in Daoist history, Highest Clarity and Numinous Treasure (Lingbao 靈寶), flourished in the middle ages and have since been subsumed under the other two schools. In addition, there are other, smaller movements and lineages such as the tradition of Thunder Rites (*leifa* 雷法) and various forms of internal alchemy (*neidan* 內丹).

The textual tradition is represented by the Daoist canon of the early Ming dynasty and various collections created since then (see Komjathy 2002). It is important to note, however, that along with the obvious issues in dealing with translations of ancient texts, there is a strong tradition of secrecy in Daoism. This has resulted in many texts using analogy and code in their descriptions of practices, and even on occasion being deliberately scrambled in order to protect the secrets of certain sects or authors. Indeed, many of the texts we can access today were not originally intended for uninitiated readers. Thus care must be taken in the interpretation of classical Daoist texts and, where possible, texts should be interpreted in conjunction with the living tradition. That being said, standard psychological research practices should also be taken into consideration.

The Secret of the Golden Flower

One Daoist textual source already relatively well known to Western psychologists is the *Secret of the Golden Flower* (*Taiyi jinhua zongzhi*). An important text of the Dragon Gate (Longmen 龍門) lineage of Complete Perfection (see Esposito 1998), it was received from the immortal Lü Dongbin 呂洞賓 in a spirit-writing séance possibly as early as 1668 (see Mori 2002; Despeux 2008b). However, due to multiple versions of the text and different stories concerning its production, its exact origin remains unclear. The earliest extant copy is from 1775 (see Mori 2002; Esposito 2008).

The contents of the text relate primarily to meditation techniques—it is essentially an instructional treatise. It is a good source for psychological study since it states that its purpose is to elucidate points hidden by secrecy and metaphor in the past. It uses comparatively clearer language and more concrete examples than many earlier texts. The current study aims to conduct a qualitative analysis of the *Secret of the Golden Flower* in order to elucidate the main points presented in this important Daoist text. The text was chosen because it expresses its message more clearly and explicitly than many other Daoist texts and because, despite potential misunderstandings about its contents, it is one of the most well known Daoist texts within Western psychological circles.

The text was popularized in the West by Jung's commentary on a translation of it by Richard Wilhelm. They first coined the title *The Secret of the Golden Flower* (Wilhelm and Jung 1962). Given that this was an early translation, and that Jung had limited access to accurate information about Daoism (indeed much of Western understanding of Daoism has only come about in the past twenty years or so; see Kirkland 2004), there are several issues with this early presentation. Wilhelm appears to have chosen to leave part of the text out, as his translation includes only eight chapters as compared with thirteen in all six known editions of the text, and is also missing part of the first chapter (Cleary 1991; Esposito 2008). Furthermore, according to Cleary (1991), Wilhelm took considerable liberties in translating the text, and this certainly appeared to be the case when the first author conducted his own translation. Perhaps not surprisingly given these facts, the accuracy of Jung's commentary has also been questioned (see Cott and Rock 2009).

It is also noteworthy that the *Secret of the Golden Flower* discusses many constructs that Jung largely ignores in his commentary. While other authors may interpret the text differently or discuss different aspects, until a structured analysis of the whole is conducted, many aspects remain uncertain. That is to say, opinions regarding what exactly the text discusses may be extrapolated from other texts, perhaps erroneously, or may simply be an interpretation that is not grounded in Daoist material at all. Therefore, a systematic qualitative analysis should demonstrate what exactly the text presents and what it does not. The current analysis thus aims first, to provide definitions derived from the text of all the major constructs it discusses; and second, to elucidate the relationships between these constructs, also derived from the text itself. In addition, the words of the text are used explicitly in the results of the analysis, providing further evidence for readers to see for themselves what exactly the text presents.

Methodology

The present study used a composite methodology consisting of aspects of map analysis, thematic analysis, and grounded theory. This methodology adhered to the following procedural steps:

- Before beginning the analysis, we read the text from start to finish several times in order to gain a familiarity with its content.
- We extracted psycho-spiritual constructs as well as passages describing their nature from the text, then organized them into a set of primary constructs for more detailed examination.
- Following this, we again searched the text for references to relationships between these primary constructs. This allowed us to reorganize the primary constructs: to collapse those equated with each other in the text under a single heading and arrange all those remaining into groups according to their relationships as described in the text. These groups became the primary "themes" of the analysis.
- Subsequently, with these themes in mind, we again examined the text to elicit any relationships between primary themes, as well as to crosscheck them for validity.
- Finally, we organized all this information into a conceptual map, depicting the primary teachings of the text.

The overarching phenomenon under examination turned out to be a form of personal transformation called "turning the light around" (*huiguang* 回光). This was apparent in five themes, two dealing with the general process and three with specific procedures and outcomes in an apparent stage-like progression. They are: 1) refining the material soul (*po* 魄)[1] into the spirit soul (*hun* 魂) and consciousness spirit (*shishen* 識神) into primordial spirit (*yuanshen* 元神); 2) refining of the illumination of consciousness (*shiguang* 識光) into the illumination of inherent nature (*xingguang* 性光); 3) harmonizing the breath; 4) the interaction of water and fire; and 5) and the interaction of Heaven and Earth. Let us now look at each of these in turn.

From Material to Spirit Soul

The spirit soul exists in the celestial heart-mind. It is yang, it is light and clear *qi*. This comes of itself from great emptiness, it shares the same substance with the primal origin. (2:115-19)

All forms of lust move *qi*. They are all the material soul's doing. This is precisely what the consciousness spirit is. (2:126-128)

---

[1] For pragmatic reasons, English translations of Chinese terms have been used here. However, given that any English term is only a partial representation and carries its own preconceived ideas (e.g., the word 'soul'), the authors recommend anyone wishing to engage in a serious study of Daoism should learn the Chinese for these key concepts and communicate in these terms.

If conceptual thought is not cut off, the spirit will not arise. If the heart-mind is not empty, the medicine will not form. (10:114-117)

Therefore, the practice of turning the light around is the means of refining the spirit soul, is the means of preserving the spirit, is the means of governing the material soul, is the means of cutting off conceptual thought. (2:86-89)[2]

Huiguang literally means "turning around," "returning," "reverting," or "revolving" (*hui* 回) "light," "radiance," or "illumination" (*guang* 光). It describes a process of recovering what is considered a natural state through a gradual refining from the coarse and crude to the fine and subtle.

The process begins with refining the products of ordinary experience or normal waking consciousness to gain access to the ingredients for enlightenment and immortality. The text discusses six constructs relating to this process, which can be arranged into two groups. The first group (see Fig. 1, right circle) contains the products of ordinary human experience, consciousness spirit (*shishen*)[3], which develops from, and functions in association with, the material soul (*po*), which in turn is housed within the body-self (*shen* 身). They stand in contrast to primordial spirit (*yuanshen*), concealed in the spirit soul, which in turn is housed in the celestial heart-mind (*tianxin* 天心; see left circle). The process of reverting one's radiance means to refine the material soul by interrupting the ordinary stream of conceptual thought or consciousness.

The refined material soul will bring about pure yang and revert to being pure spirit soul, which in turn allows primordial spirit to come to the fore and assume its original and rightful position. In other words, consciousness spirit forms a pair with the material soul. It is directly described as lust and desire but, based on other passages of the text, probably includes all conceptual, evaluative thought.

The material soul and the conscious spirit rule all ordinary psychological experience, but with the help of meditation their activities can be interrupted and refined back to a state that allows the primordial spirit and spirit soul to recover their dominance. Thus is personal transformation effected in the text.

The material soul is the substance of conceptual thought; conceptual thought develops through it. It is yin in nature and continues after death as the person's "ghost"—as contrasted with yang, the quality of the living. Yin and yang appear in the text in two ways:

---

[2] All translations are the work of the first author. The first number here indicates the chapter, the second the passage number as indicated by any punctuation in the original texts, excluding commentaries.

[3] Consciousness here, and throughout this chapter, is intended to indicate the day-to-day, discriminating, conceptual mind.

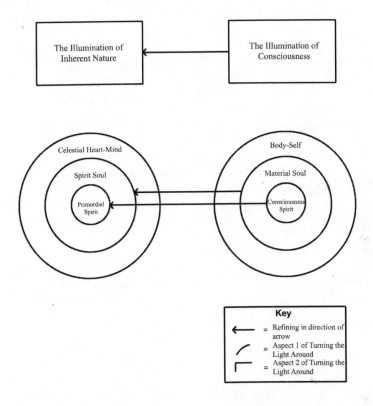

Fig 1.: The Interrelation of the Celestial and the Human.

1) they should complement each other in perfect harmony, such as heaven (yang) and earth (yin) balancing each other and merging into one; 2) yin is undesirable and should be completely refined to produce pure yang, which is desirable. The material soul is described as yin in the latter sense. Its main residence during life is the personal body-self (*shen*) which, as the text states, is created by intention—the personalized attention to ego-related concerns. It will fall away as meditation practice intensifies and is not mentioned as playing a particularly important role in turning the light around.

Primordial spirit, aside from being contrasted with consciousness spirit, is one of the traditional Three Treasures; essence (*jing* 精), energy (*qi*), and spirit (*shen*). According to *The Secret of the Golden Flower*, unlike essence and *qi*, the primordial spirit lasts for eternity. To gain access to it, one must follow the meditation practice, interrupt the consciousness spirit, and refine the material soul. This, as the text emphasizes is not mere quietism but the engagement of undivided concentration.   The practitioner thereby gains access to the infinite. In transpersonal psychology terms, the direct experience of primordial spirit may result in a temporal transcendence of the personal.

The spirit soul, according to the text, houses the primordial spirit. It appears to relate to the conscious experience of something, as in seeing or dreaming. One may speculate that the spirit soul is, therefore, the vessel through which experience of the world is possible for the primordial spirit. The spirit soul in turn resides within the celestial heart-mind and is described, in contrast to the material soul, as being yang *qi* that is obtained from the cosmos.

The celestial heart-mind, moreover, houses the spirit soul, and is equated with the earth intent. It is described as akin to a house where "the light" is the master, and thus may be the staging ground for turning the light around.

The specific procedure for this theme is to refine the material soul and interrupt conceptual thought. This is achieved through the meditation technique of turning the light around. Conceptual thought is seen as entanglement in the world of form and senses and as damaging to the spirit. Thus, the practitioner is advised to reverse this "leakage," which may mean to keep experience and attention focused inward, rather than the ordinary outflow of interaction with the phenomenal world. The consciousness spirit seems to be conceptual thought, and thus to interrupt it probably means to achieve a meditative state wherein conceptual thoughts cease to interfere with the mind.

If this is achieved, the true nature of the primordial spirit may be revealed. However, practitioners would still need to be aware of states such as "submersion in darkness," which may also be experienced as the lack of conceptual thought. To understand precisely what the material soul and the spirit soul are, may require direct experience, probably with the guidance of a master. Indeed, the text itself states that, while it is attempting to elucidate the practice of meditation, the guidance of a master is still necessary. Thus, this text alone is not sufficient to practice the techniques described.

The Daoist construct of "soul," it becomes clear, is much more concrete than comparative ideas in other religions and more consciously manipulated in praxis (e.g., solidified, crystallized, refined, reverted). The apparent goal of the practice, moreover, seems vastly different from comparative Western practices or psychological interventions. If we consider the consciousness spirit and material soul being in control to be the ordinary experience of a reasonably well adjusted individual, then many Western approaches, such as cognitive-behavioral therapy, are arguably geared toward reestablishing this situation. In contrast, this is simply the starting point for turning the light around, with the primary goal being something far loftier and ultimately spiritual.

To us, it seems like a process of finding that aspect of oneself that is not dependent on behavioral conditioning, cognitive development, or any other learning theory, and giving this aspect of the self precedence over the thinking, discriminating self in day to day awareness. It is not a regression to animal instincts or base impulses and desires, but the embodiment of a part of oneself that is connected with something greater, be it represented by humankind, nature, the earth, the universe, or words like "Dao" or "God." It is once again clear then, how this practice might be of interest to transpersonal psychologists considering, for example, Daniels's (2005) "short way" of defining transpersonal psychology as being essentially about the spiritual aspects of human experience.

Consciousness to Inherent Nature

> When you reach the pass of inherent nature [*xing*] and life conditions [*ming*] you forget intention [*yi*] and conceptual thought [*shi*]. With intention and conceptual thought forgotten, you see fundamental reality. (13:22-23)

> If you turn [the light] around for one hundred days [see Fig. 2, Stage 1], then essence and *qi* will naturally be sufficient and true yang will spontaneously appear. In the midst of water you will spontaneously have true fire [Fig. 2, Stage 2]. By means of this you can grasp the practice, by natural order [*ziran*] they will copulate, by natural order the fetus will be produced [Fig. 2, Stage 2]. At that moment I was in the heaven of no conceptual thought and no knowing, and it was as if the infant child were already complete [Fig. 2, Stage 3]. (9:10-18)

This theme is the other general aspect of turning the light around. It is discussed in terms of two constructs; the illumination of inherent nature, and the illumination of consciousness. Ordinarily, the illumination of inherent nature is constantly being transformed into the illumination of consciousness due to coming into contact with the objects of experience (including psychological phenomena such as memory, logic, etc.).

The process as described in the text is to interrupt this and reverse it, stilling the constant stream of conceptual thought and its objects via meditation, to allow the illumination of inherent nature to become full and clear. This is represented by the arrow from the box on the right of Fig. 1 to the box on the left in Fig. 1.

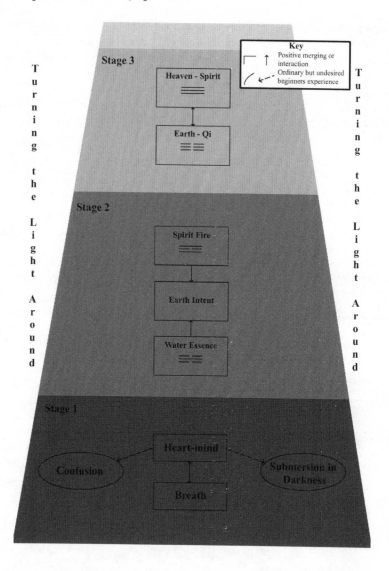

Fig. 2: Procedural Stages 1, 2, and 3.

The illumination of inherent nature may be related to what is sometimes called the "pure consciousness event" (PCE; e.g., Forman 1990) and thus turning the light around may be a method of achieving this state. The PCE can be defined as a wakeful yet phenomenologically contentless (i.e., non-intentional) consciousness (Forman 1998). The existence of such states has been debated (e.g.,

Almond 1988) and thus the process of turning the light around may prove interesting as a new avenue for research into the possibility of the PCE. The text states that if ordinary conceptual thought is forgotten, basic reality is seen, which seems to indicate that ordinary conscious experience obscures fundamental reality. Furthermore, it would appear that achieving the illumination of inherent nature is not only a goal in itself but also the means to success in the rest of the processes described in *The Secret of the Golden Flower*. The presentation of the two constructs and the process relating to them is outlined below.

The illumination of consciousness (*shiguang* 識光) is related to the consciousness spirit of the previous section. It is the ordinary, day-to-day psychological experience. The illumination of inherent nature is what exists spontaneously prior to the categorical discrimination of conceptual thought. Once conceptual thought and perception become involved, the illumination of inherent nature becomes the illumination of consciousness.

The illumination of inherent nature (*xingguang* 性光) becomes the illumination of consciousness and consequently results when the illumination of consciousness is refined or reverted through meditation. That is to say, when ordinary conceptual thought is interrupted and stilled, the illumination of inherent nature will present itself. This is not literally light, but is akin to the unformed "substance" of consciousness. Thus, the illumination of inherent nature may be considered a "pure" or unmediated consciousness. Only when the conceptual mind is "forgotten" does the illumination of inherent nature become accessible. Consequently, deliberate meditation will not produce the illumination of inherent nature; it can only be achieved through an effortlessness indicated by the classic Daoist concept of nonaction (*wuwei* 無為).

The procedure in this theme is to revert the illumination of consciousness back into the illumination of inherent nature through a process of "forgetting." Once the ordinary workings of conceptual thought have been interrupted, "fundamental reality" can be experienced. What exactly this "fundamental reality" is certainly merits further investigation; however, as *The Secret of the Golden Flower* does not delve into this topic in particular detail, "fundamental reality" was not captured as a theme or construct in the present analysis.[4] It is again important to note here that the text makes a distinction between erroneous states such quietism or submersion in darkness and what here is referred to as "forgetting conceptual thought." This theme also highlights the relationship between all of the other aspects mentioned in the text. Turning the light around is the general process; however, there are levels within this process and the next

---

4 One text that may be useful in investigating the nature of "fundamental reality" from a Daoist perspective is perhaps the *Wuzhen pian* 悟真篇, which has also been translated by Cleary (1987) under the title *Understanding Reality*. Of course it is not certain that "reality" is taken to mean the same thing in the *Wuzhen pian* and the *Taiyi jinhua zongzhi*.

three sections will outline these levels. Harmonizing the breath is the beginning process of stabilizing the awareness and producing the foundation, which is the water essence. After this "hundred days of foundation" the adept will have "true illumination" which is fire spirit, and the interaction of water and fire can take place. The result of this interaction is purified spirit and purified *qi*, pure yang and pure yin, Heaven and Earth. The interaction of Heaven and Earth is "true intercourse;" it is also a form of "bathing" and "incubation." This is the culmination of mental stillness or clarity.

Harmonizing the Breath

Now when the heart-mind forms a thought, that thought is the presently existing heart-mind. This heart-mind is illumination, it is medicine. (10:24-27)

Breath in setting up the foundation does not refer to inhalation and exhalation. Breath is one's own heart-mind, and one's own heart-mind is breath. It is primordial spirit, primordial *qi*, primordial essence. (9:25-32)

What is scattered [*san*] can be gathered in, what is in discord [*luan*] can be put in order. If one is submerged in darkness, then stupor comes from this, obscurity comes from this. Confusion still has a direction, but to arrive at the point of submersion in darkness, one is completely at the whim of the material soul. In confusion the spirit soul is still present, but to arrive at the point of submersion in darkness, pure yin is in complete control. (4:133-43)

This theme, along with the next two, represents the stage-like progression that occurs through the more general practice of turning the light around. "Harmonizing the breath" is the beginning stage, where conceptual thought is still predominant. Thus, the technique of resting the breath on the heart-mind and the heart-mind on the breath is used to help still conceptual thought. This is represented in Fig. 2 as the double-headed arrow between heart-mind and breath. The problems that arise at this beginning stage of turning the light around are confusion and submersion in darkness, represented by the ovals connected to heart-mind by broken arrows.

Discussed in terms of the material soul, confusion and submersion in darkness are not constructs in the same sense as, for example, spirit soul or breath, but are included in Fig. 2 more as "states of being" that can occur at this stage. That is to say, where constructs such as spirit soul seem to be attributed some sort of metaphysical reality in the text, confusion and submersion in darkness are described as processes that may occur, or the state of experiencing that process. The method for curing submersion in darkness and confusion, according to the text, is simply to rest the breath on the heart-mind and the heart-mind on the breath until both heart-mind and breath become pacified.

The presentation of the four constructs and the process relating to them appears below.

The heart-mind (*xin* 心) permeates all five themes of this analysis. In the first theme, there is the celestial heart-mind, which shares the character *xin*. It also matches the earth intent, which in turn may be related to the "ancestral chamber." Furthermore, both the celestial heart-mind and the heart-mind in this theme are said to "house" the spirit. The first line of extract at the start of this section is also reminiscent of the previous theme, not only in the heart-mind being equated with illumination, but also in the process of forming a thought and that thought being the substance of the heart-mind. Thus, the illumination of inherent nature and the illumination of consciousness may be two aspects of heart-mind. In the interaction of Heaven and Earth, although the heart-mind was not explicitly extracted as a construct *per se*, clarity of mind is described as being necessary in the procedure section and heart-mind is even equated with spirit at this stage. It is important to note here that heart-mind does not refer to the physical heart or brain but is more akin to the substance of consciousness and is in fact equated with the illumination (*guang*) that is turned around or revolved (*hui*).

Breath (*xi* 息) here is not the physical respiration but something more subtle associated with both the breathing and the heart-mind. Indeed, the two components of the Chinese character for breath are "oneself" or "one's own" and "heart-mind." The text, in fact, states that the breath and the heart-mind are one, although it also discusses them separately so it is not entirely clear what the distinction is. This may be another point where experiential knowledge is necessary, possibly under the guidance of someone who has already mastered the technique. It also states that the "true breath" only becomes perceptible after a certain level of subtlety is achieved and maintained for a period, whereupon the "substance of the mind" can be perceived.

Confusion (*sanluan* 散乱) is one of two obstacles that practitioners face at this stage. The characters mean "scattered," "dispersed" (*san*) and "trouble," "disorder," "confusion" (*luan*). The state they indicate is a lingering presence of the material soul, which causes the spirit to race and the mind to be distracted. It is, compared with submersion in darkness, relatively easy to cure because, although one might not be aware of it during day–to-day life, during meditation it will become obvious, at which point confusion itself becomes a cure for confusion. That is to say, once the practitioner becomes aware that they are distracted or confused, they can return to concentrating on meditation.

Submersion in darkness (*hunchen* 昏沈) is a more serious problem than confusion: the text states that here the material soul is in complete control. The characters mean "dark," "dim," "disordered" (*hun*) and "submerged," "sunken," "caught up" (*chen*). In this state of *hunchen* the spirit is dim and the mind cloudy, so that it is not easy to recognize that one has fallen into it, making it harder to emerge. The text suggests getting up and taking a walk as a potential aid in dealing with submersion in darkness, but ultimately it states that the solution to both this and confusion is "harmonizing the breath." The text also makes a distinction between (1) submersion that the practitioner can become aware of, and (2) submersion that the practitioner cannot become aware of and from which he thus never emerges.

The procedure for this theme begins with methods for dealing with the two obstacles of submersion in darkness and confusion. The text then moves on to discuss a method of "letting go," which was also important for refining the illumination of consciousness into the illumination of inherent nature. The practitioner relaxes and lets go of conceptual thought, but not so much so as to fall into submersion or to be unable to allow the mind to "listen to" the breathing. The text goes on to say that, just as the breath is not the physical respiration, "listening" is not auditory but a mental process of resting the attention on the breath. This progressive process of gradually letting go whilst maintaining a certain level of awareness on the breath leads to deeper and deeper levels of stillness (*jing* 靜), which is eventually necessary for the completion of the interaction of Heaven and Earth. It also leads to the acquisition of "true illumination," the fire spirit, and the water essence, all of which are necessary for continuing on to the next stage. The significance of one hundred days is not entirely clear based on the text alone, as it states that one hundred days is not in fact one hundred days. Again, this may be a point that requires clarification by a teacher.

Water and Fire

What is meant by water essence? This is the true unified *qi* before heaven. Fire spirit is illumination. Earth intent is the central palace, the celestial heart-mind. Fire spirit is the function, earth intent is the form, water essence is the foundation. (2:57-63)

Next use the two eyes to illuminate the palace of water inwardly. Where the flower of illumination arrives, true yang will emerge in response. As for fire, it is yang outside but yin inside. It is the form of heaven, but with one yin inside ruling it. (8:61-64)

The one yin ruler [in the trigram Kan—Fire] pursues colors and follows sounds, while the one yang [in the trigram Li—Water] withdraws hearing and arrests sight. (11:9-10)

This theme is the second in the stage-like progression that results from the general process of turning the light around. The three constructs here are acquired through completion of the previous stage. Water essence (*jingshui* 精水) is the unified *qi* that emerges when the illumination returns to the ancestral chamber through completion of harmonizing the breath. Fire spirit (*shenhuo* 神

火) is the real light that is achieved after the "hundred days of setting up the foundation," which is harmonizing the breath. Earth intent (*yitu* 意土) is related to the heart-mind and may even be the evolution of it. Water (i.e., water essence) is represented symbolically as yin outside and yang inside; fire (i.e., fire spirit) is represented as yang outside and yin inside.

The goal of this stage is to achieve pure yang, by replacing the yin inside the trigram Kan (Fire) with the yang from inside the trigram Li (Water). Earth intent is the mediating factor within this process, maintaining the central balance. The interaction of Water and Fire is represented in Fig. 2 by the arrows from fire spirit and water essence into earth intent. The method for doing this is to use fire spirit, which is the representation of the light at this stage, to arouse the yang within water. When fire spirit meets water essence, the yang *qi* within water will respond by itself. The one yang from the trigram Water and the two yang from Fire will then join to make three yang lines, which form the trigram Qian 乾 (Heaven), a necessary ingredient of the next stage of the process.

On a more psychological level, yin within Fire controls the spirit and lets it pursue sense experience. This relates to the material soul, the consciousness spirit, and the illumination of consciousness. If this yin is replaced with the yang from Water, spirit becomes stable. This is associated with the spirit soul, the primordial spirit, and the illumination of inherent nature. The presentation of the three constructs and the process relating to them is outlined below.

Water essence, then, is a form of *qi* that is yang within yin. Earth intent is the representation of the heart-mind at this stage. It is interesting to note that earth intent and fire spirit may, in fact, be different aspects of the same thing, the former being substance and the latter function. Water essence would then be the foundation on which this "thing" is based, but what exactly this "thing" constitutes the text does not specify.

As regards the procedure at this stage, the text describes in detail the process of arousing the yang from Water and joining it with the yang from Fire. Fire is described as being pure yang in substance but with yin inside controlling it. It may be possible to say that it is this yin that causes, for example, the consciousness spirit to develop. Indeed, the material soul, which the consciousness spirit develops based upon, is described as being yin in nature. However, if this single yin can be replaced with a single yang, that from Water, then the spirit will become calm and the process of reversal will begin to occur by itself. It is perhaps noteworthy that the language of the text seems to give these yin and yang energies a more distinctly physical reality than simple psychological constructs.

That is to say, this theme seems to be referring to subtle energies that have an existence somewhere in between the purely psychological and the grossly physical. The existence and nature of these energies merit further attention by transpersonal psychologists in that they appear to transcend the psychological realm and may be some sort of mediator between the mental and the physical. Some research does exist concerning subtle energies such as *qi* (see Chen 2004); however, in the absence of further research with the living Daoist tradition, the existence and nature of subtle energies in the methods outlined herein remain unverified.

Heaven and Earth

Practice turning the light around and the *qi* of Heaven and Earth, yin and yang, can not help but be consolidated. (3:3-4)

This is heaven entering into the midst of earth, the time when the multitude mysteries return to their root. This then is precisely the consolidated spirit entering the *qi* cavity. (8:139-141)

You will suddenly see white snow flying in the sixth month (i.e., in the height of summer), and if you complete the three alterations you will moreover see the glorious shining wheel of the sun. (8:3-4)

White snow flying refers to the true yin in the middle of Fire about to return to Earth. (8:198-200)

The wheel of the sun refers to the one yang in Water shining gloriously and returning to Heaven. Taking from Water to fill in Fire is herein. (8:203-06)

Water and Fire are yin and yang, yin and yang are inherent nature and life conditions, inherent nature and life conditions are body-self and heart-mind, body-self and heart-mind are spirit and *qi*. (11:11-14)

This theme represents the final stage in the progression of turning the light around. There are two constructs involved in this final stage: the trigram Qian (Heaven) which represents spirit and the trigram Kun 坤(*Earth*) which represents *qi*. These two constructs are again products of the previous stage. Through the interaction of water (water essence, Water) and fire (fire spirit, Fire), the single yin line from the trigram Kan and the single yang line from the trigram Li trade places to produce the trigrams Qian (three yang lines) and Kun (three yin lines). That is to say, Heaven and Earth are the products of the interaction of Water and Fire. At this stage, the spirit is nurtured within *qi* and "heaven enters earth." This is represented in Fig. 2 by the double headed arrow between Heaven - spirit and Earth - *qi*. It is achieved through a supreme level of psychological clarity and stillness. It is also called "bathing" or "washing the thoughts," and is the culmination of the reversion from conceptual thought to inherent nature spoken of throughout this analysis. The presentation of the two constructs and the process relating to them is outlined below.

Qian is the trigram representing heaven (*tian* 天), the power of pure yang. The discussion of this stage in *The Secret of the Golden Flower* is more metaphorical and abstruse than the prior stages, possibly because it is further from conceptual thought. Heaven is the result of replacing the yin in Fire (i.e., fire spirit) with the yang from Water (i.e., water essence). It is a representation of spirit, but the spirit that is now no longer drawn outward by sense experience but is instead turned inward and centered. It is most likely the same as the primordial spirit, and thus seems to refer to the infinite within the practitioner.

Kun is the trigram representing earth (*di* 地), the power of pure yin. Earth is the result of replacing the yang from Water with the yin from Fire. This is a representation of *qi*, but again it is *qi* that has been transformed since the previous stage. How exactly the *qi* in this theme is different from the previous theme is not entirely clear based on the text alone and may again require experiential understanding and the guidance of a teacher to recognize.

The procedure at this stage is essentially one of supreme mental quietude. There is no active work other than sitting in quietude and emptiness; heaven enters earth spontaneously of itself. The text warns that if this does not occur spontaneously (i.e., if deliberate attention is involved), then Heaven and Earth will not join properly and will after a time separate by themselves. For those familiar with the terms, the text makes allusion to the interaction of water and fire as being the "microcosmic orbit" (*xiao zhoutian* 小周天) and the interaction of Heaven and Earth as being the "macrocosmic orbit" (*da zhoutian* 大周天) (see Darga 2008).

Conclusion

The practices discussed in *The Secret of the Golden Flower* may be summarized as follows. The general practice of turning the light around can be described in two themes. The goal of the first is to refine the consciousness spirit into the primordial spirit and the material soul into the spirit soul, through a process of reversing the direction of attention from the external to the internal world. The second aspect of the general process of turning the light around is described as a refining of the illumination of consciousness into the illumination of inherent nature, again through the same process of reversal, a complete withdrawal of attention from the objects of conceptual thought.

The Secret of the Golden Flower elaborates on this general process of turning the light around by describing a stage-like progression consisting of three parts. The first stage is a clarification and stilling of mental processes through the technique of "harmonizing the breath." The second stage involves both a mental and energetic aspect, represented by the metaphor of the interaction of water and fire. Practitioners reach the third and final stage through the culmination of mental quietude and results in the incubation of the spirit in the *qi*, which is represented metaphorically by heaven entering earth.

This paper has presented preliminary definitions of the major constructs discussed in *The Secret of the Golden Flower* as well as the relationship between them. The primary constructs can be organized into five themes, and the relationship between these five themes has been discussed. Although this should not be considered an absolute presentation of the major themes of *The Secret of the Golden Flower*, the above results should allow those unfamiliar with the text to clearly understand the primary procedures discussed in the text including the constructs involved.

It should be clear from the current analysis that prior investigations of *The Secret of the Golden Flower* by Western psychologists, such as Jung's commentary (Wilhelm and Jung 1962), have failed to consider all the important constructs discussed in the text and the relationships between them. It is certainly true, however, that this analysis was hampered by some limitations. While *The Secret of the Golden Flower* tends to use clearer language in explaining the procedures captured in the present analysis, it still relies on metaphor at times and there are several constructs, such as the water essence, that may require experiential knowledge in order to truly understand them.

It would therefore be edifying, in accordance with the suggestions of Cott and Rock (2009), to verify the results presented herein with the other primary source of Daoist material, the living Daoist tradition. Thus, interviews might be conducted with, for example, members of the *Longmen* school who practice the turning the light around method, and this data could then be analyzed and compared with the results of the present study.

It may also be useful to conduct similar analyses to those conducted in the present study on other Daoist textual sources. This might allow for triangulation of results regarding constructs presented herein, such as the spirit soul and material soul, as well as adding new constructs not discussed in *The Secret of the Golden Flower*. A corpus of material could thereby be formed as a reference for psychologists wishing to understand a particular construct based on the qualitative analysis of Daoist textual sources.[5] Other future studies might include more detailed phenomenological analyses of single constructs, such as the illumination of inherent nature or the primordial spirit, and comparisons of these results with the results of phenomenological analyses of constructs from other traditions, such as Buddhism or Eastern Orthodox Christianity. Quantita-

---

[5] We do not suggest that this is the only way to understand Daoist constructs, it is merely one source of information that might be useful.

tive studies of the effects of practices such as turning the light around on mood, subjective well being, etc., may also be edifying. However, the authors would recommend these types of studies be conducted with the assistance of the living Daoist community, rather than based on textual sources alone.

The results of the present analysis should have revealed that there is potentially a great deal of material in Daoist sources that may be of interest to transpersonal psychologists. The overall goal of the practice of turning the light around seems to be an integration, first of the parts of the self (e.g., breath, heart-mind, essence, *qi*, spirit), and ultimately of all duality, as represented by the polar opposites yin and yang. Thus, arguably the goal of the practice is to transcend the individual ego in the form of the consciousness spirit and the illumination of consciousness, and move toward an identity with something that is infinite, i.e., the primordial spirit.

Needless to say, this overall goal may be considered transpersonal in nature, and there are also numerous specific references to what might be considered transpersonal experiences. For example, the identification of the self with the primordial spirit, which is said to be infinite, may represent a case of "survival of consciousness" if the self is deemed to be conscious. Depending on the definition of "ego," "forgetting conceptual thought" may represent a movement away from ego and thus a "trans-ego experience." Any one of these could be examined in greater detail to learn more about the variety of transpersonal experiences, and there are not only thousands more texts like *The Secret of the Golden Flower* but also thousands of living, practicing Daoists around the world. It is hoped that the present analysis will elicit greater interest in Daoism from psychologists and lead to new and valuable research.

Bibliography

Almond, 1988. "Mysticism and its contexts." *Sophia* 271:40-49.

Chen, K. W. 2004. "An analytic review of studies on measuring effects of external *qi* in China." *Alternative Therapies in Health and Medicine* 104:38-51.

Cleary, T. 1987. *Understanding Reality*. Honolulu: University of Hawai'i Press.

_____. 1988. *Awakening to the Tao*. Boston: Shambhala.

_____. 1991. *The Secret of the Golden Flower: The Classic Chinese Book of Life*. New York: Harper Collins.

Cott, C., and Rock, A. 2008. "Phenomenology of N,N-Dimethyltryptamine use: A thematic analysis." *Journal of Scientific Exploration* 223:359-70.

_____. 2009. "Towards a transpersonal psychology of Daoism: Definitions, past research, and future directions." *International Journal of Transpersonal Studies* 28:119-33.

Daniels, M. 2005. *Shadow, Self, Spirit: Essays in Transpersonal Psychology*. Exeter: Imprint Academic.

Darga, M. 2008. "Zhoutian." In *The encyclopedia of Taoism*, edited by F. Pregadio, 2:1287-89. London: Routledge.

DeSilva, 2000. *An Introduction to Buddhist Psychology*. Lanham: Rowman and Littlefield.

Despeux, C. 2008a. "Yangsheng." In *The Encyclopedia of Taoism*, edited by F. Pregadio, 1148-50. London: Routledge.

Despeux, C. 2008b. "*Fuqi*." In *The encyclopedia of Taoism*, edited by F. Pregadio, 428-29. London: Routledge.

Engelhardt, U. 2000. "Longevity techniques and Chinese medicine." In *Daoism Handbook*, edited by Livia Kohn, 74-108. Leiden: E. Brill.

Esposito, M. 1998. "The different versions of *The Secret of the Golden Flower* and their relationship with the Longmen school." *Transactions of the International Conference of Eastern Studies* 43:90–110.

Esposito, M. 2008. "*Taiyi jinhua zongzhi*." In *The encyclopedia of Taoism*, edited by F. Pregadio, 961-62. London: Routledge.

Forman, R. K. C.,. ed. 1990. *The Problem of Pure Consciousness*. New York: Oxford University Press.

Forman, R. K. C. 1998. "Introduction: Mystical consciousness, the innate capacity, and the perennial philosophy." In *Innate capacity: Mysticism, psychology and philosophy*, edited by R. K. C.Forman, 3-42. New York: Oxford University Press.

Hartelius, G., M. Caplan, and M. A. Rardin. 2007. "Transpersonal psychology: Defining the past, divining the future." *The Humanistic Psychologist* 352:1-26.

Kirkland, R. 2004. *Taoism: The Enduring Tradition*. New York: Routledge.

Kohn, L. 1987. *Seven Steps to the Tao: Sima Chengzhen's Zuowanglun*. Sankt Augustin/ Nettetal: Monumenta Serica.

_____, ed. 1989. *Taoist Meditation and Longevity Techniques*. Ann Arbor: University of Michigan, Center for Chinese Studies.

_____. 2008a. "Meditation and visualisation." In *The encyclopedia of Taoism*, edited by F. Pregadio, 118-20. London: Routledge.

_____. 2008b. "Mysticism." In *The encyclopedia of Taoism*, edited by F. Pregadio, 120-22. London: Routledge.

_____. 2010. *Sitting in Oblivion: The Heart of Daoist Meditation*. Dunedin, Fla.: Three Pines Press.

Komjathy, Louis. 2002. *Title Index to Daoist Collections*. Cambridge, Mass.: Three Pines Press.

Miller, James. 2008. *The Way of Highest Clarity: Nature, Vision and Revelation in Medieval Daoism*. Magdalena, NM: Three Pines Press.

Mori, Yuria. 2002. "Identity and lineage: The *Taiyi jinhua zongzhi* and the spirit-writing cult to Patriarch Lü in Qing China." In *Daoist Identity: History, Lineage, and Ritual*, edited by L. Kohn and H. D. Roth, 165-84. Honolulu: University of Hawai'i Press.

Nisbett, R. E. 2003. *The Geography of Thought: How Asians and Westerners Think Differently. . . and Why*. New York: Free Press.

Robinet, I. 1997. *Taoism: Growth of a Religion*. Stanford: Stanford University Press.

Sancier, K. M. 1996. "Medical applications of qigong." *Alternative Therapies in Health and Medicine* 2:40-46.

Wilhelm, R., and C. G. Jung. 1962 [1931]. *The Secret of the Golden Flower: A Chinese Book of Life*. London: Routledge and Kegan Paul.

Wong, E. 1997. *Teachings of the Tao*. Boston: Shambhala.

Daoism, Psychology, and Psychosomanautics

Elliot Cohen

Psychology today is multi-paradigmatic and consists of a variety of different approaches, which means that Daoism needs to carefully select a suitable partner for a genuine dialogue. An appropriate method for this might be to go back to the historical and etymological roots of psychology that relate to both psyche and pneuma (soul and breath), concepts also prominent in Daoism and already explored in analytical and transpersonal psychology. The key aspect then is the notion of transformation, leading to the question: "To what extent psychology may have to transform away from reductionist modes and positivistic epistemologies to authentically engage with Daoist principles and cultivation practices?" Another positive aspect is the recent development of psychosomanautics in an attempt to move toward more holistic, transformational, and experiential ways of studying and teaching psychology.

> The psychologizing of Eastern contemplative disciplines can rob these disciplines of their spiritual substance. It can pervert them into a Western mental health gimmick, and thereby prevent them from introducing the sharply alternative vision of life they are capable of bringing us. (Welwood in Coltart 1993, 26)

This may not appear to be the most optimistic quote to begin a comparative study, and lay the foundations for an authentic dialogue, between Daoism and psychology; yet it does serve as an important caution. The key word in the above quote is "can," and that it is not an inevitable "will" should actually serve as a cautious encouragement.

In David McMahan's (2008) *The Making of Buddhist Modernism* he explores the various transformations of Buddhism from a living religious tradition in the East to something approximating a secular philosophy/psychology in the West. Particularly striking examples of this phenomenon may be encountered in Stephen Batchelor's (1997) *Buddhism without Beliefs* and, the more recent autobiographical, (2010) *Confessions of a Buddhist Atheist*. The Western tendency appears to be one of demystifying the mystical, and reducing all metaphysical "speculation" into either metaphorical imagery or psychological categories (see Cohen 2011).

So might we be contributing towards the making of a Daoist Modernism? Is this an inevitable consequence of Daoism's entering into a dialogue with Western psychology?

Personally, I don't believe this to be the case. Daoist scholarship has already, arguably moved beyond the earlier Orientalist assertions of there being two Daoisms (Kirkland 1992, Clarke 2000); the pure, original, philosophical tradition versus a later, degenerate, religious tradition. Daoism is now generally recognized for what it is; a rich and complex mixture of historically and culturally located philosophies, liturgies, ethical teachings, meditation techniques and cultivation exercises (Kohn 2001).

In conferences and papers past I have repeatedly made the point that a psychology that endeavors to enter into an authentic dialogue with Daoism must be one that is critically informed, spiritually literate, cross-culturally capable and embodied (seeking to move beyond dualistic models). This would be a psychology that reaches out in a spirit of genuine openness and curiosity; not one that reaches in with a view to scavenging psychological insights devoid of their cultural context and deeper meanings.

Before we begin to explore how dialogue has already been taking place it is important to recognize the various incarnations of, and approaches within, psychology. It is important to recognize that psychology is not a unified discipline, and it is my contention that certain approaches are simply better equipped to understand and relate to Daoism than others (see Cohen 2009; Cott and Rock 2009)

Psychology the Science

Psychology is most commonly thought of as constituting a science of "mind and behavior." In its emulation of the natural sciences, psychology often adopts a positivist epistemology; concerning itself with measurement and prediction; quantitative data and statistical analyses. These instrumentalist tendencies allow psychologists to perceive themselves as "hard scientists" in the same manner as physicists, chemists and biologists. With regard to biology, the advent and rapid advancement of brain mapping technologies (e.g. fMRIs), Neuropsychological paradigms are fast becoming the dominant paradigms in explaining, and accounting for human behavior and consciousness (Horton and Wedding 2008); whilst cognitive science commonly employs the increasingly familiar language of information processing and endeavors to explain our perception and behaviors in terms of mechanisms and schemas; with models of memory and attention etc. typically appearing in flowchart form (Sternberg and Mio 2008).

Psychology undergraduate textbooks cite Wilhelm Wundt as being the founding father of modern scientific, or experimental, psychology; opening the first psychological laboratory in the University of Leipzig in 1879, and conducting some of the first controlled experiments; endeavoring to make psychology into an objective science (Rieber and Robinson 2001). The current, consistent popularity of experimental psychology, neuropsychology and cognitive science all bear faithful testament to these beginnings.

The origins of modern Chinese psychology, as a Western import, may be traced back to the educational reformer Cai Yuanpei, who also studied at Wundt's laboratory and was himself to establish the first psychology laboratory in Beijing University in 1917 (Jing 1994). Later Soviet inspired, and simultaneously Westernized, Chinese psychology was to typically adopt positivist paradigms that left little room for spiritual questions, let alone cultivation.

So, what might such a psychological science (Chinese or Western) have to say, or even to do, with Daoism? At first there seem to be so many separations and distances with regard to language, world-view and methods that it might seem an impossible task to begin a meaningful dialogue. Yet dialogue has been, and is still, occurring between Daoism and psychology, and this book is one such important example and milestone.

To further contextualize this book we might begin by considering the increasing general interest Western psychologists are showing in understanding the Chinese people's behavior and psyche (Bond 2010); an understanding that seems increasingly urgent as China's economy and influence continues to grow in her increasingly swift journey towards becoming the world's new leading superpower.

In mainland China the three religions of Daoism, Confucianism and Buddhism are being carefully and cautiously re-examined for their possible use in further promoting and realizing the CCP's vision of a "harmonious society" (Kuhn 2009, 31) and filling the spiritual void that rapid economic expansion and material acquisition appears to have created (or rather revealed). We may also do well to consider more recently emerging indigenous forms of Chinese psychology (particularly popular in Taiwan) that seek to restore and proudly reclaim their Daoist (and Confucian) roots (Kim et al. 2006).

It may then further relieve the reader to learn that the "scientific psychology" I described in previous paragraphs is, in reality, only a part of what psychology is (and only a part of what it does), just as the natural sciences are only a part of the broader scientific venture (including the Human and Social Sciences). Psychology has both its experimental and experiential dimensions.

Integral theorists are fond of employing the popular Jain/Buddhist parable of the blind men and the elephant. Each man grabs a part of the elephant and believes that he, and only he, has and understands the whole. One man feels the ear of the elephant and believes it to be a fan; another man grabs the elephant's leg and is certain that it is a pillar etc. All the while the elephant remains standing in their midst, unaffected, undiscovered and unidentified. The Jain principle of *anekāntavāda* or non-one-sidedness (Singh 2001, 5423), reminds one of the importance of being interdisciplinary; being willing and able to adopt multiple perspectives and standpoints; integral to any authentic dialogue.

One may immediately apply this to our study of psychology and recognize that even if one's happiness is explained as being related to (or correlated with) the metabolizing of the monoamine neurotransmitter Serotonin (5-HT), this gives us little insight into the actual sensation of, or reason for, our being happy.

During the 2009 Daoist Studies Conference I was one of a panel discussing "Daoism and Contemporary Psychotherapy." I recall how at one point of the concluding group discussion the conversation moved towards recent breakthroughs in Neuropsychology. Meditative states may now be identified as corresponding to alpha, theta, and delta brain waves (as measured by an EEG). The practice of meditation (Goleman 2003) or certain Daoist cultivation practices may indeed be seen to affect brain function and chemistry and provide their practitioners with a "measurable" sense of wellbeing (Sandlund and Norlander 2000). Suddenly Tong Wai-Hop, head of the Hong Kong Daoist Association interjected to remind us that despite all these intriguing findings these methods were all essentially "alien" to Daoism. He was, and is, quite right!

Before we start attempting to use ultrasound technology in order to locate the *shengtai* 聖胎 sacred embryo, we would do well to remember where the authority has traditionally resided within the Daoist (and Buddhist) traditions to recognize various attainments and realizations. The perfected (*zhenren* 真人) was not (and is not) the "real/authentic Man or Woman; True Man or Woman; Perfected" (Miura in Pregadio 2008, 1265) on the basis of an fMRI scan or his or her score on a psychometric evaluation. If technology and instrumentalism begins to replace traditional teachings and transmissions then Daoism will quickly become absent from the dialogue.

Although most psychology governing bodies may continue to stress more positivist approaches and methods; many humanistic, transpersonal and integral movements have been, and continue, recovering and re-emphasizing psychology's earlier explorations of consciousness, experience and the making of meaning/s.

> The word *psychology* means the study of the psyche, and the word *psyche* means mind or soul. In the *Microsoft Thesaurus*, for *psyche* we find: "self: atman, soul, spirit; subjectivity: higher self, spiritual self, spirit." One is reminded, yet again, that the roots of psychology lie deep within the human soul and spirit. (Wilber 2000, vii)

Returning to the Breath

Martin and Barres (2004) provide a fascinating glimpse of the shifting intellectual trends and nomenclature over recent centuries, concerning the study of self and personal identity. Prior to psychology there existed the earlier eighteenth-century field of pneumatology. Beginning as a philosophy of spirits (including the human spirit) in the eighteenth century, it gradually transformed into a science of the human mind. By the mid nineteenth century it had been replaced with psychology (Martin and Barres 2004, p70-71). Today one would rarely encounter pneumatology outside the study of religion and theology, where it is now specifically related to the Christian concept of the Holy Spirit.

It may interest the reader to know that *pneuma* is the ancient Greek word not only for spirit, but also for breath. The term that succeeded it, "psychology," also has ancient Greek origins in the equally evocative term *psyche* that likewise denotes soul and breath. Psyche is also a Goddess of the Olympian pantheon, who remains the figurehead (logo) of the British Psychological Society; depicted as winged and bearing a lantern.

Psyche's legend tells of her courtship with the God of love, Eros (or Cupid), whilst she was still a mere mortal. Lucius Apuleius (Apuleius and Adlington 2007) recounts the tale in his *Metamorphoses*. The various trials and labors of love, dutifully performed by Psyche, led to her eventual deification and ascension into the ranks of the immortal gods of mount Olympus.

A common symbol for Psyche is the butterfly; in fact Psyche's wings are the wings of a butterfly. One need not be an analytical psychologist in order to appreciate the potent metaphor of transformation contained in the hidden and silent journey from cocooned caterpillar larvae (seemingly dead and inert) into a vibrant and beautiful butterfly. Her journey from mortality to immortality may also explain why Psyche herself was sometimes the subject of the ancient mystery religions of Greece (Gollnick 1992, 10); typically centered around, and concerned with, themes of rebirth and immortality.

That psychology has its roots in the study of spirit/breath and themes of (the quest for) immortality may justifiably serve as a source of optimism for those seeking to pursue a meaningful dialogue with Daoism. Yet these same ancient origins also house the beginnings of the mind-body dualism that is still a persistent property of, and problem in, Western philosophy and science.

The philosophers Pythagoras, Socrates, Plato and Aristotle are all typically included in introductory discussions concerning psychology's roots in antiquity. These seminal thinkers all addressed the interaction between the body and mind and the quest for (possibility of) immortality. Pythagoras's belief in the soul also included teachings on reincarnation; whilst the soul itself was conceived of as a harmony embedded in mathematical ratios and resonating to the music of the spheres (Kahn 2001).

Much of what we know of Socrates's thought was transmitted to us through his student Plato; who is arguably responsible for some of the more drastic forms of dualism. In Plato's (360 BCE) *Timaeus* the human being is divided into a tripartite soul (appetite/spirit/reason); with the immortal *nous* or pure reason. As the head was believed to contain the fire of Psyche, pure reason and rational thought were elevated over the waters of emotion and the earth of our physicality. Platonic doctrine typically viewed the human body as being a prison or a tomb for the human soul.

By contrast, Aristotle identifies Psyche as "the first entelechy of a physical organized body potentially possessing life" (O'Brien 2005, 216). Although the idea of Psyche as an entelechy may appear to reinforce dualistic tendencies, Aristotle was to somewhat soften these stark divisions between body and mind by demonstrating their interrelatedness in terms which may immediately be appreciated by anyone familiar with Daoist terminology.

"Continence and Incontinence: Pleasure" is the title of Book VII of Aristotle's *The Nicomachean Ethics* and contains the following passage: "Outbursts of anger and sexual appetites and some other such passions, it is evident, actually alter our bodily condition, and in some men even produce fits of madness" (Aristotle, Ross and Brown 2009, 122). Perhaps the above might be appreciated as some of the first, pioneering steps towards a psychosomatic theory. Yet today we still find ourselves, in the twenty-first century, struggling with what we term the "mind-body problem."

In the West, the metaphysical explorations of the ancients and pre-moderns were gradually replaced by the physicalist/materialist paradigms of the natural sciences, in the age of modernity. The modernists gradually sought to transform the immaterial soul of Psyche into the material mind; an emergent property, or by-product, of brain function; whereas the postmodernists continue to try to reduce both the metaphysical and material realms into socially constructed discourses (until the only things we are left to talk about is how we talk about things).

The task now falls to humanistic, transpersonal, and integral psychology movements to try and restore psychology's soul; navigating between the two hegemonies of scientism and postmodernism.

In turning to Daoism, we return to the breath, the *pneuma*, but this time within a different cultural and historical context. The *pneuma* of the ancient Greeks arguably belongs to metaphysics; whereas the whole concept of *qi* transforms the West's mind-body problem into a bodymind continuum; avoiding the extremes of either materialism or idealism: *qi*, pneuma, also called "breath, energy, and vital force" (Pregadio 2008, 796), "is an energy which manifests simultaneously on the physical and spiritual level; *qi* is in a constant state of flux and in varying states of aggregation. When *qi* condenses, energy transforms and accumulates into physical shape" (Maciocia 2002, 37).

A question that I often raise is how are Westerners (and psychologists in particular) to make sense of the central role *qi* plays in Chinese thought, medicine and Daoist cultivation practices. Many Westerners still seem concerned with trying to classify *qi* in either a physical or a spiritual (metaphysical) category. Questions arise such as: "Is *qi* a real force or is it all in the mind?"

This is not a question that should be answered, but rather a question that should be questioned, laden as it is with ontological assumptions. The "real" is reduced to and equated with physical, tangible, measurable qualities; whereas the "mind" is portrayed (or more accurately dismissed) as an unreliable realm of fantasy and phantasm. The consequences of this way of thinking can still be seen in the commonly negative associations many people make with term "psychosomatic," or the still much maligned "placebo effect;" effects that are ironically very real indeed (Harrington 1999).

The recent edition of the *Journal of Daoist Studies* (2010, Vol.3) cited seventeen recent studies that sought to demonstrate measurable physical or psychological effects of *qi,* ranging from neural repair to stress reduction.

The nature and purpose of this work is both praiseworthy and informative; however, one must remain vigilant that the continued study of, and work with, *qi* is not made subject to, or on condition of its demonstrability according to purely positivistic, reductionist modes; modes that are themselves compromised by inherently dualistic perspectives. In particular, one is reminded of the work of Yan Xin and his recent creed "save qigong with science" that suggests that without the support of, or validation from, Western science the very future of qigong is in doubt.

An additional possibility may include the study of *qi* being relegated solely to the domains of parapsychology, and that *qi* is studied as a potential form of psychokinetic energy (Heath 2003, 197). This would not necessarily benefit our understandings of Daoist cultivation as parapsychology is itself a "controversial science" (Broughton 1992) struggling between the competing needs of believers and the demands of the skeptics.

The subtle movements of the mind, in the way of thoughts, or the various physical movements of the body (one's emotions and motions) may all be viewed as movements of *qi*. This becomes particularly evident in traditional Chinese medicine (TCM) where certain excesses of emotion are listed amongst the "internal causes of disease," including anger, joy, sadness, worry, fear and shock (Maciocia 2002, 129).

Immediately one may appreciate the more central role *xin* 心 heart-mind plays in TCM; whereas in the West, body and mind still tends to become subject to the separate specialties of psychologists and physicians respectively.

Before beginning more comparative studies between Western psychology (or psychologies) and Daoism, I believe it is important to summarize the central role *xin* 心 heart-mind plays in Daoist cultivation. In particular, the *xin*'s integral relationship to the Three Treasures (*sanbao* 三寶) of essence, energy and spirit.

These Three Treasures may be understood as constituting the bio-psycho-spiritual make-up of the human being. One may immediately note that these constituents are studied and placed together, rather than being separated out into separate categories and disciplines, i.e., physiology, psychology, and theology.

Jing is most commonly translated as one's "essence" and is often related to the generative, sexual energies. "Libidinal energy" may be an appropriate term to employ as it contains psychological, emotional and biological (instinctual) components and connotations. As we have already defined *qi* we are left with the immaterial, transcendent soul- *shen* defined simply as "spirit" (Pregadio 2008, 879) with its various divine associations and relation to heavenly realms.

Much of Daoist cultivation concerns the directing, channeling up and transmutation of *jing* into *qi* into *shen*. In the inner alchemical practices of *neidan* 內丹 (specifically the inner breath- civil fire) the source, or means, of this transmutation is one's *yi* 意 or intention:

> The *neidan* notion of yi (intention) can only be understood in relation to the notion of *qi* (vital breath or pneuma); together, they represent the inner link between body and mind… The yi is described in alchemical texts as the rider of *qi*, similar to a conductor who orchestrates the movement of *qi* within the body. (Esposito in Pregadio 2008, 1158)

The success of one's practice of *neidan* depends on attaining (or realizing) interchangeability and ultimate union between *xin*, *yi* and *qi*; of one's heart-mind and energized intention. It is for this reason that I term Daoist cultivation practices as psychosomanautic practices (both navigating and directing the bodymind) as opposed to simply Daoist psychology.

It is vital that any dialogue on the part of psychology with Daoism take into account this holistic world-view and avoids trying to force Daoism into either materialist or idealist camps. In fact these more holistic and embodied approaches appear to reflect changing and newly prevailing Western attitudes (Clarke 2000, 98).

Sexual Energy and Sanity

Sigmund Freud struggled throughout the latter part of his career to have his "facts" about the human psyche and unconscious recognized and validated by his psychiatric and psychological peers. Freud clearly thought of himself as a natural scientist, but the scientific status of psychoanalysis remains, to this day, an area of contention and debate. The truths of psychoanalysis were drawn not only from Freud's own self-analysis and from case studies, but also from Freud's detailed and comprehensive study of world art and literature; he was even to write "wherever I go I find a poet has been there before me" (Colangelo 2002, 192).

For many, psychoanalysis is a hermeneutic method and process, still commonly referred to as "the talking cure" (Lichtenberg 1994, ix); Jacque Lacan went as far to describe psychoanalysis as "une pratique de bavardage" (Chaitin 1991, 1) – "a babbling practice." Lacan also reflected on the scientific status of psychoanalysis in a rather creative and surprising manner. Rather than asking how psychoanalysis could become more "scientific" he asked how our current concepts of science might need to change in order to include the truths and discoveries of psychoanalysis (Johnston 2010). Perhaps I am doing something quite similar in this chapter by asking what transformations Western psychology and psychotherapy may need to undergo in order to be able to enter into an authentic dialogue with Daoism; rather than seeking to force Daoist concepts into Western psychological categories.

That a bodily disturbance (extreme cases ranging from muteness to paralysis) may have its root in a psychological disturbance (e.g. repressed desire, guilt or anger) rather than any biological origin, is an example of a typical "textbook" insight gleaned by the psychoanalytic procedure. However, Freud appreciated that his central theories identifying and emphasizing the "sexual etiology" of neurosis would be considered to be quite "unpalatable" (Petocz 1999, 21) by many of his contemporaries, and also by much of Viennese society.

In the 1940s and 1950s psychoanalysis in the US was often encountered in the form of "psychosomatic medicine" and was practiced by medical doctors who had received psychoanalytic training (this the American Psychoanalytic Association had insisted, against Freud's (1969) wishes).

One may have already noted the striking similarities between psychoanalytic and psychosomatic theory and TCM's identification of the "internal causes of disease." It would also be amiss of me not to mention the work of Georg Groddeck, of whom Ken Wilber writes:

> That Freud directly took the concept of the id from Georg Groddeck's *The Book of the It*, which was based on the existence of a cosmic Tao or organic universal spirit. That.. well, it is a long story, all of which powerfully reminds us that the roots of modern psychology lie in spiritual traditions, precisely because the psyche itself is plugged into spiritual sources. (Wilber 2000, ix)

Although Wilber may slightly overplay Groddeck's influence on Freud's particular conception of the id, there was clearly a mutual admiration between Sigmund Freud and Georg Groddeck; the self described "wild analyst" (Alexander et al 1995, 315). Groddeck's name is still associated with psychosomatic medicine, of which he is often credited as a pioneer; as one who sought to bring the body back into psychotherapy.

Freud's theories concerning libidinal energy and drives were to be enthusiastically taken up and developed further by his student Wilhelm Reich; who actively sought take psychoanalysis to what he believed to be its logical conclusion, whilst simultaneously seeking to ground his theories in the natural sciences. "Psychoanalysis must one day be established on an organic basis. This was a genuine Freudian intuition!" (Reich 1960, 40).

Sadly Wilhelm Reich's name is frequently missing from psychology courses, articles and textbooks. When he does receive a (brief) mention both his theories and sanity are commonly called into question. Reich was to take Freud's ideas concerning libidinal energy quite literally and sought to utilize this "energy" for humanities wellbeing, self-knowledge and betterment.

Reich was to locate the orgasm, or more specifically "orgiastic potency," as being the means to break through the physical, psychological and emotional boundaries, or "armoring" (the restricting, hardening, deadening patterns) associated with the neurotic personality. As with Groddeck, Reich was to emphasize a fully embodied human being and as such therapy sessions involved physical components: "There can be no doubt that the most important goal of causal analytic therapy is the establishment of orgiastic potency, the ability to discharge accumulated sexual energy completely" (Reich 1960, 38).

He called this energy "orgone" and theorized that it existed, flowed, and functioned above and beyond our personal libidinal drives and was also a cosmic, primordial energy. Orgone as an underlying, animating, flowing and unifying principle may immediately strike one as being a Westerner's recognition and description of what the Chinese had called *qi* for centuries. However, Reich's understanding of, and claims concerning, Orgone were to be quite distinct from a traditional Chinese/Daoist understanding of *qi*:

> I am well aware of the fact that the human race has known about the existence of a universal energy related to life for many ages. However, the basic task of natural science consisted of making this energy usable. This is the sole difference between my work and all preceding knowledge. (Reich ND)[1]

Frustratingly (for psychologists interested in Daoism), throughout his work, Reich makes no specific mention of *qi*. Despite asserting an awareness of humanity's knowledge of a "universal energy" he provides little evidence of any

[1] This quote was taken from the archives of Orgone Institute, and is quoted on the homepage (biography section) of website of the Wilhelm Reich Museum: Orgonon in Maine http://www.wilhelmreichmuseum.org/biography.html accessed 16/09/10

actual awareness, or knowledge, of previous energetic models (e.g. *qi* or *Prana*) to historically inform or contextualize his discovery of Orgone.

It is a telling sign that Reich believes his distinguishing contribution will be to make this energy "usable," thereby ignoring the many preceding and fruitful centuries of Chinese medicinal and martial arts, qigong and Daoist calisthenics. This might be seen as evidence of Reich's ethnocentrism, and his arguably euro-centric perspective may also be encountered in his epistemological preferences. It is clear that Reich sincerely believed the methods of the natural sciences were the most appropriate for exploring and utilizing this universal energy; as can be seen in his writings on "orgone physics" and "cosmic orgone engineering."

Throughout Reich's work one may encounter the semiotics of science; detailed graphs, illustrations and equations; all in order to legitimate and position his findings within a positivistic framework. Despite some early encouraging correspondences with Albert Einstein (Raknes 2004, 74), widespread scientific recognition would elude Reich for his entire career.

Retrospectively it may be tempting to assert that Freud had identified a psychic force equivalent to the *jing*, whereas Reich might be credited with being one of the first Westerners to develop a concept closely resembling *jing*'s transformation into *qi*. There are, however, striking differences between Reich's Orgone (OR) and Daoist energy models with a view to utilization and continence; specifically the traditional Daoist emphasis on conservation as opposed to Reich's emphasis on release. Importantly both Freud and Reich clearly denied anything resembling the *shen*.

Freud was well-known to be openly antagonistic towards (although fascinated in) religion and spirituality (Palmer 1997, Ward 1993); whereas Reich saw his work, "orgonomic functionalism," as a middle way between the two undesirable extremes of "mechanistics" and "mysticism" (Reich 1960, 10).

Reich's work remains as a warning, for all and any who would attempt to bring the concept of a "universal energy" into the psychological or natural sciences. The very word "energy" when used outside of a strictly materialist context may immediately be seen to raise accusations of "pseudoscience" or worse still "flakiness" and quickly lose one any scientific respectability and standing; contemporary "energy psychologists" remain located very much on periphery of the discipline.

Had Reich been less hostile, and more open, towards the spiritual dimension, he may well have found a more sympathetic audience and home in the early, emerging transpersonal psychology movements; he might even have also discovered some kindred spirits from amongst Daoist and Hindu adherents who also recognized and maintained the existence of a universal cosmic energy.

Analytical Psychology and Alchemy

"I shall not commit the fashionable stupidity of regarding everything I cannot explain as a fraud" (C.G. Jung). This vow still remains the motto of the UK's Society for Psychical Research and serves to demonstrate Jung's openness to both spiritual and paranormal possibilities.

Carl Jung was, at one point, identified by Freud as "my successor and crown prince" (Steele and Swinney 1982, 218), before he was to separate himself from traditional psychoanalysis by playing down the centrality (or "dogma") of sexual etiology and unashamedly elevating the spiritual dimension. Jung's conception of libidinal energy was to move beyond the sexual into something bearing far more resemblance to *yi* intention.

Jung is perhaps of singular significance to psychologists who are interested in Daoism, primarily because he is one of the first psychologists to make a serious study of Daoism and explicitly relate its systems of internal alchemy to processes of psychological healing and transformation.

Jung's analytical psychology is commonly understood as being one of the first clear articulations of a transpersonal psychology. His term *überpersönlich* (Daniels 2005, 20), "above or beyond the person," refers to his theory of a collective unconscious which carried with it clear spiritual implications.

The client is encouraged to move beyond his/her small and fragmented sense of self, to access and encounter the transforming archetypes of the collective unconscious; but this does not lead to any kind of extinction or cosmic absorption but rather the emergence of a newly healed and unified Self. Hence the attraction to alchemy where the various contradictions and complexes within one's ordinary being are transformed and transmuted in the furnace of self awareness and realization (carefully guided by the analyst), in a process Jung termed individuation (Young-Eisendrath and Dawson 2008, 301).

J. J. Clarke (2005) has already provided an illuminating history of Jung's dialogue with Daoism (and Eastern spirituality in general); ably describing his attraction to Daoist cosmology and his formative friendship with Richard Wilhelm, translator of the *Yijing* and the *Taiyi jinhua zongzhi* (The Secret of the Golden Flower). It is in Jung's forewords and extensive notes accompanying Wilhelm's translation of the latter Daoist cultivation manual--which also included the *Huiming jing* (Book of Consciousness and Life) that give the clearest indication of how Daoist thought directly impacted Jung and directed his interests:

> I shall only emphasize the fact that it was the text of *The Secret of the Golden Flower* that first put me in the direction of the right track. For we have in medieval alchemy the long-sought connecting-link between Gnosis and the processes of the collective unconscious, observable to us to-day in modern man. (Jung in Wilhelm 1962, xiv)

That analytical psychology should also contain a rich alchemical lexicon (Jung 1968) and speak of the recognition and harmonizing of conflicting forces within the psyche may appear as fertile ground for dialogue between Daoism and Western psychology. Yet one must also examine and ask how Jung may have understood, and reinterpreted, some of the Daoist concepts—one important example being the "sacred embryo" and possibility of immortality. It appears that Jung was more concerned with the psychotherapeutic benefits a belief in immortality brought his older patients, rather than believing it to be an attainable goal or reality (Jung in Wilhelm 1962, 125).

And to what extent may it be said that the *shengtai* the "embryo of sainthood, sacred embryo" (Darga in Pregadio 2008, 883) that the *neidan* practitioner seeks to conceive and gestate is purely symbolic in nature?

The historic division between the external alchemical practices and internal alchemical practices may be excitedly seized upon as representing a movement from the actual to the metaphorical; from the actual ingestion of actual elixirs to equivalent adoption of meditative postures, breath work and saliva swallowing with accompanying visualizations. Immediately one should recognize that *neidan* still represents a distinctly embodied practice rather than being solely psychological in character and accept that its fruits were unlikely to have been understood or experienced in either purely psychological or symbolic terms: "The embryo represents a new life, true and eternal in its quality, generated by the inner alchemical practice" (Darga in Pregadio 2008, 883).

That this embryo is conceived of as an actual living breathing entity that survives physical death appears quite clear in the Daoist sources that Jung had read. However, from the perspective of analytical psychology the Daoist concept of the immortal embryo may well be seen as symbolic; relating specifically to the archetype of rebirth (Jung 1986); the emergence of the Self through an experiential journey of individuation.

A Jungian may view as particularly intriguing that the Daoist's visualizations of conceiving and then gestating the immortal embryo centre beneath our navel (in the lower *dantian*); beneath the original, simultaneously physical and symbolic mark of separation from our mother (from *the* mother). This psychological separation, or freedom, from the mother would likely be understood by Jungians as being part of the heroic journey towards selfhood; and what better way to symbolize this process than by "symbolically" giving birth to one's Self.

Indeed Jung appears reluctant to believe that the Daoist authors of *The Golden Flower* or the *Huiming jing* believed in the actual physical existence of such a "sacred embryo," which he relates to the "pneumatic man" (Jung in Wilhelm 1962, 125) of European antiquity, or in immortality as an actual achievable possibility:

> My admiration for the great Eastern philosophers is as genuine as my attitude towards their metaphysics is irreverent. I suspect them of being symbolical psy-

chologists, to whom no greater wrong could be done than to take them literally.
(Jung in Wilhelm 1962, 129)

One may also encounter similar sentiments and tendencies in Western practitioners of, and writers on, Daoist cultivation; wherein profound spiritual experiences are quickly, and perhaps more safely, rendered symbolic. In Michael
Winn's chapter on "Daoist Internal Alchemy in the West" the question is
pointedly raised "Are Immortals Real?" (2009, 186).

Winn provides a dramatic description of a seemingly paranormal encounter with a Daoist immortal. The account includes references to divine light,
altered states of consciousness, channeling and Atlantis, but concludes:

> The point of sharing this story is not to convince anyone that my personal ex-
> perience is an objective or verifiable truth. It is to demonstrate that the field of
> archetypal forms in the collective Chinese psyche is fully available to Westerners.
> (Winn 2009, 187)

On the one hand Winn does not dismiss his experience as being unreal, or
purely imaginary, but at the same time he allows the reader the option of psy-
chologizing his experience into more generally acceptable symbolic formulas,
or archetypal forms. His final assertion would seem to mirror Jung's own belief
that "the human psyche possesses a common substratum transcending all differences in culture and consciousness" (1995:83, 85-6). (Jung quoted in Clarke
2000, 121-122).

Yet despite the universality of the archetypes Jung stresses the importance
of working within and from one's own historical, cultural and religious context:

> Of what use to us is the wisdom of the Upanishads or the insight of Chinese yoga,
> if we desert the foundations of our own culture as though they were errors out-
> lived and, like homeless pirates, settle with thievish intent on foreign shores? (Jung
> in Wilhelm 1962, 144)

One would think Jung would be equally horrified at the rapid rise of Christianity in China (Uhalley and Wu 2001) for similar reasons.

What Jung couldn't appreciate, or foresee, was how with the rapid advent
of communication technology, the role of market forces and globalization, the
perceived "Otherness" of Eastern spirituality would eventually become part of
the familiar, everyday landscape and experience of Westerners; attending
weekly yoga or Tai Chi classes at the church hall (perhaps before going out for
some Indian or Chinese takeout).

Humanistic Nonaction

From conversations concerning cosmology and energy we move our discussion to the relative stillness and seeming simplicity of being and becoming; from the personal and collective unconscious back to our present awareness.

The psychotherapeutic forms emerging from Humanistic Psychology were to stress the "being" of human beings. The work, thought and being of Carl Rogers was to find expression in, the still highly popular, Person-Centered Therapy (PCT).

Rogers's empowering and dialogical approach to the "person" (as opposed to the patient) was heavily influenced by the work of Martin Buber. Buber's own emphasis on being and authentic relating, in his classic *I and Thou*, was to be enthusiastically taken up by many in the Humanistic movement. Significantly, a decade prior to publishing *I and Thou*, Buber had published a translation and commentary on the *Zhuangzi* (Herman 1996, ix).

Both Buber and Rogers expressed an abiding interest in Daoist thought. I deliberately specify "thought" as their conception of Daoism appears to have more in common with literati traditions; focusing almost exclusively on the *Daode jing* and *Zhuangzi*. For Buber's and Roger's Daoism appears as an ancient and evocative philosophy of being, rather than a living religious tradition.

Rogers quotes both from Buber's writings on Daoism and from the *Daode jing*, identifying his own personal favorite saying as:

> If I keep from meddling with people, they take care of themselves,
> If I keep from commanding people, they behave themselves,
> If I keep from preaching at people, they improve themselves,
> If I keep from imposing on people, they become themselves. (1980, 42)

The above quote typifies the attitude and approach (the way of being) of *wuwei* "nonaction, non-interference; non-intervention" (Kohn in Pregadio 2008, 1067). The humanistic and person-centered approach, is also characteristically non-directive, an approach that sought not to impose upon others, whilst emphatically trusting in the client's capacity to self regulate and heal; as such it seems to embody many of the principles of *wuwei*. When Fujio Tomoda sought to accurately translate and convey the process of PCT to his Japanese colleagues he also deliberately emphasized the principle of *wuwei* (Cummins 1996).

Wuwei may, at first, appear to be a strange strategy for a Western psychotherapist to adopt, as most typically the person undergoing therapy may well be waiting to be directed, assessed or analyzed; and he or she may well wonder what they are paying for if such direction, assessment or analysis isn't forthcoming.

From the humanistic and person-centered perspective, imposing labels, dichotomies (sane/insane), psycho-pathologizing and seeking to "direct" the client all actually serves to further alienate and disempower the client; creating dependence on the psychotherapeutic process (and/or the therapist). The PCT therapist will seek, instead, to create a therapeutic space in which the client will receive "unconditional positive regard," allowing him or her simply to "be" and to "become" without excessive interference. Free of imposition the client is free to rediscover their own being and recover their own naturalness and spontaneity.

This in turn leads us to include the Daoist concept of spontaneity (*ziran*): "To act spontaneously is to have no intention of one's own, to let the natural force that is within everything work freely" (Robinet in Predagio 2008, 1303). In Rogers's 1989 classic *Becoming a Person*, he recounts one of the defining (seemingly failed) therapeutic encounters that was to inform his approach:

> Finally I gave up. I told her that it seemed we had both tried, but we had failed, and that we might as well give up our contacts. She agreed. So we concluded the interview, shook hands, and she walked to the door of the office. Then she turned and asked, "Do you take adults for counseling here?"

> When I replied in the affirmative, she said, "Well then I would like some help" She came to chair she had just left, and began to pour out her despair about her marriage, her troubled relationship with her husband, her sense of failure and confusion, all very different from the sterile "Case History" she had given before. Real therapy began then and ultimately it was very successful. (1989, 11)

That Rogers willingly admits defeat and "gives way" to the client, appears to be the catalyst that facilitates the "real" psychotherapeutic process. Rogers's previous attempts to impose his own insights and interpretations on the client are met with resistance, and the therapy reaches an impasse. Rather than seeking to force a route through this impasse, Rogers's acknowledges its presence and respectfully retreats. His retreat appears to allow his client to advance, and so the therapy progresses. It is, at this point, tempting to draw comparisons to push-hands (*tuishou*) and the watercourse way and present PCT as being its psychological equivalent.

Yet, admittedly, however far one may progress in one's personal psychotherapy, however in touch one becomes with one's being, the end result of PCT, analysis or even a Daoist based cognitive therapy (Young et al 2008) simply isn't the same as the intended goal of Daoist cultivation; "psychological adjustment is not liberation" (Jack Kornfield, Ram Dass and Mokusen Miyuki in Welwood 1983, 33-42).

> At the end of the psychotherapeutic process, the client does not expect to be able to enter water without getting wet, enter fire without getting burned, fly among the clouds, live as long as Heaven and Earth, or exhibit any magical powers. By the same token, sages, perfected, and immortals have little interest in be-

ing well adjusted to society. On the contrary, their *raison d'être* is to overcome the limitations of the world and to be outsiders and eccentrics, or in some cases far-sighted leaders who are far ahead of the crowds. (Cohen 2009, 158-59)

Psychosomanautics

A small classroom of fifteen students (none of whom had had any experience of qigong) are standing with their legs shoulder length apart, hands open and arms raised to chest height in front of their torsos in the "holding the ball of light" posture. The only other instruction they are given is to "gently attend" to their breath, without intentionally lengthening or shortening it. In a short period of time several common sensations are reported; "heat," "tingling" and "magnetism."

In the proceeding seminar the students offer various explanations for what had just happened. The power of suggestion was quickly ruled out, as I hadn't (consciously) "primed" the group to have any of these particular sensations. After much discussion the conclusions were reached that this had either been an experience "manufactured" by the mind, or else an ordinary physical experience that had been imbued with some psychological (semiotically charged) significance; in either case it had potently demonstrated a key psychosomatic principle.

These students were the first to take part in the new psychonautics module at Leeds Metropolitan University. Psychonautics refers to the means of exploring, or navigation of, inner space (the mind/consciousness). Although the term is sometimes associated with artificial means of achieving altered states of consciousness (via psychoactive, hallucinogenic or entheogenic substances) I believe it is more properly and productively understood when placed in the context of spiritual disciplines and cultivation practices.

It is in the above sense that Robert Thurman's translation of the *Tibetan Book of the Dead* describes yogis as "psychonauts" (1994, 10), as do Freke and Gandy (2003, 9) when describing the spiritual practices of the ancient Gnostics.

Conventional psychology is most commonly taught in a passive manner, as the *logia* or "study of" the mind and behavior. Conventional psychotherapy invariably involves elucidating techniques that allow for a client's "appropriate" adjustment to the prevailing norms and values of the surrounding society. To actually seek to navigate and transform the mind, via psychonautics, is I contend, something quite different.

In Susan Blackmore's (2003, 2006) work on consciousness she frequently questions how studying consciousness affects/transforms consciousness. However, the psychology most commonly taught in institutions of higher education typically avoids experiential/subjective approaches to its subject matter, preferring and adopting a more "objective," distanced and detached stance. As a result students are studying consciousness without ever being required to become personally conscious of consciousness.

W. Braud's (1998) "Integral Inquiry: Complementary ways of knowing, being and expression" is particularly relevant to this discussion, with a view to adopting his approach of "knowing through becoming":

> . . . a researcher can take an even bolder step, as well, in the direction of a truly transpersonal methodology. Such a step involves paying full attention to *what is known directly by the eye of the spirit*; this type of knowing seems to require a change or transformation in the investigator's *being*. It requires that the investigator *become* what is being studied and to know it as *subject* rather than as object. (Braud and Anderson 1998, 51)

It is in this spirit that Harold Roth's "meditation lab" (Roth 2010, 15) at Brown University allows Religious Studies students the opportunity for such first-person, experiential knowledge of the religious and meditation texts that they are studying.

One of the key objectives of the psychonautics module is that students be encouraged to actually explore (and even positively transform) their consciousnesses through actively engaging with tried and tested meditative techniques and practices. When one colleague (a Sociologist) raised the question of yoga, the reality and role of the body, and somanautics, became immediately evident. Somanautics would likewise involve cultivating an enhanced awareness of the body's physicality and physiology.

That this consciousness is embodied (Hartley 2004, Stam 1998) is a fact that many psychologists have missed or often omitted; forgetting the *soma* in the pursuit of the *psyche*. In order to move beyond the tired, dualistic models (the "mind-body problem") and work towards recognizing a bodymind continuum, the term psychosomanautic was utilized.

It is further highlighted that this bodymind does not exist in a social, cultural, political or historical vacuum; which brings us much closer to an integral approach and understanding (Wilber 2000). The additional recognition that different cultures describe and explore the bodymind in different ways encourages us to develop more cross-cultural and linguistic sensitivities and competencies.

Genuine dialogue should be transformative of all parties involved; it should lead to an opening to, and adoption of, new perspectives. It is my hope that psychosomanautics represents a transforming (or perhaps restored) psychology to authentically encounter and engage with the various Daoist traditions and cultivation practices.

As my previous discussions have hopefully demonstrated, Daoism has already been interpreted and transformed, often by Western psychologists;

mainly in the analytic and humanistic traditions. Perhaps it is time that we allow the Daoists an opportunity to interpret and transform psychology and psychotherapy in ways that further and deepen our understandings of ourselves and of one another.

Bibliography

Apuleius, L., and W. Adlington, 2007. *The Golden Ass*. San Diego: NuVision Publications.

Alexander, F., S. Eisenstein, and M. Grotjahn. 1995. *Psychoanalytic Pioneers*. Piscataway: Transaction Publishing.

Aristotle, Ross, D., and L. Brown, L. 2009. *The Nicomachean Ethics*. Oxford: Oxford University Press.

Batchelor, Stephen. 1997. *Buddhism Without Beliefs: A Contemporary Guide to Awakening*. New York: Riverhead Books.

_____. 2010. *Confessions of a Buddhist Atheist*. New York: Spiegel and Grau.

Blackmore, Susan. 2003. *Consciousness: An Introduction*. Oxford: Oxford University Press.

_____. 2006. *Conversations on Consciousness*. Oxford: Oxford University Press.

Bond, M. H. 2010. *Oxford Handbook of Chinese Psychology*. Oxford: Oxford University Press.

Braud, W. and Anderson R. 1998. *Transpersonal Research Methods for the Social Sciences: Honouring Human Experience*. Thousand Oaks: Sage Publications.

Broughton, R. 1992. *Parapsychology: The Controversial Science*. London: Rider and Co.

Chaitin, G. 1996. *Rhetoric and Culture in Lacan*. Cambridge: Cambridge University Press.

Cohen, Elliot. 2009. "Daoism and Psychology." *Journal of Daoist Studies* 2:151-62.

_____. 2011. "From the Bodhi Tree, to the Analyst's Couch, then into the MRI Scanner: The Psychologisation of Buddhism." Annual Review of Critical Psychology 8:97-119.

Colangelo, J. 2003. *Ebodied Wisdom: What Our Anatomy Can Teach Us About the Art of Living*. Lincoln: i Universe.

Cott, C., and Rock, A. 2009. "'Towards a Transpersonal Psychology of Daoism: Definitions, Past Research, and Future Directions." *International Journal of Transpersonal Studies* 28:119-33.

Clarke, J. J. 1994. *Jung and Eastern Thought: A Dialogue with the Orient*. London: Routledge.

_____. 2000. *The Tao of the West: Western Transformations of Daoist Thought*. London: Routledge.

Cummins, R. D. 1996. "Person-Centered Psychology and Taoism: The Reception of Lao-tzu by Carl R. Rogers" *International Journal for the Psychology of Religion* 6.2:107-26.

Freke, T., and T. Gandy. 2003. *The Jesus Mysteries*. London: Element.

Freud, S., and J. Strachey. 1969. *The Question of Lay Analysis: Conversations with an Impartial Person*. New York: W. W. Norton.

Goleman, D. 2003. *Destructive Emotions: A Scientific Dialogue with the Dalai Lama*. London: Bantam Press.

Gollnick, J. 1992. *Love and the Soul: Psychological Interpretations of the Eros and Psyche Myth*. Waterloo, Ont.: Wilfrid Laurier University Press.

Harrington, A., ed. 1999. *The Placebo Effect: An Interdisciplinary Exploration*. Cambridge, Mass.: Harvard University Press.

Hartley, L. 2004. *Somatic Psychology: Body, Mind and Meaning* .Hoboken: Wiley-Blackwell.

Heath, R. 2003. *The PK Zone: A Cross-Cultural Review of Psychokinesis*. Lincoln: i Universe, Inc.

Herman, J. 1996. *I and Tao: Martin Buber's Encounter with Chuang Tzu*. Albany: State University of New York Press.

Jing, Q. C. 1994. "Development of Psychology in China." *International Journal of Psychology*, 29.6: 667-75.

Horton, A., and D. Wedding, eds. 2008. *The Neuropsychology Handbook*. New York: Springer Publishing.

Johnston, A. 2010. "Turning the Sciences Inside Out: Revisiting Lacan's 'Science and Truth'." In *Concept and Form: The Cahiers pour l'Analyse and Contemporary French Thought*, edited by Peter Hallward et al. London: Verso Books.

Jones. E. 1974. *The Life and Work of Sigmund Freud*. London: Penguin.

Jung, C. G. 1952 *Psychology and Alchemy* London: Routledge

_____. 1959. *Four Archetypes: Mother, Rebirth, Spirit, Trickster*. Translated by R. F. C. Hull. Princeton: Bollingen Foundation.

Kahn, C. 2001. *Pythagoras and the Pythagoreans: A Brief History*. Indianapolis: Hackett.

Kim, U., K. Yang, and K. Hwang, eds. 2006. *Indigenous and Cultural Psychology: Understanding People in Context*. New York: Springer.

Kirkland, R. 1992. "Person and Culture in the Taoist Tradition." *Journal of Chinese Religions*, 20.

Kohn, L. 2001. *Daoism and Chinese Culture*. Cambridge, Mass.: Three Pines Press.

Kuhn, R. 2009. *How China's Leaders Think: The Inside Story of China's Reform and What this Means for the Future*. Hoboken: John Wiley and Sons.

Lichtenberg, J .1994. *The Talking Cure: A Descriptive Guide to Psychoanalysis*. Hillsdale: The Analytic Press.

Maciocia, G. 2002. *Foundations of Chinese Medicine: A Comprehensive Text for Acupuncturists and Herbalists*. London: Churchill Livingstone.

Martin, R. and Barres, J. 2004. *Naturalization of the Soul: Self and Personal Identity in the Eighteenth Century*. London: Routledge.

McMahan, D. 2008. *The Making of Buddhist Modernism* New York: Oxford University Press.

Mori, Yuria. 2002. "Identity and Lineage: The *Taiyi jinhua zongzhi* and the Spirit-Writing Cult to Patriarch Lü in Qing China." In *Daoist Identity: History, Lineage, and Ritual*, edited by L. Kohn and H. D. Roth, 165-84. Honolulu: University of Hawai'i Press.

O'Brien, J. A. 2005. *The Truths Men Live By: A Philosophy of Religion and Life*. Whitefish: Kessinger Publishing.

Palmer, M. 1997. *Freud and Jung on Religion*. London: Routledge.

Petocz, A. 1999. *Freud, Psychoanalysis, and Symbolism*. Cambridge: Cambridge Univ. Press.

Pregadio, F., ed. 2008. *The Encylodpedia of Daoism*. 2 vols. London: Routledge.

Raknes, O. 2004. *Wilhelm Reich and Orgonomy: The Brilliant Psychiatrist and his Revolutionary Theory of Life Energy*. Princeton: American College of Orgonomy Press.

Rieber, R., and D. Robinson, D., eds. 2001. *Wilhelm Wundt in History: The Making of a Scientific Psychology*. New York: Springer.

Reich, W. 1960. *Wilhelm Reich Selected Writings: An Introduction to Orgonomy*. New York: Farrar Straus Giroux.

Rogers, C. 1980. *A Way of Being*. New York: Mariner Books.

_____. 1989. *On Becoming a Person: A Therapist's View of Psychotherapy*. New York: Mariner.

Roth, H. 2010. "Early Taoist Contemplation and its Resonance in the American Academy." *The Dragon's Mouth* 2010/1:10-18.

Sandlund, E., and T. Norlander. 2000. "The Effects of Tai Chi Chuan Relaxation and Exercise on Stress Responses and Well-Being: An Overview of Research." *International Journal of Stress Management* 7. 2:139-49.

Singh, N., ed. 2001. *Encyclopedia of Jainism*. Vol. 20. New Delhi: Anmol Publications.

Stam, H. , ed. 1998. *The Body and Psychology*. London: Sage.

Steele, R., and S. Swinney 1982. *Freud and Jung: Conflicts of Interpretation*. London: Routledge.

Sternberg, R. and Mio, J. 2008. *Cognitive Psychology*. Belmont, Calif.: Wadsworth.

Thurman, R. 1994. *The Tibetan Book of the Dead: Liberation Through Understanding in the Between*. London: Thorsons.

Uhalley, S., and X. Wu, eds. 2001. *China and Christianity: Burdened Past, Hopeful Future*. New York: M. E. Sharpe.

Ward, I., ed. 1993. *Is Psychoanalysis another Religion: Contemporary Essays on Spirit, Faith and Morality in Psychoanalysis*. Northampton: Freud Museum Publications.

Welwood, J. 1983. *Awakening the Heart: East/West Approaches to Psychotherapy and the Healing Relationship*. Boulder: Shambhala.

Wilber, K. 2000. *Integral Psychology: Consciousness, Spirit, Psychology, Therapy* Boston: Shambhala.

Wilhem, Ric hard, and C. G. Jung. 1962 *The Secret of the Golden Flower: A Chinese Book of Life*. New York: Harcourt, Brace and World.

Winn, Michael. 2009. "Daoist Internal Alchemy in the West." In *Internal Alchemy: Self, Society, and the Quest for Immortality*, edited by Livia Kohn and Robin R. Wang, 181-200. Magdalena, NM: Three Pines Press.

Young-Eisendrath, and T. Dawson, eds. 2008. *The Cambridge Companion to Jung*. Cambridge: Cambridge University Press.

Immortality and Psychology in Mortal Life

REGGIE PAWLE

Several aspects of mind in the realization of Daoist immortality are relevant to the psychology of ordinary mortals in this world. They include: the functions of mind utilized in cultivation practice, the relationship of mind to body and to the world, the understanding of mind itself, and cultural considerations regarding mind. These aspects are relevant both to mental pathology and to psychological healing in daily life. Daoist ideas of life energy, yin-yang, nature, causality, and nonaction can be successfully applied in a psychological context. They are also comparable to yoga, Buddhism, Freudian psychology, and Jungian psychology, especially with regard to adapting their key concepts to the psychotherapeutic situation while yet maintaining regard for specific cultural concerns.

Daoism is not a psychology, but a religion. There are many differences between the two fields. The activities and methods of a Daoist monastery and a mental hospital have little in common. However, a basic commonality between both is the mind. Daoism, as do all human activities, engages the human mind, and naturally does so in particular Daoist ways. Psychology focuses specifically on the study of the human mind. For psychology, interest in Daoism stems from what can be learned about the human mind by studying the practices and teachings of Daoism.

The primary theme of this chapter is the relevance of Daoist practices and theory to psychotherapy with ordinary people around the globe who are grappling with the problems and challenges of life. Within this basic theme, there are two focal areas to be considered as both are highly relevant. First: which important functions of mind are engaged in Daoist practices and how are these functions engaged? Here the focus is on the conscious mind, but other parts, specifically the unconscious and the higher mind, are also considered. Second: how is the Daoist engagement of mind activated in the context of Chinese culture? This is important because both psychology and Daoism originated in their own, unique cultural contexts. In addition to the differences between the fields of psychology and religion, there are also cultural gaps that need to be taken into consideration, if psychotherapy is to benefit from a study of Daoism. Un-

derstanding the respective cultural backgrounds is a starting point to understanding the relevance of mind in Daoism for ordinary mortals.

Psychology and Daoist Culture

Psychology originated in a European cultural context. Particularly important for
a discussion of Daoism is the view that arose in Europe that the body and
mind were different parts of a human being and that they could be treated
separately. The ideas of René Descartes (1596-1650) are a prime expression of
this view. He attempted to resolve a conflict between the Catholic Church and
science by dividing the world into matter and mind, matter being the realm of
science and mind being the realm of religion (Tarnas 1991). As the cultural
strength of science increased from the time of Descartes, Freud, Jung, and others expressed the view that mind was also best studied by science, rather than
being the domain of religion. This led to the birth of psychology. Thus, psychology arose out of a cultural context that came to view mind by itself, separate from body or soul, as being a specific focus of scientific study.[1]

The cultural context in which Daoism arose and has flourished is very
different. In China (and in Korea and Japan) mind has not been viewed separately from the body, but rather has been viewed as part of a bodymind-spirit
inseparable system. Any one part is viewed and worked with in terms of its
relationships with the other parts. The Western psychological sense of mind as
a focus of scientific study has been de-emphasized, so there has not been a
tradition that has led to mind being a specific focus of study.

One result of this is that mind has been cultivated through a variety of
methods that Western psychology would not consider strictly psychological,
such as training the body, regulating the breath, and harmonizing the flow of
energy. Another result is that functions of mind have often been spoken of in
either non-mental ways (meaning in terms of their related or connected body/
behavior/spirit/environmental aspects) or less precise (meaning less of the
specific attributes of mental functions) psychological ways. An example of the
first is that in Chinese medicine emotions were connected to the internal organs and were spoken of in terms of the functioning of their respective organ.
An example of the second is that emotions were not distinguished from
thoughts; they were viewed as the same event, as reflected in the Chinese word
xin, which literally means "heart-mind."

---

[1] See Tarnas 1991 for an account of the history of Western thought from a Western
perspective. See Yuasa 1993 for an Asian perspective.

I used the wording "less precise psychological ways." However, it also can be said that mental functions are seen more precisely in their connections to other mental and non-mental phenomena. The concept of *xin* asserts that emotions and thoughts function together synchronistically. A person thinking based on this idea would say that what gives the effectiveness to the popular Western cognitive-behavioral psychotherapy (Beck, Emery, and Greenberg 2005) is this synchronistic interaction of thoughts and feelings. If you change one, you necessarily change the other. This reflects what Nisbett (2003) refers to as the Chinese tendency to see things in connection or relationship to other things, that is, to see things holistically.

Daoism generally has reflected this Chinese cultural view of mind. Mind is often spoken of indirectly and symbolically. Symbols in Daoist texts can have a plurality of meanings as Daoist texts can express several simultaneous levels of meaning (Robinet 1993, 52). The view is that everything takes place synchronistically on different levels at the same time. Mind viewed in this way functions in complex resonance in different systems on different levels—body, spirit, environment, cosmos—and cannot be viewed as a separate entity. This is a view of mind that is fundamental to understanding mind from a Daoist perspective.

One way that practice in Daoism is described is as the cultivation of the "Daoist body." Some aspects of this Daoist body can be understood as symbolic of mental functions. When mind is referred to directly, for example, by Zhang Boduan of the Southern School (Lu 2009), generally what is discussed are mental states and mental practices rather than functions of mind. In addition to the cultural influence, that Daoism is also a religion contributes to this orientation to mind. Daoism has a soteriological goal of immortality and is not focused on detailing the functions of mind. However, this is precisely what gives value to psychology for the study of Daoism. Daoism has the potential to provide new understandings of mind that reflect both cultural and religious considerations. Through this study psychotherapy can be broadened and thus be applicable to more diverse people worldwide.

Immortality Mind

Every psychology has what I call the "root of mind." What I am referring to as the "root" is the key function of mind, the mental function that a particular psychology focuses on as the important or pivotal function in psychotherapeutic work. Identifying the root of mind of a psychology serves both as a way to understand a psychology and to compare this psychology with other psychologies. For example, Freud asserted that the "drives," which he said were demands made on the mind by its connection with the body that activate mind, of a person were fundamental (Freud 2001). Jung believed that the complexes of the unconscious, which he called "archetypes," were fundamental to mind (Jung 1968). Other Western psychologists, such as Hans Kohut (1971), have asserted that it is a person's relations with others that are the pivotal function.

Turning to Asia, in the psychology of yoga consciousness itself, without any "form" such as drives, archetypes, or relationships, is viewed as the critical factor of mind (Rao 2008). In the psychology of Buddhism it is the self, or the "ego" in modern psychology terminology, that is focused on as the fundamental factor in mind (Pawle 2003; 2009).

What Daoism focuses on as the root of mind is what is cultivated in order to realize its goal of immortality. This appears variously as the life force, the life impulse, or the vital principle within a person. Radically Daoism asserts that if ordinary mortals cultivate their inherent life force to the extent that life completely permeates a person's bodymind, certainly longevity and maybe even immortality is possible. A person's life force is seen as the key to their health— mind, body, and spirit. Thus, the key to the psychology of mortal life from a Daoist perspective is the life force that is inherent in every human being.

Immortality seems in many ways of little or no relevance to the masses of people around the globe living ordinary mortal life. It is even seems absurd to spend much time with it. How many immortals has the average person met? Everyday daily life, with its challenges, sufferings, and happiness, is the concern of most people. Fundamentally psychology, despite its countless volumes of illegible texts, is oriented to this concern. Daoism also, to have a place in the world, must be relevant to these concerns of mortal life.

One approach in psychotherapy to working with an ordinary person's concerns is to focus on how a person can improve their mental functioning from ordinary to more positive functioning. This is juxtaposed with an approach that focuses on the below ordinary functioning of a person and tries to improve their functioning to ordinary. Daoism, with its goal of immortality, is implicitly a very positive psychology. It is saying, "To deal with your life concerns, what you need to do is to nurture the life force within you. Doing so, you can live better and longer, and maybe you don't even need to die."

This Daoist focus on life also distinguishes it from the India-originated yoga and Buddhist practices. Both of these assert that a person's desire to live is an attachment that must be let go of in order to realize their goal. Daoism, however, asserts that letting go of the attachment to life is not necessary. Rather what is needed to harmonize this attachment with the life force that permeates the universe.

The history of Daoism is full of discussions about whether immortality is universally attainable or only the fate of a select few (Penny 2000, 123). For ordinary mortals what is important is not whether immortality actually is a possibility, but rather how in this present condition, in this present life, to live healthily. Immortals embody that the more a person harmonizes their life with their life force, with the root of their mind, the healthier their life will be.

How are those who have become immortal described? While there are many attributes ascribed to Immortals, for ordinary mortals what is most relevant is that Immortals are described as humans who are free of that which bonds the ordinary person. They are fully alive, full of light, humor, and energy. Schipper describes them as "liberated elves" (1993, 166). Kohn writes they are in a "state of radiance and surging activity" (2009a, 12). Particularly relevant, they are truly happy and at peace. How Immortals embody this happiness is the Daoist cultivation practice of life and is a most positive psychology. For ordinary mortals how this is done is most relevant.

Daoist Immortals provide ordinary mortals with a vision of mental health and the way to it. Basic to this vision is an expression of the Chinese cultural view that everything is interconnected. Mind is non-separable from body, spirit, and the cosmos. In Daoism the life force within each of us is seen as both the same life force in all of us and that which interconnects the world. The source and the substance of this life force is said to be Dao, that which is nameless and beyond human comprehension. Dao appears in the world as "the natural way of things" (Wong 1997, 23). The way to mental health is to model oneself on Dao and how it appears in the world through the rhythms of nature.

Daoists look to nature for patterns and correspondences, to the patterns of the wind and the water, to the patterns and movements of the stars, to time in its cycles of days and seasons, to the flow of energy, and then find these same patterns and flows replicated within their own body and mind. Harmonizing with these patterns and flows, internal and external, is the beginning of Daoist cultivation practice and also the beginning of psychological health.

The basic way that mind functions according to Dao can be understood according to the idea of yin-yang. Originally yin meant the shady side of the slope of a hill and yang meant the sunny side of the slope (Kaptchuk 2000). Yin is associated with darkness and passivity, while yang is associated with light and activity. A mountain always has both, but which side is yin or yang depends on the relationship of the mountain with the sun. This relationship is always changing and moving. This movement is cyclical, orderly, rhythmical, and not vague. In any moment a person using their everyday mind can determine what of the mountain is yin and what is yang.

Movement according to yin-yang is how mind in Daoism is understood to operate. This movement is the energy of nature and the life force, called *qi*, in mind. The process of mind functions in yin-yang polarities. Basic expressions of this functioning are sunny (light, positive) and shadow (dark, negative) both being part of mind, so the activity of mind is seen as a play of non-conscious and conscious. Pathology is when the polarities are split, health is when they are integrated. Carl Jung viewed mind functioning as polarities and found support for this understanding in yin-yang (Clarke 1994).

Before I wrote that the psychology of Daoism is a positive psychology. While Daoism is positive oriented, it also strongly asserts that mind and life are a mixture and balance of opposing forces. From a Daoist perspective, Western positive psychology often comes across as unbalanced, as if it is trying to deny negative experience. While the Daoist orientation is positive, its means are utilizing both positive and negative. In the yin-yang sense Daoism is more an integral psychology than it is a positive psychology.

Mental and Ego Functioning

The way that the process of mind functions as yin-yang is through resonance, a basic Chinese medicine idea (Kaptchuk 2000). Resonance is a type of causality (how events occur) that is based in the idea of yin-yang. Resonance means that causality occurs within a system by evoking, by one part evoking a similar part in the other. One aspect of yin-yang is that in each yin, there is a little bit of yang, and vice versa. So yin evokes the yin in yang and this is how a system functions. This evoking occurs through resonance, when the yin resonates with the yin within yang and vice versa. This provides people with an easy way to understand their mental experience and is very helpful in certain situations. For example, I only respond to events according to my psychological character. When I get angry, it is because something outside of me has occurred that stimulates the part within me that corresponds to the outside event. This part within me is evoked from the non-conscious (both higher and lower) mind through correspondence into the conscious mind. If there is no such part within me, I will respond differently. Somebody else may very well respond to the situation quite differently from my response. Thus, if I want to change my mental experience, I need to change those related parts within myself. This is what I refer to as Daoist correspondence psychology.

Basic to this functioning of mind is harmonizing mind with the process of nature. Particularly important is the role of the ego, a Western psychological term. The ego has three important mental functions: (1) conscious identity, (2) subjective sense, and (3) executive or coordinator of mind. All of these functions need to not intervene with the patterns and flow of nature, but rather allow the patterns of life to manifest naturally. From a Daoist perspective this is a fundamental psychological challenge for all human beings and is the first step to mental health.

This functioning of the ego is spoken of as "nonaction" (*wuwei*) in the *Daode jing*. The ego in Daoism is more like a liaison than an executive. Through nonaction the ego harmonizes with Dao so that the natural patterns and flows of mind are manifested. In the *Daode jing* it is written, "By acting without action, all things will be in order" (1963, 103). Rather than the ego being a doer, when it is nonactive and becomes an empty center of mind, then the original movement of the life force is free and the mind as whole becomes alive with *qi*, the mysterious, invisible life force that pervades all things. Mind becomes tranquil, thereby allowing harmonization with, blending with, adjusting to, being the patterns of nature. *Qi* links all parts of body and mind and its cultivation for immortality is where Daoist practice develops its uniqueness.

This nonactive conscious mind can be easily experienced in its basic form if a person sits quietly, focuses on their breathing, and allows the conscious mind to be awareness only without thoughts. What is required is the intention to do this. If a person does this, then mind is "brought into order" naturally, using an East Asian and a Daoist expression.[2] In other words, mind settles down, using the corresponding American expression. A well-known phenomenon in many forms of meditation, it is rarely addressed in psychology: if the conscious mind concentrates on one thing, thinking slows down and can even stop.[3] If a therapist explains this to people and encourages them to practice it, a relaxation of body and mind occurs naturally. In Daoism this is referred to as the beginning of practice, in which the conscious mind is active. This action leads to nonaction in its fulfillment. Nonaction here is described as the completely "unmoving mind," a mental state of deep calm that is preparatory to embodying Dao (Lu 2009, 82).

Key to the conscious mind functioning as balancer and liaison is volition. Daoist cultivation does not occur without active volition. Volition is a person's will, the focusing of their intention on an object. How volition functions is most important. People can use volition as an independent force that tries to strongly and forcefully make something happen. A second use is utilizing volition in tandem with other parts of the body and mind. Volition in Daoism is used in this second way, as a gentle guide, a function that helps mind adjust to Dao.

This use of volition has a cultural context. A clear explanation of this context is found in Kuriyama (2002, 10-11), where he compares drawings of the body, one by the Chinese Hua Shou (dat. 1341), the other by the Belgian Vesalius (dat. 1543). It is easy to see the different use of volition. The drawing by Vesalius shows clearly the muscles of the body. Muscles can be controlled directly by volition, as in I can control when my hand opens and closes. The drawing by Hua Shou, however, shows the meridians, the intersections of the passageways of *qi* in the body. These meridians cannot be controlled directly

---

2 This expression can be found often in Daoist writings, as in the previous *Daode jing* quote. I have also noticed how my Japanese students repeatedly describe their experience of meditation as having brought their "mind into order."

3 For examples, see Gunaratana (2002, 70) and Lu (2009, 82).

like muscles. Rather, they can only be influenced through having a healthy bodymind and cooperating with the flow of *qi*, gently directing its flow in the desired ways that are inherently natural.

Volition in Daoism, while within this cultural context, has its own utilization. One use is as a mental guide for the flow of *qi* in the bodymind. In this guiding intention is coordinated with breath. Breath is *qi* or pure matter-energy (Schipper 1993, 34). It is through breath that the conscious mind discovers *qi* and then is able to use gentle volition to guide *qi* through the bodymind, thereby integrating a person with the energies of the cosmos. For those who wish to de-stress, Daoist breathing practice is highly recommended. Stress is one of the primary symptoms of psychological imbalance in Chinese medicine (Hammer 1990, 13) and breath is a basic antidote.

Intention is also used in Daoist cultivation joined by imagination as visualization. This is the conscious use of visualizing images with the purpose of transforming mind. Kohn defines Daoist visualization as "the mental focus on specific scene or sequence of events, such as energy flows, deities, cosmic patterns, saints' lives, or potential future events" (2009a, 140). Visualization opens the conscious mind to more subtle aspects, thereby allowing the corresponding energies of the non-conscious mind to manifest. Visualization is part of the beginning of Daoist cultivation, but the goal is to surpass this activity (Schipper 1993).

In utilizing intention and imagination in this way, another conscious mind function that is coordinated with these two is attention. This is a basic element in Daoist practice (Schipper 1993) and is cultivated while correspondingly the analytical or thinking function of mind is intentionally not cultivated. Attention is the focus of the conscious mind on an object. Concentration is sustaining attention to this object over time. The ability to concentrate is necessary for Daoist practices such as visualization and breathing, so it must be developed. Doing so requires active volition. The more a person is interested in the object of attention, the easier it is. However, there are always periods when boredom or other factors take over the mind. And these times are integral to developing concentration ability. The key to attention development is sustaining attention when a person has lost interest in the object. At such times the conscious mind is full of thoughts with corresponding visuals and emotions that have nothing to do with the intended object. If the practitioner repeatedly shifts their attention from this mental content back to the intended object, then concentration ability develops. Additionally, a lack of thinking and a calmness of mind will also develop.

Thinking and the Senses

While the Daoist adept is trained to sustain attention, simultaneously they are also trained to let go of thinking and discrimination. This is another basic way that the conscious mind is used in Daoist cultivation. The *Zhuangzi* emphasizes that mind tends to analyze, to discriminate, to make judgments, all of which if engaged too much will tangle a person up and result in becoming lost in a maze of desires and complications. Such a person tends to over-value their sensory experience and not know their true nature (see Watson 2003).

A beginning step to being healthy in the conscious mind is to let go of the thinking activity. Freedom from the constraint of conceptual thinking is what Laozi called "the thaw" (Schipper 1993, 201). Zhuangzi called this the "fasting of the heart-mind" (Watson 2003, 53), describing an emptying of the mind of all analytical thought and discrimination while learning to listen to the inner spirit rather than the outer senses. This is also a "double oblivion (*jianwang*)," letting go of mental projections that are believed to be reality and letting go of one's attachment to the functions of the conscious mind (Kohn 2009b, 12; 2010). The practice of forgetting the conscious mind is "sitting in oblivion," in which everything is put outside oneself and then a person is "able to enter where there is no life and no death" (Watson 1964, 79).

This approach to the thinking mind, however, does not deny a role for thinking in daily life. Humans need to be able to understand how Dao works and be able to function on the basis of this understanding. In Daoist practice this is what Kohn refers to as "cosmological reorientation" (Kohn 2009b, 13-17). Part of the beginning of Daoist practice is studying ideas of the self and world and how these are part of the larger rhythms of nature. Practitioners "learn to appreciate the cosmological patterns of the universe and see the world in terms of interrelated patterns, calendar cycles, complex numerologies, and intricate networks of abstract symbols" (Kohn 2009b, 13). This is part of aligning and adjusting one's identity to being a process rather than being a solid entity.

The style of thinking that is utilized in this Daoist study is an expression of the view that mind functions according to correspondences. Daoist study uses "correlative thinking" (Kohn 2009b, 14), which is the repetition of a simple pattern in different cases. Basic to the simple pattern used is the relationship or the association of the parts of the pattern. To think in this way is to look for patterns by examining the correspondences of different parts. My view is that correspondence thinking is the style of the unconscious. The unconscious is not rational or conceptual, but instead functions on the basis of one thing resonating with another thing. Dreams, for example, are only understandable in their associations, what an object seems like, what an object resembles.

The relevance of correspondence thinking for Daoism to psychology is that by engaging correlative thinking, the practitioner is training their conscious mind to align with the non-conscious parts of mind. This leads mind to be harmonious with the patterns of nature and leads to health. If a person stays only within conceptual thinking, it will be impossible for them to realize Dao. Thus, psychotherapy needs to encourage and facilitate associative thinking. This has been a part of Western psychology since Freud pioneered "free association" (saying whatever spontaneously comes to one's mind), so it is not unique to Daoism. It is, however, a foundational part of a correspondence psychology.

Pattern of Mind

What, then, is the basic pattern of mind that many consider a fundamental issue in psychology? More often referred to as the "structure of mind," this "gives an individual his or her distinctive shape, governing the regularity of behavior, events, and relationships within an individual life" (Greenberg and Mitchell 1983, 19). In the context of the correspondence psychology of Daoism, pattern is a more appropriate term than structure. This issue is very important for clinical work as a therapist's understanding of mind is a fundamental part of how they observe, interpret, interact, and work with their client. When different views on the pattern of mind are compared, answers to basic psychotherapeutic questions such as what is pathology and what is healing emerge.

Often the basic pattern or structure of mind is viewed in three parts. Parts are distinguished from functions in that parts are areas or fields of mind within which specific functions, like attention and volition, are active. Freud asserted that the basic structure of mind was superego, ego, and id. Jung saw mind as conscious mind, personal unconscious, and collective unconscious. In yoga the mind is viewed as supraconscious, conscious, and subconscious (Vishnudevananda 1960). In Yogacara Buddhism, the parts of mind are the six senses, the thinking mind, and the storehouse unconscious (Kochumuttom 1982).

To understand a Daoist pattern of mind, mind should be approached through the principle of correspondence. Mind is patterned the same way as is the body as is the world as is the universe. The basic pattern of the universe is expressed in *Daode jing* 42 (Chan 1963), where it is written that from Dao came the One (unity of the universe), which produced the Two (yin and yang), which produced the Three (interaction of yin and yang), which then produced the myriad beings (the world). In Chinese cosmology, which Daoism subscribes to, this interaction of yin and yang is manifests in continuously moving energetic cycles that have five phases, which are rising yang, peak yang, yin-yang in balance, rising yin, and peak yin. These are the "five prime movers" in the world (Saso 2000, 212). In the human body they are associated with five storage organs (yin) and five processing organs (yang), each of which has many correspondences that include emotions and the senses (see Kohn 2008). The pattern that is expressed here is that the Three form the basic way of functioning and this way moves in five basic phases.

One way that this basic pattern is applied in Daoism is in internal or spiritual alchemy cultivation practice (*neidan*). There are many systems of neidan and the details vary from system to system. For example, the most important points in neidan are the three cinnabar or elixir fields (*dantian*) (Neswald 2009). However, the specific location of these elixir fields varies according to different systems of practice (Komjathy 2009).

In *neidan* the three (interaction of yin and yang) is consistently represented as the number "3," notably indicating the Three Treasures of life (vital essence, primordial *qi*, and original spirit), while the number "5" is used for the five movers or phases (Saso 2000). These three principles of life are each associated with one of the three elixir fields. Correlated to mind the three elixir fields express basic parts of mind and the five phases express basic functions of mind. The terms "fields," "phases," and "movers" are good ways to describe mind from a Daoist perspective, as they express the parts and functions of mind being processes rather than solid entities.

It is in the elixir fields that the immortal elixir forms and is nourished by Daoist adepts. The lower field is gender specific (Valussi 2009). It is the "Essence Chamber," the storage center of *qi* in the body. In men it is generally found in the abdominal region and is referred to as the "Ocean of *Qi*." In women, the "lower" center is found in the Cavity of *Qi*, which is between the breasts. The middle elixir field is in the heart region and it houses original spirit (*shen*) (Saso 2000). The upper elixir field is in the head region and it houses primordial breath (also called Taiji—Great Ultimate—or hundun--Primordial Chaos; see Saso 2000).

The lower field corresponds to the Daoist lower mind in psychological terminology. This is the storage part of mind, out of conscious awareness, yin in nature, and shadowy. Primarily it stores "essence" (*jing*), a concentrated form of *qi* that is primal energy and is essential to the activity of all life. Essence in its most concrete form appears as sexual energy, in a man as seminal essence and in a woman as menstrual blood (Kohn 2008). This is the instinctual part of mind in a generative sense: from here the primal life force appears in a form that fuels the bodymind. It is provocative that the lower mind is viewed as having gender differences, a view that receives little attention in psychology.

The lower field also houses what is referred to in Daoism as destiny (*xingming*), meaning a person's biological and material elements. Psychologically this corresponds to a person's basic character constitution, that which makes a person who they are in life (Kohn 2009a). This is the central point around which all of the body is organized (Schipper 1993), so correspondingly it is also the center of gravity of mind. When destiny or the lower mind is cultivated, the result is a "full stomach" (Lu 2009, 82), meaning that a person's foundation in the world becomes firm and fills with recovered primordial *qi*.

The middle field corresponds to the Daoist middle mind. It is where *qi* recovered from essence is refined into original spirit (*shen*). Its general location at the heart indicates a connection to the heart-mind (*xin*), a person's conscious mind. In the Heavenly Master sect the symbol of spirit is the "Heavenly Worthy of Numinous Treasure" (*lingbao*) who stands for the liaison spirit between Heaven and Earth. "The term *ling* refers to half of a talisman kept in the heavens while *bao* indicates the precious half buried in the earth" (Saso 2000, 196). This corresponds to the liaison function of the conscious mind.

In its liaison function, in the words of Zhang Boduan, the conscious mind needs to become "empty mind" in order to realize one's true, original nature (Lu 2009). Empty mind is non-active mind. The healthy functioning of conscious mind, rather than being either yin or yang, is that of inner clarity and utmost emptiness. If all thoughts and ideas are ceased (the "fasting of the heart-mind") and a deeply peaceful mind is established, then it is possible for the true inherent nature of consciousness to be revealed as spirit. Psychologically inherent nature corresponds to a person's identity. This asserts that there is a level of identity hidden deep within consciousness that is out of ordinary awareness and is not easily accessed by ordinary conscious mind activity. Rather than using the senses and the intellect, to realize one's identity the conscious mind needs to open to and harmonize with the non-conscious mind.

The upper elixir field corresponds to the upper mind in Daoism. This is the field of Dao, described variously as emptiness, pure immortal spirit, primordial chaos (*hundun*), pure yang spirit (*yangshen*), and light energy. It is personified in the "Heavenly Worthy of Primordial Beginning," who stands as a symbol for primordial breath, the basic life-giving substance within the bodymind (Saso 2000, 196). This is the field where the original spirit of a person becomes concentrated after the conscious mind is purified and stilled. Original spirit is then transformed into pure immortal spirit.

Psychologically this field corresponds to the higher functions of mind, aspects of mind that transpersonal psychology attempts to explore and integrate into psychology. This part of mind involves the higher functions of human beings. These include spiritual aspects and higher yang energies, but they also involve ordinary functions of the conscious mind that need to be oriented to this higher mind. Included in this orientation are intention, self-reflection, cultivation of virtue, conscience, self-transformation, awareness of potentials, and benevolence. These qualities are referred to as aspects of a person's non-corporal or spirit soul (*hun*) (Kaptchuk 2000).

Comparative Perspectives

Having examined the Daoist pattern of mind, we can now begin to compare it with the understanding of the mind in other systems, as outlined in the chart below. Part 1 in Daoism shows the upper level of mind, functioning as a higher energetic level of the life force and comparable to the superego in Freud and the conscious mind in Jung. This Daoist upper mind includes possibilities for mind and mental health that are not part of either the Freudian or the Jungian systems. It reflects a Daoist understanding of person quite different from Western conceptualizations.

Part 2 shows a level of mind that serves as an intermediary function (except in the Jungian system where the emphasis is on the interaction of conscious/unconscious), but with some variation as to what and how it mediates. In Freud, it mediates between social concerns and the drives; in Yogacara Buddhism, it mediates between the unconscious and the senses; in yoga, the focus is more on the intellectual and rational functions, which need to be trained so the higher mind can function. All this stands in contrast to the Daoist emphasis on the middle mind as nonaction, so mind can conduct *qi* or the life force.

Part 3 shows how all these systems contain similarities in the lower mind. However, the Daoist emphasis on life force appears in the generative function of the lower mind, the Ocean of *Qi* and the Cavity of *Qi*, which serves a person's health in daily life. The idea of destiny (one's basic character) can be seen in particular to have similarities with the Jungian archetypes, although more on a personal level rather than a collective level.

	Freud	Jung	Yoga	Yogacara	Neidan
Part 1	Superego = Social Concerns, Values	Conscious Mind = Ego	Supraconscious Mind = Intuition Higher faculties	Six Senses	Primordial *qi*, Yang, Light, Chaos
Part 2	Ego = Executive; Identity Subjectivity	Personal Unconscious = Personal Archetypes	Conscious Mind = Intellect, Rational	Manas = Thinking, Reified Self	Conscious = Liaison, Spirit & Heart-Mind
Part 3	Id = Drives, Repression	Collective Unconscious = Collective Archetypes	Subconscious Mind = Instincts, Emotions	Alayavijnana = Stores seeds, origin of mind states	Ocean/Cavity of *Qi* = yin, dark, essence, *qi*, destiny, assimilation
Root	Drives	Archetypes	Consciousness	Self/Ego	Life force

A comparison of mental patterning as based on this chart that can be fruitfully applied in psychotherapy concerns the understanding of psychological pathology and psychological healing. How a psychotherapist diagnoses and what they recommend for healing is most relevant to all therapy clients. The Daoist system views pathology as interference with the way of nature and healing as the cultivation of the life force. There are many possible applications of the Daoist cultivation practices of life and immortality in psychotherapy with ordinary mortals around the globe.

A simple approach to applying Daoist practices to everyday mind is to focus on three basic practices, that of regulation of the body, breath, and mind. The three are interrelated and if they are cultivated together, the result is asserted to be longevity and supreme happiness (Watson 2003). Important to regulation of the body are body postures, exercises, and diet. Through regulating breath, harmonization of mind with body and spirit and the conducting of *qi* (primal energy) are facilitated. Mind is regulated through tranquilization, the ways of non-intervention, and concentration.

Regulation in Daoism expresses some basic ideas for psychotherapy. The first is that healing begins with action by the conscious mind. The ordinary mind tends to be active, so the approach here is that the first step is to use that activity tendency rather than to try to willfully change it to nonaction. A second idea is that people themselves need to do something. They will not heal if they take a passive approach, such as simply taking medication. A third idea is that once a person has brought healthy ordinary functioning to their mind, then they need to let go of control and become nonactive. Full healing only occurs through conscious mind functioning as a liaison, so a person needs to learn to go with the flow of nature.

Mind, breath, and body are one in the Daoist way. A person needs to pay attention to their body and listen to it. This is somatic psychotherapy. Usually the conscious mind is the last part of mind to feel various influences. For example, the symptoms of stress or anger appear in the body often before the person is aware they are stressed or angry. Daoism with its internal emphasis and bodily practices greatly enhances a person's internal sensitivity.

Mind needs to be stable and tranquil before Daoist cultivation can precede. How this is accomplished is directly relevant to everyday mind. One of the primary ways that the Daoist approach to the thinking is relevant to everyday life is to aid people to let go of their obsessions. The Daoist adept who sits in oblivion is not mentally nonfunctional, but rather has reordered and transformed the functions of mind through putting priority on awareness and engagement in the present. When a person "acts in oblivion," a term I am using here in association with "sitting in oblivion," in daily life, they are whole body and mind engaged in awareness of the present, in the immediacy of experience, with attention free to be utilized as is appropriate for the situation. Attention to experience directs a person to life as it is, which in Daoism is said to be where true spontaneity arises (Schipper 1993).

Attention to experience is an ordinary mental function. However, in Daoism attention is cultivated and raised to higher levels of functioning. This occurs through learning to concentrate, by sustaining attention through learning to shift attention back to the object of concentration. I often recommend attention-shifting to clients, especially those with attention deficit hyperactivity problems. In the case of daily life it means returning one's attention to one's activity in the moment. If a person engages attention-shifting repetitively, my clients report this helps both their task efficiency and their calmness of mind. One Japanese word for neurosis is *toraware*, which literally means "prisoner" or "to be caught." This is the idea that the cause of neurosis is a person's attention being "caught" by something. They then go around and around in their thinking mind obsessing about what they are caught by, thereby becoming a prisoner within their own mind. The cultivation of concentration is based on the idea that basic to mental health is free attention, attention that functions as needed according to the situation.

Letting go of thinking also has implications for cognitive-behavioral psychotherapy. This therapy focuses on re-structuring a person's thinking habits and self beliefs from unhealthy to healthy. Daoist ideas have been utilized in trying to develop a Daoist cognitive-behavioral therapy approach (Tseng, Chang, and Nishizono 2005). While there is value in this type of work, from a Daoist point of view there are also limitations and cautions. Cognitive-behavioral therapy focuses on replacing negative with positive habits, which sometimes creates a struggle within the person, a kind of dualistic approach. Daoism is a non-dualistic approach to mind and focuses more on thinking that reflects cognition of experience as it is. Healing comes from reordering and then transforming the functions of mind. Thus, reprioritize: emphasize attention, de-emphasize thinking, and then change the quality of each. Most importantly, Daoism, with its focus on the long term (long life and immortality) asserts that full healing comes only in transcending one's cognitive mind. Working within thinking patterns is a first step in healing. Full health cannot occur by just working within the conscious mind.

One of my Asian clients attended a Western drug detoxification center at which the therapy was based on cognitive-behavioral work. His comments were that while it was extremely helpful in getting him off drugs, it was also "too Western," limited in depth, too rational, hard for daily life, and he was much relieved by a more Daoist approach. Tseng ("Integration and Application for Therapy" in Tseng, Chang, and Nishizono 2005, 271) writes similarly, stating that most Western therapies value rational and cognitive approaches to understanding problems and how to deal with them, while most Eastern therapies, including Daoist approaches, stress the importance of actual experience without cognitive understanding.

The movement of energy in life-sustaining ways is basic to Daoist cultivation. One aspect of energy cultivation that is highly useful for ordinary people is the *neidan* reversal cultivation or backward-flowing method. Commonly people direct their energy down the front of their body and outward toward sensory desired objects. Daoism asserts that this results in a gradual wasting of the life force until it is used up. Those seeking immortality cultivate the reversal of this movement. Instead of throwing energy out of and off oneself, they seek to retain it within and circulate it up the back of the body to the head. In this way energy begins to flow harmoniously within a person and longer life is possible. This is specifically applicable to daily life by identifying one's habits, both physically and mentally, that throw off energy rather than circulate it. A person then replaces these unhealthy habits by repeating new habits in the Daoist way of mind.

Conclusion

Even ordinary mortals can sense and life Daoist immortality through the cultivation of their inherent life force. This living is not eternally focused, but rather centers on transforming bodymind in the present life. If the average person intuits and trusts their life force, and lives according to its inherent forms and patterns, their bodymind will be transformed in healthy ways. The relevance of immortality is in life, in the cultivation of the primal life force that is pulsing at the root of each and every living being. This is where Daoist immortality is the most applicable to the everyday mind of the ordinary mortal. Those who are suffering are trapped within their suffering experience. Daoist practices with the Daoist understanding of mind provide a way for ordinary mortals to transform their suffering into health and happiness.

I have discussed both practical applications for the client in psychotherapy as well as a theoretical view for the psychotherapist to work with the client. This has been an attempt at participating in the development of a psychology with Daoism. Further developing of this psychology will broaden the scope and effectiveness of psychotherapy in the world today.

Bibliography

Beck, Aaron, Gary Emery, and Ruth Greenberg. 2005. *Anxiety Disorders and Phobias: A Cognitive Perspective.* Cambridge: Perseus.

Chan, Wing-tsit. 1963. *Tao-te Ching.* New York: Bobbs-Merrill.

Clarke, John. 1994. *Jung and Eastern Thought: A Dialogue with the Orient.* New York: Routledge.

Freud, Sigmund. 2001 [1915]. "Instincts and their vicissitudes." In *The Standard Edition of the Complete Psychological Works of Sigmund Freud*, 14:117-40. London: Vintage.

Greenberg, Jay and Mitchell, Stephen. 1983. *Object Relations in Psychoanalytic Theory*. Cambridge, Mass.: Harvard University Press.

Gunaratana, Bhante. 2002. *Mindfulness in Plain English*. Boston: Wisdom Publications.

Hammer, Leon. 1990. *Dragon Rises, Red Bird Flies*. New York: Station Hill Press.

Jung, Carl. 1968. *Man and His Symbols*. New York: Dell.

Kaptchuk, Ted. 2000. *The Web That Has No Weaver: Understanding Chinese Medicine*. New York: Contemporary Books.

Kochumuttom, Thomas. 1982. *A Buddhist Doctrine of Experience: A New Translation and Interpretation of the Works of Vasubandhu the Yogacarin*. Delhi: Motilal Banarsidass.

Kohn, Livia, ed. 2000. *Daoism Handbook*. Leiden: E. Brill.

_____. 2008. *Meditation Works: In the Daoist, Buddhist, and Hindu Traditions*. Magdalena, NM: Three Pines Press.

_____. 2009a. *Introducing Daoism*. London: Routledge.

_____. 2009b. "Modes of Mutation: Restructuring the Energy Body." In *Internal Alchemy: Self, Society, and the Quest for Immortality*, edited by Livia Kohn and Robin R. Wang, 1-26. Magdalena, NM: Three Pines Press.

_____. 2010. *Sitting in Oblivion: The Heart of Daoist Meditation*. Dunedin, Fla.: Three Pines Press.

Kohut, Hans. 1971. *The Analysis of the Self*. New York: International Universities Press.

Komjathy, Louis. 2009. "Mapping the Daoist Body: Part Two – The Text of the *Neijing Tu*." *Journal of Daoist Studies* 2:64-108.

Kuriyama, Shigehisa. 2002. *The Expressiveness of the Body and the Divergence of Greek and Chinese Medicine*. New York: Zone Books.

Lu, Xichen. 2009. "The Southern School: Cultivating Mind and Inherent nature." In *Internal Alchemy: Self, Society, and the Quest for Immortality*, edited by Livia Kohn and Robin R. Wang, 73-86. Magdalena, NM: Three Pines Press.

Neswald, Sara Elaine. 2009. "Internal Landscapes." In *Internal Alchemy: Self, Society, and the Quest for Immortality*, edited by Livia Kohn and Robin R. Wang, 27-53. Magdalena, NM: Three Pines Press.

Nisbett, Richard. 2003. *The Geography of Thought: How Asians and Westerners Think Differently. . . and Why*. New York: Free Press.

Pawle, Reggie. 2003. "The no-self psychology of Zen Buddhism: Causality, attachment, and the manifestation of fundamental aliveness." Ph. D. Dissertation, UMI Dissertation Services 3080423.

_____. 2009. "The ego in the psychology of Zen: Understanding reports of Japanese Zen masters on the experience of no-self." In *Self and No-self: Continuing the Dialogue Between*

Buddhism and Psychotherapy, edited by Dale Mathers, Melvin Miller, and Osamu Ando, 45-55. London: Routledge.

Penny, Benjamin. 2000. "Immortality and Transcendence." In *Daoism Handbook*, edited by Livia Kohn, 109-33. Leiden: E. Brill.

Rao, K., Anand Paranjpe, and Ajit Dalal, eds. 2008. *Handbook of Indian Psychology*. New Delhi: Cambridge University Press India.

Robinet, Isabelle. 1993. *Taoist Meditation: The Mao-shan Tradition of Great Purity*. Translated by Norman Girardot and Julian Pas. Albany: State University of New York Press.

Saso, Michael. 2000. *The Teachings of Taoist Master Chuang*. Eldorado Springs, Col.: Sacred Mountain Press.

Schipper, Kristofer. 1993. *The Taoist Body*. Translated by Karen Duval. Berkeley: University of California Press.

Tarnas, Richard. 1991. *The Passion of the Western Mind: Understanding the Ideas That Have Shaped Our World View*. New York: Ballantine.

Tseng, Wen-Shing, Suk Choo Chang, and Masahisa Nishizono, eds. 2005. *Asian Culture and Psychotherapy: Implications for East and West*. Honolulu: University of Hawai'i Press.

Valussi, Elena. 2009. "Female Alchemy: An Introduction." In *Internal Alchemy: Self, Society, and the Quest for Immortality*, edited by Livia Kohn and Robin R. Wang, 142-64. Magdalena, NM: Three Pines Press.

Vishnudevananda. 1960. *The Complete Illustrated Book of Yoga*. New York: Bell.

Watson, Burton. 2003. *Zhuangzi: Basic Writings*. New York: Columbia University Press.

Wong, Eva. 1997. *The Shambhala Guide to Taoism*. Boston: Shambhala.

Yuasa, Yasuo. 1993. *The Body, Self-cultivation, and Ki-energy*. Translated by Shigenori Nagatomo and Monte Hull. Albany: State University of New York Press.

The "Unconscious" in West and East

Thoughts on Siri Hustvedt's "Shaking Woman"

ELISABETH FRIEDRICHS

In her 2010 bestseller The Shaking Woman: A History of My Nerves, *Siri Hustvedt describes how she experienced uncontrolled convulsions that remained unexplained by standard medical approaches. Exploring them further, she reflects on her close relationship to her deceased father, analyzes her dreams along the lines of Freud, and concludes that her best bet is to integrate the "shaking woman" as part of herself. Traditional Daoist texts similarly deal with the subject of translating different parts of the personality from the unconscious into the conscious realm, e.g., Zhuangzi's butterfly dream and the mystery in the work of Ge Hong. Daoists do this by focusing on self-cultivation, which can be understood as an early form of psychotherapeutic intervention. They have various exercises for balancing and cultivating qi, essential for the promotion of a harmonious condition of body and mind. Modern seekers such as Siri Hustvedt may well learn from the various Daoist techniques, thus enhancing established Western methods, such as dream work and writing.*

In her 2010 book *The Shaking Woman,* American writer Siri Hustvedt describes the process of how she dealt with her fits of uncontrolled shaking. She takes the reader on a grand tour of basic ideas of philosophical and psychological/psychoanalytical thinking in Western science and its concept of the relations between, body, soul and spirit. Involved for many years in Columbia University's Program of Narrative Medicine for psychic patients, she is also well versed in medical literature.

Her detailed and precise description makes it possible to look at her symptoms also from the perspective of Chinese medicine. So let me take the liberty of developing my ideas about her "case," focusing on the importance of the "unconscious" in Western thought and Daoist bodymind cosmology. At the same time I do not wish to suggest that either of the two systems is better than the other, but am working more toward thinking in terms of mutual inspiration.

In 2007, two and a half years after the death of her father Lloyd Hustvedt (1922-2004), who she had been very close to, Siri Hustvedt had to give a speech in his honor. The occasion was the planting of a northern fir tree in the garden of the university where her father had taught at the Norwegian Department for almost forty years. While delivering the speech, her body started to shake heavily from the neck down—her head was not involved. At the end of the speech the shaking stopped. Similar seizures continued to occur repeatedly. Since then, she has dealt with them differently, simultaneously transforming her experience in literature.

The seizures are beyond the ordinary, medical categories of modern diagnostics and consultations. For this reason, Hustvedt takes it on herself to find out the causes of these highly disturbing events. Even as late as the publication of her book she is still not completely seizure-free so that each section of her work takes the reader on an exploratory journey into the subtly changing understanding of the specific nature of her continued seizures.

Western Psychoanalysis

Making ample use of Western psychoanalytic literature, specifically Freud, the author brilliantly describes the appearance of unconscious content in her consciousness, relating how forgotten experiences in her own life and that of her father came back to the surface. Like her father, she is recognized as a person who can think clearly and formulate her ideas well. The seizures, she writes, always start with the "act of speaking." She wonders: "Is it connected to a memory?" (2010, 100) and promptly remembers an experience she had shortly before her father's death when she had returned home and was back in her old room:

> As I lay there, thinking of my father, I felt the oxygen line in my nostrils and its discomfort, the heaviness of my lame leg, from which a tumor had been removed years before, the pressure in my tightened lungs, and a sudden panicked helplessness that I could not move from the bed on my own but would have to call for help. For however long it lasted, only minutes, *I was my father.* The sensation was both overwhelming and awful. I felt the proximity of death, its inexorable pull, and I had to struggle to leap back into my own body, to find myself again. (124-25)

Looking back, she remembers that when she first prepared the memorial speech after her father's death, she had just interrupted her work on a book entitled *The Sorrows of an American*, in which she describes the traumatic experiences of her father as a soldier in the Pacific.

> For the book, I borrowed my father's words, in which he tells about the murder of a Japanese officer, and recorded the passages he had written about his flashbacks, one in particular: a trembling fit he had as he listened to a hymn in the chapel on the St. Olaf College campus, not far from where I found myself the afternoon I shook so hard I thought I would fall down. (126)

With her shaking seizures Hustvedt thus expresses not so much her own experience, but that of her father. She asks herself whether this might suggest that some elements in her deep attachment to her father were never properly dealt with. Her considerations, moreover, reflect the differentiation between mourning and melancholy as described by Sigmund Freud in his 1917 essay "Mourning and Melancholy" (Ger: *Trauer und Melancholie*). He distinguishes different kinds of grief and notes that for anyone who is in mourning for another has thus suffered a conscious loss, the outside world is gray and meaningless. However, if he or she remains healthy on the inside, the mourner has a clear and open connection with the loved one and there are no unsolved conflicts. This is significantly different from melancholy:

> In melancholia, however, the afflicted person has powerful identifications with the dead person, some of which are unconscious, and the loss becomes internal, not external—a psychic wound. (126)

Many characteristics Freud describes are today seen as symptoms of clinical depression. Hustvedt cannot find any of them in herself, she does not suffer from thoughts of punishing or diminishing herself, has no particular guilt feelings or the need to impoverish herself. Still, she wants to find out whether her seizures could possibly be understood as an expression of a "psychological wound," of unresolved issues with her dead father that fester in her unconscious.

To get to the roots of her condition, she finally decides to undergo psychoanalytical therapy. On the very day when she makes this decision, which she perceives as deep and far-reaching, she teaches a writing class in the psychiatric section of the hospital and discusses, in response to a student's demand, themes like fear and sadness. The following night she has a dream which she finds highly significant:

> A doctor . . . tells me I have cancer. . . . The cancer is inoperable. I am dying. There is nothing to be done, he says. I wander away from the physician, and it is only then that I become intensely aware of the tumors under the skin at my throat and around my neck, bulging protuberances that move under my fingers when I touch them and that confirm my terminal state. . . .

> Well, I think to myself, I've always known that the book I am writing wouldn't be a long one, but now I will have to . . . end it sooner than I had expected. I am dying. It will be the *last* book I write. This makes me terribly sad— not desperate, as I would have been in waking life, but, unutterably, deeply sad. . . .
>
> As is true of many dreams, this one collapsed my day into a curious, dense little parable. Even before I crawled out of bed, I understood that my dream tumors referred to the malignant tumor the doctors removed from my father's thigh . . . the leg I had felt so intensely during my minutes of nearly complete identification with my father as I lay in my childhood bed (128)

A key characteristic of dream work in Freud is the idea of "condensation work" (Freud 2005, 265). Following this Hustvedt sees her dream as a condensed form of unconscious content, which expresses the deep connection she has to her deceased parent. She even interprets the death in her dream as that of her father:

> In the dream, I was only sad [that I had to die soon], strangely deliberate, resigned, and capable of calm meditation on my lot. In other words, it was a dream not about my own death but about my relation to another death – one I seem to be carrying around with me every day like a disease. I may be wrong, but I feel I've never been so close to the shaking woman as in that dream. (137)

It makes her "terribly sad" to have to shorten the book she is working on, which shows a connection to her own life and her work as a writer as well as to her particular physical experience. As she had noticed earlier: "But the neck is also where the shaking woman begins. A sick neck served as the perfect dream image of my symptom: *From the chin up, I was my familiar self. From the neck down, I was a shuddering stranger*" (129).

Her analyst, who also has extensive medical training, expresses strong skepticism when Hustvedt presents the theory that her seizures express her relation to her father and suggests this as the key therapeutic focus. The analyst wants to make sure that there is no physical sickness; he has her undergo an up-to-date brain diagnosis. No pathological changes are found. But the MRI, which rattles on for over thirty minutes, triggers a heavy seizure of migraine.

That makes her think: a technical-medical test supposed to find the reasons for her newly developed seizures now triggers something else, a familiar feature that has accompanied her since her youth. That is to say, her migraines are not so much an illness but form part of herself, just like the participants in her writing class in the clinic accept their psychoses as a part of who they are. She says: "The headache is me, and understanding this has been my salvation. Perhaps, the trick will now be to integrate the shaking woman as well, to acknowledge that she, too, is part of myself" (174). At the same time, the shaking woman increasingly becomes "an admittedly handicapped part of myself" (190).

She is of course aware that with this she stands in the tradition of Sigmund Freud whom she mentions several times. Yet she comes herself, and from her own inner power, to the healing recognition that the seizures are "part of herself." Since medical diagnostics tend to contribute to her increased anxiety, she decides not to continue with psychotherapy. She loses the urgency to clarify and transform the relationship to her deceased father. A key factor in this new approach is her appreciation of Freud's work on dream interpretation—even though she is completely aware of the fact that dreams can never be fully clear and that there is always a certain level of vagueness and insecurity. She says:

> In the *Interpretation of Dreams*, Freud writes: "I have already had occasion to point out that it is in fact never possible to be sure that a dream has been completely interpreted. Even if the solution seems satisfactory and without gaps the possibility remains that the dream may have yet another meaning." (130-31n130; see Freud 2005)

Dreams can help to express unconscious content and tendencies, but not everything one experiences in a dream can be completely opened up or fully interpreted. It is after all the very nature of the unconscious, as Freud already noted, that it cannot be made fully visible or understood. In *The Interpretation of Dreams* he says:

> Properly speaking, the unconscious is the real psychic; its inherent nature is just as unknown to us as the reality of the external world, and it is just as imperfectly reported to us through the data of consciousness as is the external world through the indications of our sensory organs. (2005, 482)

Freud later expanded his theory to include the concept of Id (Ger.: *Es*), a notion originally introduced by his close colleague, the family doctor Georg Groddeck (1866-1956). In his 1917 publication, *Das Buch vom Es*, he wrote:

> I hold the view that man is animated by the Unknown, that there is within him an "Es," an "It," some wondrous force, which directs both what he himself does and what happens to him. The affirmation, "I live" is only conditionally correct, it expresses only a small and superficial part of the fundamental principle, "Man is lived by It." (cited in Laplanche and Pontalis 1973, 199; see also Groddeck 1935)

The unconscious or Id is thus not only the ultimate source of Hustvedt's shaking seizures but it also contains the root of her creativity and ability to write. Any attempt to suppress or eliminate any disturbing manifestations of the unconscious may thus also lead to the transformation or reduction of other, more creative or desired aspects. Thus Hustvedt reflects on herself as a self-conscious storyteller on an island: "Around and beneath the island of that self-conscious storyteller is a vast sea of unconsciousness . . . There is much in us we don't control or will, but that doesn't mean that making a narrative for ourselves is unimportant" (198).

The Daoist Perspective

Unlike these Western perceptions of reality, consciousness, and the unconscious, in Daoist thinking the promotion of harmony in all walks of life forms the central focus. To achieve this harmony, however, Daoist masters have attributed at least as much importance to the unconscious, the hidden, the not-fully-explicable. How, then, do they speak of this phenomenon?

One way they present it is with the concept of *hundun* 渾沌, translated as "chaos," "disorder," "confusion." The classical passage about *hundun* is in *Zhuangzi* 7 where Chaos appears personified as the god of the center. He is described as lacking the seven sensory orifices in the head, i.e., he has no mouth, eyes, ears, and nostrils and thus no senses to perceive the world. The gods of the Northern and Southern Seas want to do him a favor, since he always treats them with utmost kindness. Over seven days they drill the orifices into his head: on the seventh day, Hundun dies. The message of this story is that forceful action contrary to nature, here the drilling of the holes, destroys original chaos, the primordial purity of the person. "The death of Hundun indicates the loss of Dao, the natural essence of the world, and in opposition to that the development of the artificial" (Ommerborn 2007). [1]

The great German translator of the Chinese classics, Richard Wilhelm, translates *hundun* as "the Unconscious" ("das Unbewußte;" 1977, 99) in the sense of a hidden force at work in everything natural. A hidden and not fully understandable element of human nature, then, *hundun* is a basic force common to everything natural: it can do more harm than good if we try to understand it fully.

Another way to describe the unconscious in Daoism is through the notion of vital energy (*qi* 氣). *Qi* is the basic material of all that exists, the subtle flowing force that connects all existence, over and above sensory perception. *Qi* animates life and furnishes the functional power of events; its quality and movement determine human life and well-being. Everyone receives a basic amount of *qi* from nature and needs to sustain it throughout life. To do so, people absorb postnatal *qi* into the body from breathing air and taking in food and drink. They also nurture their *qi* through emotional, social, and sexual interaction with other people and animals. At the same time they may also lose *qi*

---

[1] The edition of the *Zhuangzi* used (English and Chinese) is part of the Chinese Text Project: http://chinese.dsturgeon.net/text.pl?node=2753&if=en. Accessed May 2010.

through abuse, be it by living in a polluted environment, taking too much or not getting enough nourishment, as well as by being subjected to tensions, stress, and negative emotions.

Qi is also at work in humans as a part of the myriad beings which are—as outlined in the *Daode jing*—part of the harmonious unfolding of creation and connected to everything due to its universal power:

> The Way [Dao] gives birth to the One.
> The One gives birth to the Two.
> The Two give birth to the Three.
> The Three give birth to the myriad things.
> The myriad things support the yin and embrace the yang
> And through blending *qi* create harmony. (De Bary and Bloom 1999, 1:89)

To connect back to Dao, to find harmony with the creative source of all, Daoists recommend the recovery of the energetic connection in a process that does not suppress or eliminate but open and enhance the various aspects of the unconscious. A key practice here is "mind fasting," described in the *Zhuangzi*:

> Unify your will and don't listen with your ears but listen with your mind. No, don't listen with your mind, but listen with your *qi*. Listening stops with the ears, the mind stops with perception, but *qi* is empty and waits on all things. Tao gathers in emptiness alone. Emptiness is the fasting of the mind. (ch. 4; Kohn 2011, 107)

The result of this practice is the partial loss of identity, the dissolution of the individual, separate self into the larger flow of Dao underlying all. The Zhuangzi speaks of it as "not being there any longer as an entity." This, in turn, makes it possible for the person to relax into pure so-being and move about at ease:

> You can enter and move about in the world, but don't be concerned with fame. If invited, go and do your part; if not, just stop. Be without any obvious openings and without any poisonous feelings about the world. Just rest in yourself completely without the need to attain anything: that gets you pretty close. (Kohn 2011, 109)

Yet another Daoist concept that relates to the Unconscious is *xuan* 玄, lit. "darkness," "mystery." It appears in the *Daode jing*, which speaks of the Dao as the "gate of the mystery" (ch. 1), but is described in more detail in the work of the scholar and alchemist Ge Hong 葛洪 (ca. 283-343 CE), notably in his *Baopuzi* 抱朴子 (The Book of the Master Who Embraces Simplicity; trl. Ware 1966). Here he speaks of *xuan* as the basic force that cannot be fully understood which is yet common to all beings.

For Ge Hong "all things are permeated by metaphysical oneness, the mystery, which creates and animates all things." For him, "mystery" is synonymous with the way (ultimate reality, *dao* 道) and oneness (unity, *yi* 一). It "carries within it the embryo of original oneness; it forms and shapes the two forces [yin and yang]. . . . If something is taken from it, it does not suffer" (www.iep.utm.edu/g/gehong.htm).

In addition, both the *Zhuangzi* and Ge Hong describe the ideal state of being with the metaphor of the newborn infant or even the embryo in the mother's womb: either is completely at one with natural development, which it cannot begin to understand and to whom full understanding might even be detrimental. As Isabelle Robinet says: "Where the mystery is present, joy is infinite; where the mystery has departed, efficacy is exhausted and the spirit disappears" (1997, 82-83). Ge Hong similarly notes: "The way of *xuan* is obtained within oneself, but is lost due to things outside. Those who employ *xuan* are those who work with spirit; those who forget it are merely [empty] vessels" (www.iep.utm.edu/g/gehong.htm).

Sleep, Dream, Death

The state in which people are closest to the unconscious in Daoism is described as oblivion, a mystical immersion in the greater universe. This, not unlike the way in which the unconscious is perceived in the West, can be linked with sleep and dreaming. As Ute Engelhardt points out, "in the book *Zhuangzi* sleep occurs mainly as a metaphor for an ideal, carefree, and ecstatic existence, on the one hand, and for death, on the other" (2009, 55). The text has: "The true men of old did not dream when they slept, had no anxiety when they awoke, and did not care that their food should be pleasant. Their breathing came deep and silently" (ch. 6).

Sleep here represents freedom, openness, perfect happiness. It stands for an ideal the *Zhuangzi* represents as a form of mystic consciousness, complete oneness with the Dao. Dream, too, appears in this sense, best known in the famous story where Master Zhuang dreams that he is a butterfly and after waking up is not sure whether he is in fact a person who just dreamt of being a butterfly or maybe a butterfly dreaming that he is Master Zhuang (ch. 2).

This addresses another key topic: dream as a potential state within human beings to expand their identity and/or take on a different perspective, a new mode of being. Dreams are the gateway to transcendence, to transformation. Like Freud's unconscious, the Daoist self contains a great deal of volatile potential, of unknowing, of emptiness—leaving the nature, or even the very existence, of one's personal self in question. As Livia Kohn notes:

This famous "butterfly dream" continues the theme of the self, not so much in terms of the different parts of the body and the requirements of society but in terms of personal perception and the sense of certainty of who we are. The self, it turns out, is undefined, fluid, in transformation, a nonentity, nothing we can firmly pin down. (2011, 74)

This theme, of course, is not limited to Eastern literature. One of the best known routines of the famous Bavarian comic Karl Valentin (1882-1948) focuses on a similar theme—and was most certainly not based on a close encounter with Zhuangzi. In his spectacular "duck dream," hilariously presented in broad Bavarian dialect, a local gendarme wakes his colleague to take over his watch. The sleeper complains that this was a lousy time to be roused: in his dream he had been a duck who had found a tasty worm and was just about to bite into it. The comic dialogue then deals with the question whose wondrous dream it was—the gendarme's or the duck's?—and who would be the ultimate instance to make that judgment.

The German philosopher Ernst Bloch (1885-1977) once described this duck dream in a radio interview as semi-Chinese (1982, 85) and connected it to the scholastic Talmud debates of Judaism:

There we have the closer interconnectedness: what is dream, what is reality? Am I dreaming or am I awake? Where do I get the criteria that I am not actually dreaming right now? How do I know that I am awake? This means that dream opens up the peculiar vision of all sorts of possible categories, of a bricolage of realities. It does so without any kind of force, any necessity. Someone even called this, due to its perceptiveness and its apparent superfluousness, the Bavarian Talmud. (1982, 86)[2]

In the chapter "Dreams" of her new book *Chuang Tzu: The Way of Perfect Happiness*, Kohn similarly notes that the butterfly is often an image or metaphor for the theme of transformation and may signify the transition from life to death:

It is also a spontaneously recurring image in the dying, especially in dying children. It stands for the sense of complete freedom and release, the power of inherent transformation, the opening of ourselves to new realms, new visions, and a different dimension of reality. (2011, 74)

Death in *Zhuangzi*, of course, is nothing to be feared but just another state of existence as part of the continuous flow of Dao. Mourning, depression, and sadness—key themes in Western psychology—accordingly take on a different dimension. Thus Huizi visits Master Zhuang after the death of his wife to find him sitting comfortably on the ground, drumming and singing happily. Huizi

---

[2] Unless otherwise specified, translations are by the author.

asks him about this apparent callousness. Zhuangzi explains that he did in fact pass through an initial stage of mourning, but has since come to the realization that life and death are just different phases of cosmic transformation. He says:

> "Right after her death, I was totally bereft and deeply affected. But then I thought about her beginnings and realized that she hadn't been alive then either. Before she was born, she had no bodily form. Before she had a bodily form, she had not even a breath of vital energy.
>
> "Intermingling in undifferentiated chaos, change happened and there was vital energy. Another change happened and there was bodily form. Then another change occurred and, presto!, there she was: alive. Now there has been yet another change, and she is dead.
>
> "These changes proceed one after the next, just like the four seasons move from spring to fall, from winter to summer. See, now the person lies there, sleeping in the great chamber of the universe. If I went and mourned her by wailing and weeping, I figured I'd just show that I had no understanding of the underlying patterns of destiny. So I stopped. (Kohn 2011, 37)

Zhuangzi's way of dealing with his wife's passing can be interpreted in Freudian terms as successful "grief work" or "work of mourning". He does not show signs of "psychological wounding" or any sort of unresolved conflict with his spouse that might possibly predispose him toward melancholy or depression—or various kinds of psychological or physical symptoms such as shaking seizures. Still, the Daoist understanding of life and death, transformation and transcendence is significantly different from Western notions and has little in common with Freud's view of the world—based on traditional Judaism yet dominantly informed by modern atheism and the materialist perspective of science.

The Seizures Interpreted

Western psychologists, too, have made ample use of sleep and dream. Siri Hustvedt, unable to find out "who the shaking woman is" (2010, 186) from either the neurologist reading of the MRI or the psychoanalytical exploration of her subconscious, finds decisive insights in dream analysis. Applying her profound knowledge of Freudian psychoanalysis, she realizes that the body remembers and experiences something sub- or unconsciously that she tries to understand with her conscious mind. Thus the shaking seizures become meaningful.

Viktor von Weizsäcker (1886-1957), specialist for internal medicine and neurology, is considered the founder of German psychosomatic medicine, the so called 'Heidelberg School' of psychosomatic medicine. (Hahn and Jacob, 25). Weizsäcker himself described his form of medicine as "anthropological medicine,", and hoped—as did his disciples—that the term would express the idea that every disease is a result of the patient's life history and the environment of which he or she forms a part. It indicates that every physical experience expresses itself in the mental sphere, and vice versa.

As he says: "There is nothing organic that does not have a sense; there is nothing psychological that is without a body" (1987, 314).[3] This means that, where the conscious, intellectual grasp of a certain event or such a "sense" seems too frightful, it may well be that the body remembers. Heinrich Huebschmann (1913-1995), a disciple of von Weizsäcker, used this kind of analysis in the 1950s and 60s in connection with the medical treatment and monetary compensation of political victims under the Nazis, who laid claims of reconciliation on the German state. He found quite clearly that the human mind and consciousness refuse to remember anything that is too threatening, too close to loss of life. The inner organs of the body, on the other hand, will maintain that memory so that, for example, heart attacks may well be the late result of time in a concentration camp. As he says:

> "Every cell of the body remembers," say the French allergy specialists Ch. Richet and A. Mans. The director of a clinic for victims of politically prosecution . . . has regarded this as the cause of illnesses occurring much later" (1974, 184).[4]

Applying this line of reasoning to Siri Hustvedt's seizures, they would appear to be late manifestations of suffering experienced in connection with her father, kept out of conscious awareness but surviving in the cells of the body.

As noted earlier, Western psychosomatics go back to a large extent to Freud. Already Weizsäcker said: "I believe . . . that all major discoveries and realizations of psychoanalysis go entirely back to Freud" (Henkelmann 1986, 110). The core of this view, moreover, is the verbal dialogue with the physician, the key to any form of therapy.

Weizsäcker and his disciples do not agree just to what degree this methodological approach was used to increase the conscious awareness of patients in relation to the function of the ego. Freud, of course, was already aware of "free association" as a means of approaching the unconscious, in contrast to consciously conducted discussions. In his 1926 essay, "The Physician and the Patient" ("Der Arzt und der Kranke"), Weizsäcker notes accordingly:

---

[3] Originally published in 1934: "Nichts Organisches hat keinen Sinn, nichts Seelisches hat keinen Leib."

[4] Heinrich Huebschmann was my father and still is a tremendous inspiration today. An internist, cardiologist, and psychotherapist, he called himself—against the massive resistance of physicians' associations—"Doctor of Internal and Memory Medicine," always conscious of the importance of psychological impact and memory on the health of the body.

When the patient said to me "I am ill," I also knew directly what he meant; I did not understand because I thought something, but because I understood him. The origin of this understanding was not at all my understanding something by thinking, but that I understood someone; completely unthought, completely thoughtless I understood him . . . Because it becomes clear that understanding someone and understanding something are two completely incomparable cases. (1987, 19-20)

He also insists that "the first medical action must be a question. . . . The beginning is thus not knowing, but asking." This attitude of openness can also be described as a form of "emptiness." It comes close to a conception of "not doing" or *wuwei* as found in Daoist thought.

Huebschmann, too, was quite aware of the central importance of therapeutic not in the course of treatment. He notes:

The supreme method is the discussion with the patient. . .What is decisive is not the action of the doctor, however, but the involvement of the patient. Enabling the patient to speak and then also to reveal himself or herself genuinely is the alpha and omega, the whole secret of the method. (1952, 275)

The goal of this therapeutic attitude of nondoing as listening, according to Huebschmann, is geared primarily toward the opening of self-awareness and cannot be compared to nondoing as a dominant attitude to life—especially when related to the nondoing of people under repressive regimes such as the Nazis. As he says:

The disease, as we saw, arises not only out of the loss of drive, but also through the frustration of ideals. If this is the case, however, then the treatment does not consist of increasing the patient's adaptability, but must be directed towards self-assertion, to the assertion of the better self. During the treatment, the patient gains the strength not to *adapt* himself or herself to intolerable conditions in the environment, but rather on the contrary to *oppose* them and, along with the transformation of the self, to transform them as well. (1952, 275)

However, he is also very much aware of the value of the unconscious in diagnostics and therapy. Thus, Huebschmann uses an aphorism by Blaise Pascal as the epigraph to his book *Krankheit, ein Körperstreik*: "The heart has its reasons, of which reason knows nothing. One must imagine a body full of thinking members" (1974, 8).

The pioneers of Western psychosomatics were the first to approach physical diseases based on understanding body and mind as closely interrelated—thus taking on the perspective of Chinese medicine. They worked for the longest time on lesser physical ailments that had no obvious organic cause, calling them functional problems and finding that they responded well to psychosomatic treatments. Only in the last few years has it become acceptable that also serious and even terminal diseases such as heart conditions can be related to the living conditions and attitudes of the patient. [5]

The greater availability of training in Chinese medicine among Western physicians is another factor that may well have contributed to the intensified awareness of bodymind-soul interconnections. Acupuncture also works well on mind and spirit, which is made clear in the names of some important acupuncture points, such as Gate of the Material Soul (*Pohu* 魄戶, BL 42) and Door of the Spirit Soul (*Hunmen* 魂門, BL 47). Many psychotherapists, moreover, have come to apply exercises based on qigong both to renew their own energies as well as to assist their patients.

Thus through needling points or practicing exercises that nurture *qi,* one can gain access to the patient's feelings and underlying experiences, yet there is no need to articulate everything verbally. What is not spoken can sometimes also remain unspoken, since the natural course of change in things may also rearrange arising emotions and feelings in a harmonious way.

In addition, the seizures also make sense from the perspective of Daoism and Chinese medicine. This is where my practical background comes in. As a family doctor trained and licensed both in Western medicine and in some areas of complementary practice, I have applied Chinese medical techniques, especially acupuncture and qigong, in clinical practice for many years. I am on the board of the Medical Association of Qigong Yangsheng, serve as an editor of its journal, and have attended international conferences on Daoism regularly since 2004. I am neither a sinologist nor an expert of Daoist texts and have only limited knowledge of Chinese, but I think I can use the concepts outlined above in conjunction with my practical background to make some tentative conjectures about Hustvedt's seizure experiences.

Siri Hustvedt describes herself as a person with a lot of synesthesia (2010, 120): she is aware of many details such as colors and sounds in herself and others; she describes how she experiences her father's bodily symptoms and sufferings as her own—what others cannot comprehend. She thus has a special connection or resonance, a quality that according to the theory of the five phases can be linked with the phase metal or the inner organ complex known as "lungs." In emotional terms, the lungs are also related to "mourning;" in terms of the dynamic cycle of the five phases, they overcome or control the liver. A healthy liver is characterized by a "harmonious flow of *qi* and blood;" it is the "general among the organs."

Now Hustvedt's very active lung is under enormous stress since she is in mourning for her father. For this reason, it cannot exercise its function of curb-

---

[5] See, for example, Jochen Jordan on: "The Seat of the Soul is the Heart: Psychological Aspects of Heart Disease" (2003). (http://www.studgen.uni-mainz. demanuskripte/jordan.pdf, 03052011).

ing the liver, which corresponds to the phase wood. This leads to various malfunctions in the realm of liver: fits like migraine and other forms of seizures. Since Hustvedt has experienced these earlier, this shows that she has a pre-existent sensitivity toward the phase wood. Her dreams—disquieting and full of mourning—further illustrate how far removed she is from a state of harmony. They stand in a huge contrast to Zhuangzi's butterfly dream.

Chinese medicine has a broad spectrum of therapeutic devices. Using acupuncture points, stimulated with needles, massages, or mental energy guiding, would be a prime way of accessing Hustvedt's condition, focusing especially on points on the *qi* channels of meridians of the lungs and liver. Beyond that, even more central to Chinese medicine and essential to the practice of Daoism, is what we call self-cultivation or nourishing life (*yangsheng* 養生).

One of the prime sources on the various methods of nourishing life is the Japanese work *Ishinpō* 醫心方 (Essential Medical Methods) an important medical compendium by the court physician Tamba no Yasuyori 丹波瀨康 (912-995). The text was presented to the Japanese emperor in 984. Especially its later chapters focus on nourishing life: chapter 26 is on facial treatments, magical methods, and fasting; chapter 27 deals with breathing techniques, mental cultivation, healing exercises, clothing, and the arrangement of living quarters; and chapter 28 presents materials on sexual practices. Chapters 29 and 30 treat diets and the way of healthful eating (see Hsia, Veith, and Geertsma 1986; Hsu 2008). The book cites numerous earlier works, most importantly the fourth-century *Yangsheng yaoji* 養生要集 (Long Life Compendium; lost; compiled Stein 1999), which covers a similar spectrum of methods but also emphasizes the proper use of language.

Language as a modality of (self-) healing is an interesting feature. Hustvedt creates her own therapy through the process of writing. In her case, the writing is fully part of the Western tradition, following especially Freud and the psychoanalytic methods, where consultation is based on dialogue, rendering un- and subconscious content conscious through language. Yet at the same time the act of writing can be understood from the perspective of Chinese medicine as a therapeutic approach in the sense of "cultivating language."

Similarly, the physical methods of Chinese cultivation, the healing exercises today known as qigong and taiji quan (as well as Indian yoga), form a way of bringing unconscious content to the foreground. Moving slowly and deliberately, applying the body in a focused and conscious way, one releases tensions, patterns, and memories of the past. Just as language begins with the conscious mind and, in an act of "writing down the bones" (see Goldberg 1989), moves the person toward sub- and unconscious patterns, so slow, careful body movements—using all three major components of body posture, imagination, and breath, as my teacher Jiao Guorui would say—can unravel unconscious patterns and repressed memories.

Harmonious, slow body movements as much as the flow-of-consciousness sessions of writing can have a balancing effect on disharmonious states of body and mind. It is thus no accident that Siri Hustvedt writes fiction and interprets her dreams. She knows fully well that the fundamental character of the unconscious will only allow a certain degree of conscious understanding and awareness—both to safeguard the person and to avoid endangering the creative process of writing. She no longer experiments with other forms of Western-style therapy, not even psychotherapy, finding that they do not provide any help or support. Her whole recovery is based on writing and the internal connection to dreams.

Creative Potential

Whether seen from Western or Eastern perspective, writing and bodily exercise serve as forms of the creative process that connect to the unconscious. Their active engagement is often prompted by uncertainty, insecurity, and often-physical discomfort. Thus the unconscious comes to the fore, growing in power as creative potential.

The Daoist tradition, making use of this feature, allows unconscious or "chaos" patterns to evolve naturally and sees no need for the practice of conscious resolution, uncovering, or examination. Still, Sigmund Freud also points at the special importance of the unconscious in the creative process: "From the communications of some of the most highly productive persons, such as Goethe . . . , we learn, indeed, that the most essential and original parts in their creations came to them in the form of inspirations and reached their perceptions almost finished" (2005, 482-83). He points out, as cited earlier, that in every dream interpretation, in every dream analysis, a bit of uncertainty remains.

Toward the end of her book, Hustvedt agrees that it might be helpful to accept the shaking seizures as a part of her in the same way as she has done with her migraine attacks. They serve a useful purpose in her life, after all, bringing out her special ability of brilliant writing. In terms of Chinese medicine, this is related to the organ of the heart, seen as the seat of the spirit, which contains the presence of mind, radiance, and clarity of speech. It is also the seat of the joy widely found in Hustvedt's brightly humorous work.   Both from an Eastern and from a Western perspective her writing, the interpretation of her experiences and her dreams, can thus be understood as a method of self-healing. It is, then, that her seizures have changed since, possibly been reduced, after the completion of her book?

Bibliography

Bloch-Almanach. 1982. "Einladungen bei Ernst Bloch." NDR 21.2.1963. Radio recording of Bloch-Archive, Ludwigshafen, Inv.-Nr. 5-6/80. Frankfurt a.M.: Suhrkamp. Used by permission of the publisher.

De Bary, Wm. Th., and Irene Bloom, eds. 1999. *Sources of Chinese Tradition.* 2 vols. New York: Columbia University Press.

Engelhardt, Ute. 2009. "Schlaf und Traum in der chinesischen Lebenspflege." *Zeitschrift für Qigong Yangsheng* 2009: 52-62.

Freud,Sigmund. 1931. *Theoretische Schriften (1911-1925).* Vienna: Internationaler Psycho-analytischer Verlag.

_____. 1953. *Mourning and Melancholia.* Translated by James Strachey. London, Hogarth Press.

_____. 2005 [1913]. *The Interpretation of Dreams.* Translated by A. A. Brill. New York: Barnes & Noble Classics.

Girardot, Norman. 2009 [1983]. *Myth and Meaning in Early Taoism: The Theme of Chaos (Hun-dun).* Dunedin, Fla.: Three Pines Press.

Goldberg, Natalie. 1989. *Writing Down the Bones.* Boston: Shambhala.

Groddeck, Georg. 1935 [1917]. *The Book of the It.* London: C. W. Daniel.

Hahn, Peter, and Wolfgang Jacob, eds. 1987 *Viktor von Weizsäcker zum 100. Geburtstag.* Heidelberg: Springer.

Henkelmann, Thomas. 1986. *Viktor von Weizsäcker (1886-1957). Materialien zu Leben und Werk.* Heidelberg: Springer.

Hildenbrand, Gisela, M. Geißler, and Stephan Stein, eds. 1998. *Das Qi kultivieren, die Lebenskraft nähren, West-Östliche Perspektiven zu Theorie und Praxis des Qigong und Yangsheng.* Uelzen: Medizinisch-Literarische Verlagsgesellschaft.

Hsia, Emil C. H., Ilza Veith, and Robert H. Geertsma, trans. 1986. *The Essentials of Medicine in Ancient China and Japan: Yasuyori Tamba's Ishimpô.* 2 vols. Leiden: E. Brill.

Hsu, Elisabeth. 2008. *"Ishinpô."* In *The Encyclopedia of Taoism,* edited by Fabrizio Pregadio, 1:535. London: Routledge.

Huebschmann, Heinrich. 1952. *Psyche und Tuberkulose.* Stuttgart: Enke,

_____. 1974. *Krankheit, ein Körperstreik.* Freiburg im Breisgau: Herder.

Hustvedt, Siri. 2010 *The Shaking Woman or a History of my Nerves.* New York: Henry Holt.

Kohn, Livia. 2011. *Chuang Tzu: The Tao of Perfect Happiness—Selections Annotated & Explained.* Woodstock, VT: Skylight Publishing

Laplanche, J., and J. B. Pontalis. 1973. *The Language of Psychoanalysis.* Translated by Donald Nicholson-Smith. New York: Norton.

Ommerborn, Wolfgang. 2007. "Der Begriff 'Chaos' (Hundun) in der chinesischen Geistesgeschichte." *Zeitschrift für Qigong Yangsheng* 2007:86-91.

Robinet, Isabelle. 1997. *Taoism: Growth of a Religion*. Translated by Phyllis Brooks. Stanford: Stanford University Press.

Stein, Stephan. 1999. *Zwischen Heil und Heilung: Zur frühen Tradition des Yangsheng in China*. Uelzen: Medizinisch-Literarische Verlagsgesellschaft.

Ware, James R. 1966. *Alchemy, Medicine and Religion in the China of AD 320*. Cambridge, Mass.: MIT Press.

Weizsäcker, Viktor von. 1987. *Gesammelte Schriften*, 1926-1941. Edited by Peter Achilles. Frankfurt am Main: Suhrkamp.

Wilhelm, Richard. 1977. *Dschuang Dsi. Das wahre Buch vom südlichen Blütenland*, Düsseldorf: Diederichs.

Daoism and Positive Psychology

Healing Self, Healing Society[1]

Donald D. Davis

There are various similarities between Daoism and Western psychology, particularly a recent emphasis called positive psychology. It has paid particular attention to positive beliefs such as optimism and happy emotions, and supported research that documents the impact of a positive attitude on important mental and physical health outcomes, well-being, and longevity. All these are benefits that Daoists have pursued for centuries. Daoist-inspired practices such as meditation, qigong, *and* taiji quan, *moreover, produce similar benefits. It is quite possible that they achieve these effects by influencing positive beliefs and emotions. Scientific research designed to examine points of convergence between Daoism and psychology may yield great benefits and increase the relevance of Daoism in the modern world.*

Daoism emerged and thrived during times of social turmoil, conflict and change. Its beliefs and practices nurtured countless Chinese in their efforts to adapt and survive during these challenging times. In the process, Daoism helped individuals to flourish and, through their individual and collective efforts, contributed to the flourishing of families, communities and society. Daoist beliefs and practices may contribute as well to individual and social flourishing in the modern world. To achieve its potential impact, however, Daoism must be transmitted in a manner that maintains its essence and meaning while adapting to fit modern conditions.

The West has been trying to understand its encounter with Daoism since first contact (Clarke 2000). Early translations of classics such as the *Daode jing* revealed an extraordinarily rich tradition of Chinese wisdom that was under-

---

[1] A version of this chapter was presented as part of a panel on Daoist Psychology (Robert Santee, chair) at the Sixth International Conference on Daoist Studies ("Daoism Today: Science, Health and Ecology"), Los Angeles, June 2-6, 2010.

stood incompletely. Western translators often viewed Daoist knowledge through cultural conceptual lenses that often produced misunderstanding. Early translators were unintentionally like Procrustes, a mythical Greek robber who invited travelers to spend the night at his inn and sleep on an iron bed that was never the correct size. When they lay down, and he found them to be either too short or too tall, Procrustes would stretch them or cut off their limbs until they fit.

Like Procrustes, early translators of Daoist knowledge unconsciously stretched or cut off what they learned to fit into the bed of their beliefs. Ethnocentrism, stereotypes, religious beliefs, Orientalist fantasies, and cultural imperialism subtly and unconsciously influenced their attempt to understand and translate Daoist ideas. Moreover, scholars who lacked direct experience with Daoist self-cultivation practices produced translations that are sometimes inaccurate, sterile and lifeless.

Despite these limitations, transmission of Daoism to the West continues unabated. Transmission occurs directly through publication of its seminal texts. Most popular is the *Daode jing*, with more than 250 translations into Western languages, mostly English, French, and German (LaFargue and Pas 1998). Transmission of Daoism also occurs indirectly through its influence on the arts (Little 2000) and health care practices (Kohn 2005; 2006). Many in the West are familiar with the fruits of Daoism, for example, Chinese landscape painting, meditation, taiji quan, qigong, fengshui, Chinese medicine, and acupuncture, but they may be unaware of the Daoist roots that nourish them.

A growing group of modern scholars less influenced by the cultural biases and preconceptions held by their predecessors continues to transmit Daoism to the West. Moreover, modern scholars of Daoism are more likely to practice self-cultivation and use their personal experience to inform their study and transmission of Daoist knowledge. This personal experience enables an interpretation and understanding of Daoist knowledge more likely to capture its original meaning and yield clear discussion of its process and effects.

Cultural and national boundaries are less likely to restrict transmission of Daoism today due to the reach of globalization and technologies such as the Internet as well as inexpensive and widely accessible world travel. Internet websites (for example, www.DaoistStudies.org) provide an electronic community of Daoist scholars and practitioners that allows quick dissemination of information and knowledge to all, not just to a small group of adepts living in remote China. Global foundations exist (for example, www.LegacyofDao.org) to support dissemination of ancient Daoist knowledge and adapt it to needs of the modern world. Daoist scholars and practitioners from around the world can easily collaborate, and knowledge can now be shared at the speed of electrons circling the globe. One may now study with authentic Daoist masters after a few hours of air travel or via the Internet if one prefers not to leave home.

As in ancient China, Daoist knowledge can improve the quality of modern life. Daoism can provide a means to experience happiness and well-being, improve human relationships, reduce conflict and aggression, and encourage respect for and harmony with the natural environment, goals that are just as important now as during ancient times. For Daoism to achieve these goals, however, people today must become familiar with its beliefs and practices. We discuss two potential pathways for this transmission. These pathways emphasize common ground between Daoism and psychology and highlight the Daoist foundation of popular health practices such as taiji quan and their positive impact on important goals of psychology such as enhanced mental and physical health, well-being and longevity. We close with a call for greater collaboration between psychologists and Daoists.

Pathways for Daoism

New ideas move more easily across cultural boundaries when they fit the values, beliefs and needs of those who may adopt them and appear to provide relative advantage compared to existing practices. Daoism will be assimilated to the extent that its beliefs and practices seem helpful. Daoism is a living tradition that has often adapted to satisfy individual and social needs and will adapt as well to meet modern needs.

Daoism, of course, was created and practiced in a different world than exists today. Despite differences, commonalities exist. Like ancient Chinese people, those who live in the modern world care about health, well-being, and longevity. Both aspire to live a long life filled with meaning and purpose. Moreover, there is growing acknowledgement of the relationship between body and mind and use of integrative approaches to strengthen these links to enhance health and well-being (Wolsko et al. 2004). Integration of body and mind has played a central role in Daoist practice (Schipper 1993) and is a distinguishing feature of Daoist self-cultivation and practices such as taiji quan and qigong (Kohn 2006; 2008).

The *Neijing tu*, for example, uses a map of the body as a visual aid for self-cultivation as part of *neidan* practice, which cultivates body and mind to enhance longevity and spiritual growth (Komjathy 2008; 2009). Daoist beliefs and practices can enhance health and human flourishing in the modern world just as they have done for millennia in China. Moreover, Daoist practices that emphasize integration of body and mind in pursuit of health and longevity are likely to be popular. First, however, Daoism must find pathways for entering the modern world beyond translation of its seminal texts.

Below I present two potential pathways through which Daoism may enter the modern world. One pathway focuses on psychological research and practice, particularly a new emphasis in the West called positive psychology. The second pathway we discuss focuses on three Daoism-inspired practices—meditation, qigong, and taiji quan—that contribute to health and well-being. We discuss several points of convergence between positive psychology and Daoism-inspired practices and suggest that use of supporting evidence derived from psychological research will enhance the credibility of Daoist practices and encourage their adoption and practice in the modern world. Personal experience with the benefits of Daoist-inspired practices will foster their use.

Positive Psychology

Psychology encompasses many ideas and practices that are consistent with the Daoist experience. Psychology in the West has stimulated an interest in personal growth, which provides a means by which we can approach, understand, and appreciate Daoism and its practices of self-cultivation. Moreover, Buddhist meditation practices such as mindfulness meditation are growing in popularity and becoming incorporated into psychological research and practice because of personal experience with them and growing scientific evidence for their effectiveness (Wallace and Shapiro 2006; Walsh and Shapiro 2006).

Successful experience with Buddhist meditation practices may help Western psychologists to be more receptive to Daoism. A bridge between Daoism and psychology would allow exchange of ideas and practices that would provide benefits to both. We do not mean to suggest that Daoism is *only* psychology or that it should be forced to fit into conceptual containers taken from psychology. We suggest instead that Daoism and psychology share some important ideas and goals despite employing different terms and theories of explanation and that they may each benefit from exploring points of convergence.

In the West, the discipline of psychology focuses on the science of mind and behavior. Psychology embraces the full range of human experience including the importance of religion and spirituality (Emmons and Paloutzian 2003). Human experience results from the joint influence of characteristics of the individual (for example, physiology and brain functions, personality traits, values, attitudes, and beliefs) and characteristics of the environment in which the individual is situated (for example, family, work and social groups, organizations, and national cultures).

Psychologists employ scientific research methods to understand human experience. Examples where psychological research has enhanced individuals and societies include: prevention of suicide, improved decision making, education, child development, environmentally friendly behavior, workplace improvement, and increased awareness, happiness, health, and well-being, just to name a few (American Psychological Association 2009). Professionals who practice psychology use scientific findings to inform the manner in which they provide psychological services to the public.

Positive psychology, a rapidly growing specialty within psychology, has much in common with Daoism and provides an important focus for future research and practice that may connect the two. The foundation of positive psychology is the study of human flourishing and the human strengths that lead to optimal human functioning (Lopez, Snyder and Pedrotti 2011). Potential commonalities with Daoism include: 1. the role of thoughts and emotions in fostering happiness and well-being; 2. the connection between body and mind and its impact on physical and mental health and longevity; 3. the employment of ethics, virtues, and character strengths to guide one's life; 4. the sustaining of effective interpersonal relationships; and 5. the creation of organizations and social institutions that enable individuals to lead fulfilling and meaningful lives. All these contribute to human flourishing, and their nexus provides an important bridge between positive psychology and Daoism.

There is strong interest in positive psychology in the contribution of positive cognition and emotion to well-being and happiness and of their combined influence on mental and physical health and longevity (Peterson 2006). This dual focus on cognition and emotion recognizes the fact that thoughts and feelings are intertwined; they are jointly influenced by external and internal events and they mutually influence each other. What we think influences what we feel, and what we feel influences what we think. Together, cognition and emotion— thoughts and feelings—shape desired outcomes such as health, well-being and longevity, which are goals that are important to Daoists as well as everyone in the modern world.

Positive Cognition

Cognition is the study of mental processes as well as their content. Common topics for study include the process of attention, the manner in which sensations combine to form perceptions, storage and retrieval of information, beliefs, and concept formation. Positive psychologists have tended to focus on cognitions about the future, particularly hope, optimism and a sense of self-efficacy concerning one's ability to meet the challenges of life as well as high levels of cognition that may be construed as wisdom (Snyder, Lopez and Pedrotti 2011). Daoism has much to offer to the study of cognition, and especially its training. However, due to limited space, I will focus on optimism. This is because of its positive relationship with other cognitions such as hope and self-efficacy, its central role in shaping happiness and well-being, and its influence on longevity, a seminal interest of Daoism.

Optimism is a form of positive thinking in which good things are expected to happen in the future. Its opposite mental state—pessimism—is a form of negative thinking in which bad things are expected to happen in the future. Note that these two conditions are *mental states*—expectations and beliefs about the future—not the actual occurrence of positive or negative events. Optimism reflects what one *expects* to happen, not what *actually* happens, although life experience certainly shapes expectations. Optimism is important because it is linked to positive emotions, perseverance and resilience in the face of challenge and struggle, achievement of goals, effective problem solving, and health, well-being and longevity (Snyder, Lopez, Pedrotti 2011).

Optimism may be viewed as a disposition—an individual characteristic that is relatively constant across time and situations—or as a learned style of thinking—an individual characteristic that fluctuates across time and situations and can be influenced by life experience (Peterson 2006). Both dispositional optimism and learned optimism have been studied extensively, and both are linked to important outcomes. Comparison of identical and fraternal twins reared together and apart, which is the clearest means of assessing the influence of inherited characteristics, reveals that a predisposition to optimism is inherited, and that both the dispositional and learned aspects of optimism predict important aspects of physical and mental health. The inherited component may explain about 25 percent of the expression of dispositional optimism and predicts depression and life satisfaction in adulthood (Plomin et al. 1992).

Learned optimism, measured as a learned explanatory style for the causes of events in one's life, also has a substantial genetic component (Schulman, Keith, and Seligman 1993). Despite this inherited disposition, life experiences such as parenting, school, and training shape the possibility of learning to view the future in a positive way (Peterson and Steen 2005). Psychological interventions can change pessimists into optimists and can reduce negative symptoms such as depression in both children (Gillham et al. 1995) and adults (Seligman et al. 1988). These significant effects have been sustained for up to two years demonstrating that considerable malleability exists in the expression of optimism. This malleability suggests that optimism may be influenced by Daoism-inspired practices such as meditation, taiji quan and qigong that can change patterns of thinking.

Optimists and pessimists are different in ways that have an important impact on their lives. They vary in how they approach and define problems and challenges, as well as the manner in which they cope with adversity (Carver and Scheier 2005). For example, optimists use a different style of thinking about the causes of bad things that happen to them than do pessimists (Peterson and Steen 2005). Optimists tend to reframe stressors that may occur in daily life as opportunities for growth and change; they experience a wide range of more positive health outcomes compared to pessimists because of this reframing (Snyder and Lopez 2007, 187).

Optimistic thinking and its accompanying strategies for coping with stressful life events are positively related to: work performance (Long 1993); recovery from coronary bypass surgery (Fitzgerald et al. 1993); healing after bone marrow transplants (Curbow et al. 1993); successful coping with breast cancer (Carver et al. 1993); and greater success in reducing coronary risk (Shepperd, Maroto, and Pbert 1996). Moreover, optimistic thinking endures across the lifespan. Optimistic thinking during early life predicts superior health 35 years later; pessimistic thinking similarly predicts physical illness (Peterson, Seligman, and Vaillant 1988). Positive thoughts and expectations have been associated with an increased life span of 7.5 years, an effect that is stronger than that produced by lowered blood pressure and cholesterol, lower body mass index, and a history of no smoking (Levy et al. 2002). Optimism enhances health and longevity, important goals of Daoist cultivation.

Positive Emotions

Psychologists distinguish between different aspects of feeling in order to study more precisely their various effects. As Snyder, Lopez and Pedrotti (2011, 117-140) and Fredrickson (2001) discuss, *affect* refers to a general sense of positive or negative arousal that is the most basic element of consciously accessed feeling, is not connected to a specific object, and is relatively long lasting. *Emotion* is a feeling that is always connected to a specific object and has a "sharpened" quality that flows from personally meaningful affective experience and is shorter in duration than affect.

Mood is a "free-floating" feeling that lasts longer than an emotion. It often relates to expectations about experiencing future positive or negative experiences. High levels of positive affect and low levels of negative affect combined with general satisfaction with one's life produce *subjective well-being*, which is the long-term capacity to experience positive emotions and happiness (Diener, Lucas and Oishi, 2005). These aspects of feeling overlap in their felt experience and have in common a connection to the body through physiological arousal and the central nervous system (Watson 2005). We focus our discussion on the role of positive emotions and subjective well-being because of their consistent relationships with health and well-being. Moreover, because these terms are often used interchangeably, we use the term emotion to represent all aspects of feeling in order to simplify discussion.

Like the positive cognition of optimism, positive emotions may be dispositions that are relatively stable across time and situations or may be a more malleable means of experiencing the world that varies across time and situations and that learning and life experience may influence. Positive emotions tend to be stable over time yielding highly correlated scores measured decades apart, particularly among adults (Helson and Klohnen 1998). This stability results from the fact that the affective component of emotion—the aspect representing general physiological arousal—is in part heritable. Genetic predisposition explains as much as 40 to 50 percent of emotional expression, but life experiences such as learning and practice also exert strong influence (Bouchard 2004; Peterson 2006, 63-65).

Positive emotions are related to optimism, particularly its dispositional aspect (Carver and Scheier 2005; Lyubormirsky, King, and Diener 2005). Cultivation of positive emotions such as serenity, harmony and equanimity, because of their importance to health and longevity, has long been the focus of Daoist practice (Kohn 2001; 2005). We discuss below some interventions that have been effective in increasing positive emotions as well as describe how we believe Daoist practices may be used to manage emotional expression and cultivate positive emotions.

Psychologists have traditionally paid greater attention to the role of negative emotions such as sadness and anxiety and their contribution to psychopathology and mental illness (Seligman and Csikszentmihalyi 2000). Recent attention to positive emotions such as joy, contentment, playfulness, and serenity show they produce many important benefits (Lyubomirsky, King, and Diener 2005). Positive emotions are related to reduced anxiety and depression (Watson 2005), improved cardiovascular reactions to stress (Tugade, Fredrickson, and Barrett 2004), enhanced immunological response (Futterman et al. 2002), reduced pain and medication use among those with sickle-cell disease (Gil et al. 2004), and numerous other indicators of mental and physical health (Lyubomirksy, King, and Diener 2005).

The relationship between positive emotions and physical health benefits is sustained over time. Positive emotions were related to several indicators of health 5 years later in a sample of approximately 5000 Russian adults (Graham, Eggers, and Sukhtankar 2004). Positive emotions predicted reduced incidence of stroke among more than 2000 older adults during 6 year follow up assessment after controlling for the influence of blood pressure, body mass index, smoking history, and selected chronic diseases, with effects stronger among men than women (Ostir et al. 2001).

Not surprisingly since positive emotions are related to health benefits over time, they also predict longevity. In a study of nearly 700 Roman Catholic nuns, Danner, Snowden, and Friesen (2001) found that positive emotions measured at the time that participants entered the convent during their late teens and early twenties were strongly associated with longevity more than 6 decades later during ages 75 to 95. Those who reported experiencing the greatest positive emotions and those who reported the least differed in mortality by a factor of 2.5. The relative risk of death increased as the experience of positive emotions decreased. The influence of positive emotions on longevity is more clearly highlighted in this group of nuns because they shared the same occupation, lived in the same convents and thus experienced similar living environments, nutrition, and access to medical care, and avoided risky behaviors such as smoking and drug abuse.

A new theory that may explain these effects is known as the broaden and build theory. It states that positive emotions strengthen health and well-being through a process that triggers an "upward spiral." This involves broadened attention, perception, cognition, and actions linked to them. It also comes with an expansion of personal resources resulting from this broadening spiral of positive emotions (Fredrickson 2001; 2005; Fredrickson and Joiner 2002). In other words, positive emotions expand awareness, which then leads to actions that increase personal resources that may be used to enhance one's life.

Increased resources strengthen positive emotions, which then stimulate further expansion of the upward spiral. Over time, this upward spiral leads to significant, positive changes in mental and physical health. Effective coping skills, which are also related to the positive cognition of optimism (Carver and Scheier 2005), are one important resource that may be acquired through this broadening and building process and that may be used to enhance health and well-being. For example, adaptive coping strategies, such as active engagement and problem solving, are associated with both optimism and coping successfully with breast cancer (Carver et al. 1993) and open-heart surgery over six months later (Scheier et al. 1989). Moreover, optimistic surgery patients who dwell less on negative emotions report greater quality of life after their surgery (Scheier et al. 1989).

This brief review has shown that optimistic beliefs about the future and positive emotions contribute independently and jointly to the experience of health and longevity, two outcomes that Daoists have sought for centuries. This research demonstrates the manner in which positive psychology may inform Daoist practice by identifying characteristics such as optimism and positive emotions that may provide a focus for Daoist practice and help Daoists to achieve their goal of increased longevity. Next, we discuss how Daoism-inspired health practices of meditation, taiji quan and qigong may influence cultivation of positive mental states and emotions and thus represent a second pathway for Daoism to enter the modern the world.

Health Practices

Many Daoism-inspired practices have been created over the centuries to enhance health, nourish life, and extend longevity. Examples include physical exercises, meditation, breathing, Traditional Chinese Medicine (TCM) and acupuncture, diet and herbs, among others (Kohn 2005; 2006; 2010). Often these practices are combined together as when meditation and breathing are integrated with physical movement in taiji quan and qigong. These practices provide a second pathway for Daoism to enter the modern world.

In the United States more than 20 million people report practicing meditation, over 3 million people report using acupuncture, and nearly 3 million people report practicing taiji quan or qigong (Barnes, Bloom, and Nahin 2008; Birdee et al. 2009). Despite growing popularity, several obstacles limit wider adoption of these Chinese health practices. Many are unaware of the history and cultural context of these practices and thus are unaware of their benefits. Moreover, those who begin to learn these practices may become discouraged by the length of time required to learn them and quit practicing before they experience their benefits.

Although many qigong sets are brief and may be learned in a short time, authentic styles of taiji quan may have more than one-hundred movements and take several years to learn and many more years of diligent practice to master thus discouraging their use. Scientific evidence for the effectiveness of practices such as meditation, taiji quan and qigong may accelerate their use. We briefly summarize research examining the effectiveness of meditation, taiji quan, and qigong and emphasize outcomes also investigated by positive psychologists in order to highlight possible points of convergence between the two disciplines.

Meditation, Taiji quan, and Qigong

These practices all integrate body and mind by cultivating different combinations of attention and mental focus, breathing and body movement. Created for different purposes and possessing some unique characteristics, they nevertheless share many similarities (Kohn 2005; 2006; 2008). Indeed some believe that they are merely variations on the same theme (Cohen 1999; Jahnke 2002). They each cultivate states of mental and physical relaxation and create attitudes, emotions, and physical changes related to health, well-being, and longevity; they are forms of "meditative movement" for research purposes (Larkey et al. 2009). Therapeutic models that capture the complexity of these practices are available to guide research designed to assess their clinical effectiveness (Wayne and Kaptchuk 2008a; 2008b).

Health practices that employ Eastern approaches to integration of body and mind are receiving increased attention by researchers. Santee (2007; 2008) has shown how Daoist ideas may be used in counseling and stress management practices. The August 2009 issue of *Annals of the New York Academy of Sciences* is dedicated to reports of scientific research studies that document how meditation and breathing combined with physical exercises such as yoga can enhance health and longevity (Bushell and Theise 2009). A column in each issue of the *Journal of Daoist Studies* summarizes results from published research studies that evaluate the clinical effectiveness of Daoism-inspired practices such as qigong, taiji quan, and meditation (e.g., Davis 2010).

Research has shown that meditation can enhance physical and mental health (Baer 2003). Meditation that focuses on loving kindness and compassion has been shown to increase the experience of positive emotions, which then leads to decreased depression and increased satisfaction with life (Frederickson, Cohn, Coffey, Pek, and Finkel 2008). Meditation may achieve these effects due to the neuroplasiticity of the brain's circuitry. In other words, changes in mental states can lead to relatively permanent changes in the brain and its functions (Davidson 2000). For example, pessimistic thoughts and emotions may change brain structure and function in areas such as the prefrontal cortex and amygdala (Davidson et al. 2002). Meditation training as brief as weekly sessions for eight weeks has been shown to reduce negative emotions, strengthen immunity to illness and change brain function (Davidson et al. 2003). Self-regulation of mental and emotional states and cultivation of positive emotions is the central mechanism for achieving these benefits and, through training, positive emotional states can be made automatic and enduring across time and situations (Tugade and Fredrickson 2007). This research may explain how Daoist practices achieve their effects. The relationship between thoughts, feelings and their accompanying physiology supports the ancient wisdom of focusing on both body and mind to cultivate health, well-being and longevity.

Research has documented the ability of Buddhist meditation practices to cultivate different levels of awareness and enduring expressions of positive emotion through self-regulation of thoughts and feelings (Brown 2009). Cognitive behavioral therapy, commonly used by psychologists to treat depression and other disorders and to enhance mental health, has benefited from inclusion of various forms of Buddhist meditation practice that employ such self-regulation practices (Baer 2003). Daoist meditation practices resemble Buddhist practices, but differences exist as well (Kohn 2008). Although not yet tested empirically, Daoist meditation practices should also enhance positive emotions because of their emphasis on cultivating self-awareness and self-regulation of the body and mind. More importantly, Daoist meditation practices and exercises such as taiji quan and qigong may provide additional benefits due to their emphasis on integrating the body and mind together to cultivate and balance the body's energy (*qi*), a focus that may boost and amplify the healing process according to the principles of Traditional Chinese Medicine (Liu and Chen 2010).

Reviews of hundreds of research studies examining the effects of meditation, qigong, and taiji quan have reported numerous health benefits. Positive outcomes include: indicators of physical health and longevity, such as improvement in balance and prevention of falls; enhancement of cardio respiratory function; enhanced immune response; reduction in bone loss; and improvement in mental health outcomes such as decreased anxiety and depression and enhanced positive mood and stress management (Chen 2007; Jahnke et al. 2010; Lee et al. 2007; Ng and Tsang 2009; Ospina et al. 2007). Taiji quan and qigong are effective for specific medical conditions. They include diabetes mellitus (Chen et al. 2009), hypertension (Lee et al. 2007) and self-efficacy concerning its control (Lee, Lim, and Lee 2004), tinnitus (Biesinger et al. 2010), arthritis (Uhlig et al. 2010), reduction in chronic musculoskeletal pain associated with arthritis (Hall et al. 2009), and fibromyalgia (Wang et al. 2010). These effects come through body movement, focus on breathing patterns, and cultivation of a clear, calm state of mind (Larkey et al. 2009), which when practiced together may reduce numerous symptoms of stress (Sandlund and Norlander 2000).

As a result of this accumulating scientific evidence, physicians and prestigious medical centers now recommend practices such as taiji quan (Mayo Clinic 2009). For many, qigong and taiji quan provide an introduction to Daoist ideas, such as effortless action (*wuwei*), virtuous action (*de*), naturalness and freedom from pretense (*ziran*), harmony and balance (yin and yang), softness (*song*), tranquility (*jing*), emptiness (*xu*), responsiveness (*ying*), self-cultivation (*xiuyang*), as well as selflessness (*wusi*). They involve cultivation and use of energy in all of its forms (essence, *qi,* spirit), and enlightened mind (*ming*), as well as specific approaches to meditation such as sitting in oblivion (*zuowang*) and mind fasting (*xinzhai*). Through practices such as taiji quan and qigong, the body becomes the means for cultivating and controlling the mind and enhancing health, well-being, and longevity, and as a result serves as the gateway to enter the study and practice of Daoism. Unfortunately, the explicit connection between these Daoist ideas and practices such as taiji quan and qigong is often unknown to those who practice them. Wider adoption of these practices will enhance health, well-being and longevity, but this will not increase awareness of Daoism unless their connection to Daoism is also made clear.

Conclusion

Daoist texts such as the *Daode jing*, Daoist-inspired health practices such as taiji quan, qigong, and TCM, and various forms of meditation have become popular in the West. Scientific studies provide evidence for the ability of these practices to enhance mental and physical health, well-being and longevity. Research documenting effectiveness of Daoist practices in psychology, especially in the area of positive psychology, can contribute to further adoption of Daoism in the West. Daoism-informed practices such as meditation, taiji quan and qigong may influence mental and physical health directly through changes in physiology as well as indirectly by changing thoughts and feelings that influence these outcomes.

Use of scientific research to evaluate the effectiveness of Daoist practices does not diminish the importance of Daoist religious practices and rituals that have no focus on healing body or mind. We do not mean to imply that all Daoist knowledge should be evaluated scientifically. Nor do we mean to suggest that Daoist knowledge that does not lend itself to scientific study is less valuable. Instead, we encourage exploration of the common ground between Daoism and science, particularly psychology. Efforts to find common ground between science and Buddhism by the Mind and Life Institute under guidance of H.H. the Dalai Lama (www.mindandlife.org/) illustrate the potential success of this approach. Research in neuroscience documents the manner in which change in thoughts and feelings may alter brain structures and enhance health in a manner consistent with Buddhist beliefs and practices (Begley 2007). Research should examine the impact of Daoist beliefs and practices on physical and mental health, well-being and longevity. This evidence would speed the adoption of Daoism and enrich the science and practice of psychology.

Future research should examine the ability of Daoism-inspired practices such as meditation, taiji quan, qigong, and TCM to enhance positive thoughts and emotions and the impact of such change on health, well-being and longevity. The relationship between Daoist ethics and leadership and their ability to create positive work organizations that foster human potential provides another area ripe for future research (Davis and Kohn 2009). These efforts point to the way in which Daoist practices can be studied scientifically without conflict or contradiction with religious practice. With wider dissemination, Daoist knowledge and practice can help to heal self and society in the modern world as it once did in ancient China.

Bibliography

American Psychological Association. 2009. *Psychology Matters: Psychological Applications in Daily Life*. Retrieved from http://psychologymatters. apa. org/

Baer, R. A. 2003. Mindfulness training as a clinical intervention: A conceptual and empirical review. *Clinical Psychology: Science and Practice* 10:125-143.

Barnes, P. M., B. Bloom, and R. L. Nahin 2008. *Complementary and alternative medicine use among adults and children: United States 2007*. Atlanta: National Center for Health Statistics, Centers for Disease Control and Prevention.

Begley, S., ed. 2007. *Train your mind, change your brain*. New York: Ballantine.

Biesinger, E., Kipman, U., Schätz, S., and Langguth, B. 2009. Qigong for treatment of tinnitus: A prospective randomized controlled study. *Journal of Psychosomatic Research* 69:299-304.

Birdee, G. S., P. . M. Wayne, R. B. Davis, R. S. Phillips, and G. Y. Yeh. 2009. T'ai chi and qigong for health: Patterns of use in the United States. *The Journal of Alternative and Complementary Medicine* 15:969-73.

Bouchard, T. J. Jr. 2004. Genetic influence on human psychological traits. *Psychological Science* 13:148-151.

Brown, D. 2009. Mastery of the mind East and West: Excellence in being and doing and everyday happiness. *Annals of the New York Academy of Sciences* 117. 2:231-251.

Bushell, W. C., and N. D. Theise. 2009. Toward a unified field of study: Longevity, regeneration, and protection of health through meditation and related practices. *Annals of the New York Academy of Sciences* 117. 2:5-19.

Carver, C. S., and Scheier, M. F. 2005. Optimism. In C. R. Snyder & S. J. Lopez Eds., *Handbook of positive psychology*, 231-243. New York: Oxford University Press.

_____, Pozo, C., Harris, S. D., Noriega, V., Scheier, M. E., Robinson, D. S., Ketcham, A. S., Moffat, F. L., and Clark, K. C. 1993. How coping mediates the effect of optimism on distress: A study of women with early stage breast cancer. *Journal of Personality and Social Psychology* 65:375-390.

Chen, K. 2007. Qigong therapy for stress management. In P. M. Lehrer, R. L. Woolfolk, and W. E. Sime, eds., *Principles and practice of stress management*, 428-448. New York: Guilford Press.

Clarke, J. J. 2000. *The Tao of the West: Western transformations of Taoist thought*. London: Routledge.

Cohen, K. S. 1999. *The way of* qigong: *The art and science of Chinese energy healing*. New York,: Ballantine/Random House.

Curbow, B., Somerfield, M. R., Baker, F., Wingard, J. R., and Legro, M. W. 1993. Personal changes, dispositional optimism, and psychological adjustment to bone marrow transplantation. *Journal of Behavioral Medicine* 16:423-443.

Danner, D. D., Snowden, D. A., and Friesen, W. F. 2001. Positive emotions early in life and longevity: Findings from the nun study. *Journal of Personality and Social Psychology* 80:804-813.

Davidson, R. J. 2000. Affective style, psychophysiology, and resilience: Brain mechanisms and plasticity. *American Psychologist*, 55:1196-1214.

_____, Kabat-Zinn, J., Schumacher, J., Rosenkrantz, M., Muller, D., Santorelli, S. F., Urganowski, F., Harrington, A., Bonus, K., and Sheridan, J. F. 2003. Alterations in brain and immune function produced by mindfulness meditation. *Psychosomatic Medicine* 65:564-570.

_____, Lewis, D. A., Alloy, L. B., Amaral, D. G., Bush, G., Cohen, J. D., Drevets, W. C., Farah, M. J., Kagan, J., McClelland, J. L., Nolen-Hoeksema, S., and Peterson, B. S. 2002. Neural and behavioral substrates of mood and mood regulation. *Biological Psychiatry*, 52:478-502.

Davis, D. D. 2010. Science on qi. *Journal of Daoist Studies*, 3:231-235.

_____, and Kohn, L. 2009. *Daoism, virtues and flourishing in organizations.* Paper presented at the Fifth International Conference on Daoist Studies, Wudangshan, China.

Diener, E., Lucas, R. E., & Oishi, S. 2005. Subjective well-being: The science of happiness and life satisfaction. In C. R. Snyder & S. J. Lopez Eds., *Handbook of positive psychology,* pp. 63-73. New York: Oxford University Press.

Emmons, R. A., and Paloutzian, R. F. 2003. The psychology of religion. *Annual Review of Psychology 54*:377-402

Fitzgerald, T. E., Tennen, H., Affleck, G., and Pransky, G. S. 1993. Optimism, perceived control over stress, and coping. *European Journal of Psychology* 7:267-281.

Fredrickson, B. L. 2001. The role of positive emotions in positive psychology: The broaden-and-build theory of positive emotions. *American Psychologist* 56:218-226.

_____2005. Positive emotions. In C. R. Snyder and S. J. Lopez Eds., *Handbook of positive psychology*, 120-134. New York: Oxford University Press.

_____, Cohn, M. A., Coffey, K. A., Pek, J., and Finkel, S. M. 2008. Open hearts build lives: Positive emotions, induced through loving-kindness meditation, build consequential personal resources. *Journal of Personality and Social Psychology* 95:1045-1062.

_____, Joiner, T. 2002. Positive emotions trigger upward spirals toward emotional well-being. *Psychological Science* 13:172-175.

Futterman, A. D., Kemeny, M. E., Shapiro, D., and Fahey, J. L. 1994. Immunological and physiological changes associated with induced positive and negative mood. *Psychosomatic Medicine* 56:499-511.

Gil, K. M., Carson, J. W., Porter, L. S., Scipio, C, Bediako, S. M., and Orringer, E. 2004. Daily mood and stress predict pain, health care use, and work activity in African American adults with sickle-cell disease. *Health Psychology* 23:267-274.

Gillham, J. E., Reivich, K. J., Jaycox, L. H., and Seligman, M. E. P. 1995. Prevention of depressive symptoms in schoolchildren: Two-year follow-up. *Psychological Science* 6:343-351.

Graham, C., Eggers, A. and Sukhtankar, S. 2004. Does happiness pay? An exploration based on panel data from Russia. *Journal of Economic Behavior and Organization* 55:319-342.

Hall, A., Maher, C., Latimer, J., and Ferreira, M. 2010. The effectiveness of tai chi for chronic musculoskeletal pain conditions: A systematic review and meta-analysis. *Arthritis & Rheumatism* 61:717-724.

Helson, R. and Klohnen, E. C. 1998. Affective coloring of personality from young adulthood to midlife. *Personality and Social Psychology Bulletin* 24:241-252.

Jahnke, R. 2002. *The healing promise of qi: Creating extraordinary wellness through* qigong *and* taiji quan. New York: McGraw-Hill.

_____, Larkey, L., Rogers, C., Etnier, J, and Lin, F. 2010. A comprehensive review of health benefits of qigong and tai chi. *Health Promotion* 24.6:e1-e25.

Kiecolt-Glaser, J. K., McGuire, L., Robles, T. F., and Glaser, R. Psychoneuroimmunology: Psychological influences on immune function and health. *Journal of Consulting and Clinical Psychology* 70:537-547.

Kohn, L. 2001. *Daoism and Chinese culture.* Cambridge, MA: Three Pines Press.

_____. 2005. *Health and long life the Chinese way.* Cambridge, MA: Three Pines Press.

_____, Ed. . 2006. *Daoist body cultivation.* Magdalena, NM: Three Pines Press.

_____. 2008. *Meditation works in the Hindu, Buddhist and Daoist traditions.* Magdalena, NM: Three Pines Press.

_____. 2010. *Daoist dietetics: Food for immortality.* Dunedin, FL: Three Pines Pres.

Komjathy, L. 2008. Mapping the Daoist body: Part one: The *Neijing Tu* in history. *Journal of Daoist Studies* 1:67-92.

_____. 2009. Mapping the Daoist body: Part two: The text of the *Neijing Tu. Journal of Daoist Studies* 2:64-108.

LaFargue, M., and Pas, J. 1998. On translating the Tao-te-ching. In L. Kohn and M. LaFargue Eds., *Lao-tzu and the Tao-te-ching*, 277-301. Albany: State University of New York Press.

Larkey, L., Jahnke, R., Etnier, J., & Gonzalez, J. 2009. Meditative movement as a category of exercise: Implications for research. *Journal of Physical Activity and Health* 6:230-238.

Lee, M. S., Lim, H. J., and Lee, M. S. 2004. Impact of qigong exercise on self-efficacy and other cognitive variables in patients with essential hypertension. *Journal of Alternative and Complementary Medicine* 10:675-680.

_____, Pittler, M. H., Guo, R., and Ernst, E. 2007. Qigong for hypertension: A systematic review of randomized clinical trials. *Journal of Hypertension* 25:1525-1532.

Levy, B. R., Slade, M. D., Kunkel, S. R., and Kasl, S. V. 2002. Longevity increased by positive self-perceptions of aging. *Journal of Personality and Social Psychology* 83:261-270.

Little, S. Ed. . 2000. *Taoism and the arts of China.* Chicago: Art Institute of Chicago.

Liu, T., and Chen, K. Eds. 2010. *Chinese medical* qigong. London: Singing Dragon.

Long, B. C. 1993. Coping strategies of male managers: A prospective analysis of predictors of psychosomatic symptoms and job satisfaction. *Journal of Vocational Behavior* 42:184-199.

Lyubormirsky, S., King, L., and Diener, E. 2005. The benefits of frequent positive affect: Does happiness lead to success? *Psychological Bulletin* 131:803-855.

Mayo Clinic. 2009, October. *Yoga and taiji quan. Supplement to Mayo Clinic Health Letter.* Rochester, MN: Mayo Foundation for Medical Education and Research.

Ng, B. H. P., and Tsang, H. W. H. 2009. Psychophysiological outcomes of health qigong for chronic conditions: A systematic review. *Psychophysiology* 46:257-269.

Ospina, M. B., Bond, T. K., Karkhaneh, M., Tjosvold, L., Vandermeer, B., Liang, Y., Bialy, L., Hooton, N., Buscemi, N., Dryden, D. M., and Klassen, T. P. 2007. *Meditation practices for health: State of the research. Evidence report/Technology assessment No. 155.* Prepared by the University of Alberta Evidence-based Practice Center under Contract No. 290-02-0023. AHRQ Publication No. 07-E101. Rockville, MD: Agency for Healthcare Research and Quality.

Ostir, G. V., Markides, K. S., Peek, M. K., and Goodwin, J. S. 2001. The association between emotional well-being and the incidence of stroke in older adults. *Psychosomatic Medicine* 63:210-215.

Peterson, C. 2006. *A primer in positive psychology.* New York: Oxford University Press.

_____, Seligman, M. E. P., and Vaillant, G. E. 1988. Pessimistic explanatory style is a risk factor for physical illness: A thirty-five year longitudinal study. *Journal of Personality and Social Psychology* 55:23-27.

_____, and Steen, T. A. 2005. Optimistic explanatory style. In C. R. Snyder and S. J. Lopez Eds., *Handbook of positive psychology*, 244-256. New York: Oxford University Press.

Plomin, R., Scheier, M. F., Bergeman, C. S., Pedersen, N. L., Nesselroade, J. R., and McClearn, G. E. 1992. Optimism, pessimism and mental health: A twin/adoption analysis. *Personality and Individual Differences* 13:921-930

Sandlund, E. S., and Norlander, T. 2000. The effects of tai chi chuan relaxation and exercise on stress responses and well-being: An overview of research. *International Journal of Stress Management* 7:139-149.

Santee, R. 2007. *An integrative approach to counseling: Bridging Chinese thought, evolutionary theory and stress management.* Thousand Oaks, Calif. : Sage Publications.

_____. 2008. Stress management and the *Zhuangzi*. *Journal of Daoist Studies* 1:93-123.

Scheier, M. F., Mathews, K. A., Owens, J. F., Magovern, G. J., Lefebvre, R. C., Abbott, R., and Carver, C. S. 1989. Dispositional optimism and recovery from coronary artery by-pass surgery: The beneficial effects on physical and psychological well-being. *Journal of Personality and Social Psychology* 57:1024-1040.

Schipper, K. 1993. *The Taoist body* Translated by K. C. Duval. Berkeley: University of California Press.

Schulman, P., Keith, D., and Seligman, M. E. P. 1993. Is optimism heritable? A study of twins. *Behaviour Research and Therapy* 31:569-574.

Seligman, M. E. P., and Csikszentmihalyi, M. 2000. Positive psychology: An introduction. *American Psychologist* 55:5-14.

_____, Castellon, C., Cacciola, J., Schulman, P., Luborsky, L., Ollove, M., and Downing, R. 1988. Explanatory style change during cognitive therapy for unipolar depression. *Journal of Abnormal Psychology* 97:13-18.

Shepperd, J. A., Maroto, J. J., and Pbert, L. A. 1996. Dispositional optimism as a predictor of health changes among cardiac patients. *Journal of Research in Personality* 30:517-534.

Snyder, C. R., and Lopez, S. J. 2007. *Positive psychology: The scientific and practical explorations of human strengths.* Thousand Oaks, Calif. : Sage Publications.

_____, Lopez, S. J., and Pedrotti, J. T. 2011. *Positive psychology: The scientific and practical explorations of human strengths.* Los Angeles: Sage.

Tugade, M. M., and Fredrickson, B. L. 2007. Regulation of positive emotions: Emotion regulation strategies that promote resilience. *Journal of Happiness Studies* 8:311-333.

_____, Fredrickson, B. L., and Barrett, L. F. 2004. Psychological resilience and positive emotional granularity: Examining the benefits of positive emotions on coping and health. *Journal of Personality* 72:1161- 1190.

Uhlig, T., Fongen, C., Steen, E., Christie, A., and Ødegård, S. 2010. Exploring tai chi in rheumatoid arthritis: A quantitative and qualitative study. *BMC Musculoskeletal Disorders* 11:43-49.

Wallace, B. A., and Shapiro, S. L. 2006. Mental balance and well-being: Building bridges between Buddhism and Western psychology. *American Psychologist* 61:690-701.

Walsh, R., and Shapiro, S. L. 2006. The meeting of meditative disciplines and Western psychology: A mutually enriching dialogue. *American Psychologist* 61:227-239.

Wang, C., Schmid, C. H., Rones, R., Kalish, R., Yinh, J., Goldenberg, D. L., Lee, Y., and McAlindon, T. 2010. A randomized trial of tai chi for fibromyalgia. *New England Journal of Medicine* 363:743-754.

Watson, D. 2005. Positive affectivity: The disposition to experience pleasurable emotional states. In C. R. Snyder and S. J. Lopez Eds., *Handbook of positive psychology*, 106-119. New York: Oxford University Press.

Wayne, P. M., and Kaptchuk, T. J. 2008a. Challenges inherent to tai chi research: Part I— T'ai chi as a complex multicomponent intervention. *Journal of Alternative and Complementary Medicine* 14:95-102.

_____. 2008b. Challenges inherent to t'ai chi research: Part II—Defining intervention and optimal study design. *Journal of Alternative and Complementary Medicine* 14:191-197.

Wolsko, P. M., Eisenberg, D. M., Davis, R. B., and Phillips, R. S. 2004. Use of mind-body therapies: Results of a national survey. *Journal of General Internal Medicine* 19:43-50.

Practical Experience with Deathbringers

J. MICHAEL WOOD

One prominent aspect of Daoist psychology is found in the so-called Three Deathbringers, also known as the Three Worms, demonic parasites that strive to make us sick and shorten our lives. From practical and clinical experience, I have observed certain actions in dealing with these demon archetypes as they manifest themselves in patients with various symptoms. Based on this, I propose a theory as to their formation and dissolution, as well as a methodology leading to the ultimate resolution of this particularly destructive energy form.

I began my journey as an energetic healer with a lifelong interest in holistic healing modalities. I came from a family of chiropractors, and from early on heard many exciting stories of healing success. However, after a thwarted attempt to go to Chiropractic College and a four-year stint in the military, I joined my father in the financial planning industry for a 43-year career. During this career, I had the opportunity to school myself in several healing modalities including reflexology and neurovascular holding point techniques. I found that I could affect healthy outcomes with those who would stand still long enough for me to work on them. Over time, I developed confidence in these skills, and as it turned out they allowed me to avoid a potentially life-threatening condition.

Like many in the healing arts, I am a "wounded healer", who having proved to myself that there is more than just the scientific, western approach, determined to see if I could make a positive difference in the lives of others. My crisis came in August 1999, when I woke up to near blindness. I began to use reflexology points for the eyes, then applied neurovascular holding points and managed to clear most of the blindness with the exception of an area in my left peripheral vision. It remained annoying, but I took no further action until two days later. My best friend is an MD, and on telling her about what I was experiencing, she immediately sent me to the hospital for tests. They discovered that I had had a stroke, which showed two infarctions in the right occipital lobe apparently touching the right optical nerve, which controls left peripheral vision. The blind spot was slightly larger than the span of my hand at arms length.

Six weeks later, I had a second major event, followed by another hospital stay with all the tests amounting to over $25,000, none of which could determine why I was having the strokes. This was followed during the next six months with twelve transient ischemic attacks (TIA, i.e., baby strokes). During these attacks I would immediately use reflex points and neurovascular points, which stopped the ongoing attack within seconds. Concerned that I might have another attack in my sleep and not have the good outcome I was experiencing, I asked the neurologist why I was able to stop the attacks, but could not prevent them from happening in the first place. The answer for someone who was now in fear of his life was frightening: "Sometimes these things happen, and we just don't know why." This put me on a path of understanding the cause of my health issue instead of just working with the symptoms.

My journey to save my life began with gaining an understanding of the autonomic nervous system (ANS), and its two sensory antennae, the sympathetic (SNS) and parasympathetic nervous systems (PSNS): the fight/flight and rest/digest/heal controllers of the ANS. I determined very quickly that my life and lifestyle had been in a constant state of stress, and quite simply, the body broke down. This knowledge was the key to understanding what was going on physiologically as well as energetically and psychologically.

I began to apply the tools of calming breath and mind. In March of 2000, The TIA's and strokes stopped. I discovered that I had been the author of my near demise, but I could also be the author of a remarkable recovery. The blind spot still remained until I had the good fortune to meet and ask for the help of Master Chunyi Lin at the National Qigong Association (NQA) annual meeting in Portland, Oregon in August 2000, just about a year after the initial stroke. He was kind enough to do a treatment on me, and on opening my eyes, the blind spot had reduced by about 70 percent—verified by my neuro-ophthalmologist—in mere minutes.

At that moment I knew that my life path was to change. I wanted to pursue a course of study in qigong. To learn more about the workings of breath and the body's mechanism of holding the memory of emotions, I entered the professional program at the Hendricks Institute 2001, concurrently taking Master Lin's two courses on qigong. I practiced on anyone who would hold still – again to good effect.

In 2003, I took the Master's course through the International Institute of Medical Qigong with Jerry Alan Johnson, graduating in October. In 2004, I again took his oncology course taught in Houston. In the following year, I had the great good fortune to meet and begin training with Master Robert Peng, a Shaolin-trained healer, who taught me the "Open the Door, Remove the Thief" (SKT) technique to dissipate energetic charges around emotional issues. It involves measuring the intensity of an issue on a scale from 1 to 10, tapping on key energy points, and actively releasing negative patterns. I incorporated it with my training in mechanical and somatic breath work and medical qigong to develop an effective clinical protocol that I have successfully used clinically over 2,900 times since then.

Also in 2005, I traveled to the Celestial Masters temple on Mt. Longhu and discovered more depth and understanding of the proper use of energy in my daily practice as well as in the clinic. In 2007, I traveled to China once more, to train with Master Duan Shileong, who at the time was 100 years old—a great example of the longevity available through proper and disciplined practice of qigong.

I have encountered many adventures and experiences on this journey. I served as chair of the board of the National Qigong Association; I have taught seminars on breath work and SKT; I have directed a post-graduate course in medical qigong at Logan College of Chiropractic. In addition, I have come to attend academic meetings and presented a paper and workshop at the 6th International Conference on Daoism. All the while I have maintained a private clinical practice, and teaching courses to certify as Medical Qigong Practitioner (200 hours) and Therapist (300 hours) to over a hundred students, following the curriculum of the International Institute of Medical Qigong.

The Traditional System

The traditional Daoist understanding of the mind is based on the mainstream system of classical Chinese medicine, which works with the five phases, also commonly called "elements." Each phase (wood, fire, earth, metal, and water) is associated with a specific inner organ, notably a yin or storing organ (liver, heart, spleen, lungs, and kidneys). These organs in turn—at the core of a complex correspondence system that also includes body tissues, fluids, senses, flavors, and many more (see Porkert 1974; Kaptchuk 2000; Kohn 2005)—house five prenatal spirits (*shen*), the psychological dimension of the person.

These spirits consist of spirit proper or primordial spirit (*yuanshen*), a group of three spirit souls (*hun*), seven material souls (*po*), plus the two directional factors intention (*yi*) and will (*zhi*). They are installed as part of the energetic matrix of each yin organ during gestation. Once the child has taken its first breath, it begins to experience life through the five senses and perceptions. This life experience is the function of the will, known as postnatal *shen* or acquired spirit.

Primordial spirit resides in the heart. The individual essence that connects the person to Dao, it is the highest and noblest part of human nature. Spirit is the intangible power of Dao, which comes to inhabit the body as pure form, a body that is free from personal preferences and identities and essentially just a microcosmic replica of the greater universe. The body is thus, as the medieval

Daoist *Xisheng jing* (Scripture of Western Ascension, DZ 726) points out, the "habitation of the spirit," "the carriage of the spirit, the habitation of the spirit, the host of the spirit" (Kohn 2007, 145).

The Tang thinker Li Rong adds: "Spirit functions in giving life to embodied beings. Without this, there would be no life. . . . It is only upon borrowing spirit that embodied beings can come to life. Spirit uses them as a habitation in order to attain completion. Without the joining of the spirit and embodied beings, there would be no life or completion" (Kohn 2010, 101). "Spirit," the Tang work *Tianyinzi* (Book of the Master of Heavenly Seclusion; DZ 1026) says, is "that which "arrives without moving and is swift without hurrying, what transforms along with yin and yang and is as old as Heaven and Earth" (sect. 8). The *Neiguan jing* (Scripture of Inner Observation; DZ 641) provides more details:

> Spirit is neither black nor white, neither red nor yellow, neither big nor small, neither short nor long, neither crooked nor straight, neither soft nor hard, neither thick nor thin, neither round nor square. It goes on changing and transforming without measure, merges with yin and yang, greatly encompasses Heaven and Earth, subtly enters the tiniest blade of grass. Controlled it is straightforward, let loose it goes mad. Clarity and purity make it live, turbidity and defilements cause it to perish. Fully bright, it radiates to the eight ends of the universe. Darkened, it confuses even a single direction. Keep it empty and serene, and life and Dao will spontaneously be present. (2b)

The two kinds of "souls," next, are connected to the liver and the lungs. The liver holds the aspect of spirit commonly manifested in three aspects called spirit or cloud souls. Best described in modern terms as representatives of the parasympathetic nervous system (PNS) that support rest, digestion, and healing, they are yang in nature, link people with heaven, and support intellectual, artistic, and spiritual endeavors. [1] At death, they return to heaven, transforming into the ancestral spirit that is worshiped on the family altar. The Tang scripture *Baosheng jing* (Scripture of Preserving Life, DZ 871) describes them as "located beneath the liver; they look like human beings and all wear green robes with yellow inner garments"(1b). Although rooted in the liver, they are particularly connected to the three elixir fields (*dantian*), energy centers in the person's head, chest, and abdomen, residing on the left side of the central pillar of the body.

The names of these three wonderful aspects of human existence, who will take their leave and thus allow the body to be vacant for a period on a regular basis, are "Spiritual Guidance," "Inner Radiance," and "Dark Essence" (1a). As

---

[1] The *hun* is also the agent called back in the ritual known as "Summoning the Soul" (*chaohun* 招魂). A shaman or priest climbs to the roof of the house and calls out in all directions to the departed soul to return, depicting each region as dreary and dangerous. The rite, as much as the three-day delay of the burial, makes sure that the soul is not just on temporary leave or the person in a state of suspended animation. For original chants, see Hawkes 1959. For Han beliefs, see Yü 1987. For modern Hong Kong, see Chan and Chow 2006.

shown in an illustration in the text, they look noble and appear human in shape, are dressed in courtly garb, and should be supported in their beneficent activities. Certain physical exercises are helpful as are meditations and special incantations. When the three spirit souls are treated in this manner to bring out the best in them, they will in their turn take care that, as the *Baosheng jing* says, "there will be no disaster or affliction [to the person], and all evil demons will be subdued. The body at peace, you will attain the Dao. Then there is no more suffering or pain" (2a; Kohn 1995).

The material souls reside in the lungs. Not unlike what modern medical books call the sympathetic nervous system (SNS), which governs fight, flight, and freeze, they are yin in quality, connect the person to earth, and control basic survival instincts, such as the need for food, sleep, and sex, and in general manage the physical aspects of the individual (Jarrett 2006, 30). At death they return to earth by staying with the corpse; they are nurtured in proper burial sites and procedures as well as through sacrifices at the tomb. Also linked with the three elixir fields, they reside to the right of the central axis. One stays at the top of the head, at the point acupuncturists call Hundred Meeting (*Baihui*; GV20) and Daoists know as the Heavenly Pass. A cluster of five reside close to the diaphragm, while the last one is at the center of the feet at the first point of the kidney meridian, a major energetic gate of the body known as Bubbling Well (*Yongquan*; K1).

Unlike the noble yang spirits of the spirit souls, they are nasty and fundamentally evil creatures, beastly in shape and quite disastrous in their activities. The *Baosheng jing* describes them:

> The seven material souls consist of the energy of yin and of evil. They are basically demons. They can make a person commit deadly evils, be stingy and greedy, jealous and full of envy. They give people bad dreams and make them clench their teeth, incite them to say "right" when they think "wrong."
>
> In addition, they cause people to lose their vital essence in sexual passion and get dissipated by hankering after luxury and ease. Through them, people will completely lose all original purity and simplicity. (2a)

These souls, far from looking like human beings, are strangely formed devils, having birds' heads, only one leg, tails, abominable outgrowth, and the like. Their names are accordingly Corpse Dog, Arrow in Ambush, Bird Darkness, Devouring Robber, Flying Poison, Massive Pollution, and Stinky Lungs (3ab).

How the two kinds of souls function, moreover, is defined by essential inherent nature and original destiny, the inborn/genetic and outer/social conditions of life, two agents that represent an individuated connection to Dao. They shape the concrete fulfillment the souls will strive for—be it artistic, musical, intellectual or spiritual for the spirit souls, finding most satisfaction in food, sex, wealth, status, or comfort for the material souls. They also determine the direction the next two psychological forces take: the will (yin) and intention (yang), which function in close relation to the kidneys and spleen. They represent the general power of thinking and planning in the intention and the more focused determination directed toward a specific objective in the will.

The will in particular often takes over the central function of the primordial spirit, growing in proportion as energetic armoring for the ego. It is the psychological function that allows people to form appropriate emotional boundaries—assuming the individual has completed proper resolution of the emotional stimuli. Lack of proper resolution of these stimuli will result in seven excessive emotions, also fundamentally associated with the five inner organs: anger, euphoria, worry, grief, and fear, as well as depression or despair and the coping mechanism of disassociation. These in turn lead to a host of emotional and physical symptoms.

The will thus includes both good experiences that enhance the primordial spirit and toxic experiences that elicit the seven toxic emotions held in the five storing organs. The system can be outlined as follows:

organ	spirit	good experiences	toxic emotions
liver	spirit soul	goodwill, compassion	anger
heart	spirit	peace, order	manic joy
spleen	intention	trust, openness	worry
lungs	material soul	integrity, courage	grief, sorrow
kidneys	will	wisdom, understanding	fear, shock

If toxic emotions accumulate and are not discharged with intentional techniques taught in Daoist and qigong practice, such as the Shaolin technique called "Open the Door, Remove the Thief," the creative, subconscious mind continues to give energy and activity to them around a toxic emotional event. Each mental replay of the triggering event will strengthen and more deeply imbed the toxic emotions.

The Deathbringers

Daoist psychology is made more complex by the appearance of three semi-supernatural agents, called the three worms (sanchong) or the three corpses (sanshi)—the latter expression using the causative form of the word and thus best rendered as "three deathbringers" (Kohn 1995). They are first mentioned in Wang Chong's Lunheng (Balanced Discussions) of the second century C.E. He has: "In the human body there are three worms. They correspond to creatures that live in the marshes beneath the soil. Those we call leeches. The leeches gnaw their way through the feet of people, just as the three worms gnaw through their intestines" (16.3; see Forke 1972, 2:363).

The three worms here are real worms, placed solidly in the natural world; they are leeches, not demons. The same idea is found in the biography of the physician Hua Tuo in the *Sanguo zhi* (Record of the Three Kingdoms) of the third century: "To expel the three worms, use a green pasty powder made from the leaves of the lacquer tree. Take it for a long time, and the three worms will be expelled, the five inner organs will be greatly strengthened. The body as a whole will feel light, and there will be no white hair (*Weizhi* 29; DeWoskin 1983). Again, the three inner parasites are plainly physical beings that cause harm to the person, who can be cured by medicines.

This early medical view first developed into a more religious vision in the *Baopuzi* (The Book of the Master Who Embraces Simplicity) by Ge Hong, compiled about 320 C.E. (see Ware 1966). The three worms change and take on a supernatural character: no more mere "leeches" gnawing on human intestines, they are now officials of the celestial hierarchy, placed in the body to monitor human behavior and punish sins and transgressions. The *Baopuzi* has:

> There are three deathbringers in our bodies. Although not corporeal, they are like our inner energies, like numinous powers, ghosts and spirits. They want us to die early. After our death, they become our ghosts and move about at will to where sacrifices and offerings are laid out.
>
> On every *gengshen* day [57th day of the 60-day cycle], they ascend to heaven and file a report on our misdeeds with the Department of Destiny. Similarly during the last night of the month, the Stove God makes a journey to heaven and reports on our behavior. For the more important misdeeds, three hundred days are deducted from our lives. For lesser sins, they take off three days. (6.4b; see Ware 1966, 115-16)

While the three worms have thus graduated from a mere physical if dangerous nuisance to demonic deathbringers, their wormy nature is retained in a separate group of parasites, known as the nine worms (*jiuchong*). More organic and less demonic creatures, they are like the germs and bacteria we guard against even today yet they also work actively together with the deathbringers, who summon them to cause sickness and disease. As the *Baopuzi* says:

> If you only have a faithful heart and do nothing for your spiritual wellbeing, your pre-destined lifespan will be defective and you will come to harm. The three deathbringers will take advantage of your weak months and perilous days, of all those hours when your longevity could easily be interrupted or sickness incurred, to summon vicious energies and bring in any parasites they can find. The danger is great for anyone. . . . When the situation intensifies, illnesses are produced. (15.7a; Ware 1966, 252-53)

The three worms as deathbringers, therefore, have advanced to managerial positions. They no longer cause the harm themselves but order other noxious creatures to do so. Illnesses are still caused by physical parasites that enter the body in a moment of weakness; however, the agency that instigates this invasion is now separate and has a religious character. While the religious tradition thus supersedes the medical, it never ignores or abolishes it altogether.

The most detailed description of the three deathbringers is found in the *Baosheng jing* of the ninth century. It provides them with names, special portfolios, and specific lists of ailments. In addition, the text provides an illustration. It says:

> The upper deathbringer is called Peng Ju, also known as Ake (Shouter). He sits in the head and attacks the cinnabar field in the Niwan Palace [center of the head]. He causes people's heads to be heavy, their eyesight blurred, their tears cold. He makes mucus assemble in their noses and their ears go deaf. Because of him, people's teeth fall out, their mouths rot, and their faces shrink in wrinkles. He further deludes people so they desire carriages and horses, crave for fancy sounds and sights, and gloat over evil and filth. . . .
>
> The middle deathbringer is called Peng Zhi, also known as Zuozi (Maker). He enjoys deluding people with the five tastes and makes them greedy for the five colors. He lives in the human heart and stomach and attacks the Scarlet Palace [in the heart, the middle cinnabar field] together with its central heater. He causes people's minds to be confused and forgetful, so that they are full of troubles, dry in saliva and low in energy. Dissipated and melancholy, they follow the false and see things in wrong perspective. . . .
>
> The lower deathbringer is called Peng Qiao, also known as Jixi (Junior). He lives in people's stomachs and legs and attacks the lower parts of the body. He makes energy leak [through the genitals] from the Ocean of *Qi* [the lower cinnabar field] and thereby invites a multiplicity of ills. Attracting the robbers of human intention, he makes people hanker after women and sex. Courageous and zealous only in the pursuit of passion, people suffering from him are blindly attached to things and waste away. They have no way to control themselves and hold on to life. (7a-8b; Kohn 1995)

In modern parlance, Jerry Alan Johnson calls them Bloody Corpse Demon, White Maiden Demon, and Old Blue Demon. He sees them as three internal corpse demons, "representing the deviant manifestations of a specialized energetic development of the *po's* destructive inclinations" (2002, Vol. 2, Pg. 424). Nevertheless, he does not show the mechanics of the manifestations—unlike what I have come to encounter in my clinical practice.

Clinical Observations

Over the past two years in my clinical practice, I have come to observe an energy form that looked like it had octopus tentacles attached to various places on the body. Trying to deal with it in several patients, I noticed that using sword fingers, Five Finger Thunder Palm, and the usual toxic *qi* removal techniques of medical qigong—as taught in the International Institute of Medical Qigong—had only marginal success. On subsequent clinic visits, the energy manifestation was as apparent in the patient as during the previous visit. In discussion with Livia Kohn in August of 2009, she pointed me to her book *Health and Long Life* (2005) that included pictures of the three energetic archetypes of the deathbringers.

In the following week, I once more saw the "tentacle" in a patient I will call M. K. This time, I followed it to its source in the spiritual field of the protective energetic shield of the body, classically and hereafter called the *weiqi* field, which led me to a vision of the Old Blue Demon. It looked like "a monkey gargoyle." I was startled at first, then calmed myself and began the usual attempts to remove it as I would an energetic cluster. As in previous cases, I cleared all I could notice, but had a nagging doubt that it was totally gone. The figure materialized as M. K. described what she thought was the root of her toxic emotions and seemed linked to the issue to which it was attached. At this point, I realized that I needed a different strategy. Interestingly, the creature never paid any attention to me or my efforts: its intentions were solely focused on its connection to the patient. This has consistently been the case, both in this situation as well as in nineteen other encounters I have had with the deathbringers so far.

My experience has shown that a deathbringer forms when the patient has had deep and long bouts with the seven toxic emotions, leading to a state where they have become obsessive in nature. It seems that the patient's self-worth is attacked to point that despair is bound with hopelessness, and life loses its value. However, instead of an outward expression of suicide, the patient uses a more passive-aggressive approach that internalizes a "death wish." In conversations with such patients, it becomes apparent that they all carry a great deal of despair. Only a few express suicidal ideation verbally. They are, it seems, possessed by a "quiet killer" that slowly and thoroughly drains their life force.

From working with various patients, I have come to believe that the deathbringers are formed as follows. A splintered spirit soul, which is yang in nature, having exited through the point at the top of the head due to intense trauma, resides outside the protective energetic shield of the body. The material souls, yin in nature—and the seven toxic emotions they feed on—in a state of extreme agitation express themselves so powerfully that they break through the spiritual *weiqi* field. They then attach themselves to, and combine with, the exposed, splintered spirit souls. This results in giving form and shape to the destructive, demonic archetype of a deathbringer: exactly which one of them appears depends on the exact nature of the toxic emotions.

In other words, the deathbringer is not some "outside" entity, but a product of our own powerful toxic emotions (yin) and creative skills combined with our true life force or "soul" energy (yang). The figure as visualized is a "marker" that helps clinicians to recognize what they are dealing with. How and why this particular marker came about is beyond the scope of this paper, but as a concept, it seems to be borne out in practice by the actions of the energy as clinical resolution is achieved.

After clearing the demonic figure of its toxic, yin nature, the clear and peaceful yang nature of the spirit-soul energy does not "dissipate", but instead flows back into the body through the *Baihui* point at the top of the head (GV20). The splintered portions of the spirit soul reintegrate with its fundamental spirit as it resides in the liver and the three elixir fields. Instead of a "banishment" ritual as might be done with a spirit entity, the clinical practice required is a soul-retrieval, preceded by additional steps of removing toxic yin energy from the entity. Results are instantaneous and obvious to both patient and clinician. Though ominous looking and sounding, and seemingly mythological in nature, the clinical work is very straightforward. It is not a long agonizing process.

The deathbringers' powerful and persistent power comes from the combination of the patient's personally generated toxic will (yin) and its pirating of the spirit soul, which is part of the primordial spirit (yang). This makes it possible for the demonic manifestation to attack the body that contains it: we have met the enemy and he is us.

From my experience in disconnecting, removing, and dissipating these entities, I find that they are completely driven by will and intention. They are devoted to one purpose only—the fulfillment of a silent death wish—and they go about it to the exclusion of all distractions, including the practitioner's efforts to discomfit them. This indicates that they are not free-wheeling, outside entities, but internally generated and limited in both nature and dimension. Are they powerful? Yes, but only because of the power of the soul energy to which the toxic will have attached itself. A deathbringer is in fact nothing but a silent death wish.

This death wish is still part of the person and an expression of his or her spirit. This is why I speak of the "splintered *hun*" as opposed to "the *hun*" as an operational term or phase. It expresses the conscious out-of-body experience of such traumatized people: they feel like they are watching themselves like dispassionate observers, either doing something or having something done to them. This is an experience of a partial or splintered soul.

In severely or repeatedly traumatized persons, the emotional trauma after the experience is so great that this splintered soul can no longer reintegrate and does not know how to again root itself in the liver and in the three elixir fields. Instead, it remains outside the body, hovering at the edges of the protective energetic shield of the body.

This splintered spirit soul is generally palpable in a line extending to about four feet from the body. It is usually slanted upward at about a thirty-degree angle to the left front of the head and extends from the area of the left eye to the scalp line. The palpated energy is of a highly charged and dense nature, and can be communicated with by mind intention. I differentiate this action from that of the *hun* leaving fully at death or of it hovering nearby when a person is in a coma. In the cases of coma and splintered hun, the spirit soul is vulnerable to toxic influences, as they have no shield within the layers of the protective energetic fields.

Treatment Protocols

Though there is no "one size fits all" procedure, due to a patient's spiritual emotional and physical constitution, the protocols I use follow a similar pattern:

1. Patient Intake
—Patient provides medical history.
—Open-ended interview questions based on items noticed on chart; patient volunteers responses and explanations.

2. Breathing Mechanics
—Sequenced breathing, with focus on unique mechanical keys and visualizations, to promote true, deep abdominal breathing.
—Exhale technique (*tu*) and inhale technique (*na*).
—Purpose: provide a reliable parasympathetic response for maximum healing potential for the patient; a way to bring him or her back to a peaceful state if emotions become overwhelming.

3. Session Preparation
—Counting 1 to 10 meditation (Johnson 2002, 3:218). Purpose: This allows the practitioner to relax and sink, rooting the mind in preparation for extending the energetic field and connecting to the divine energy. It uses a rhyming pneunomic device: One-fun, Two-shoe, Three-tree, Four-core, Five-alive, Six-thick, Seven-heaven, Eight-gates, Nine-shine, and Ten-begin.

—Three invocations (Johnson 2002, 3: 220). Purpose: Also called the "divine hook-up," the three invocations are to assist the practitioner to observe the patient, void of personal thoughts, feeling and judgments.

1. The first connects the practitioner to the healing energy of the divine, roots the energy deep in the earth, and removes all negative vibrations from the his or her energy field.

2. The second connects both practitioner and treatment room to the divine healing energy and secures a sacred healing space.

3. The third envelopes the patient in divine healing energy, creating an orb to be rooted into the earth with an energetic vortex that eliminates toxic or evil *qi*.

—Sweep and purge the *weiqi* fields to remove external toxic *qi*. This is done by extending *qi*, energetically sweeping head to toe, to cleanse any toxic or evil *qi* in the external *weiqi* fields to void dragging this toxic *qi* into the internal fields when using external *qi* emission techniques.

4. Determining Deathbringer's Presence
—Determine if the disturbance is intermittently present (organ imbalance) or if it is consistent and persistent (possible deathbringer). I ask the patient's spirit to reveal any deathbringers that are present and wait for the energetic shift to clarity of vision. Each one is quite distinctive and unmistakable.

5. Observing and Identifying Potential Entities
—Upper Deathbringer: After formation, it invades and occupies the marrow from head to toe by inserting itself from behind the patient, i.e., it walks into the spine. It seems to be connected tightly to the heart as well as to the knees, which I believe indicates a significant "shock" factor in its early formation. Its removal must be done out the back, just as it came in. Trying to pull it out through the front is problematic.
—Middle Deathbringer: It generally appears in front of the body, although I have seen it sitting on top of the shoulder of a patient with severe migraines (GB21). It attaches to the patient with a dark, fibrous energetic cord.
—Lower Deathbringer: It appears in front of the patient and appears to be kneeling, extending its hands in the liver and spleen areas. The only one I have seen so far I describe in the third case below; the deathbringer's position may be different in other cases.

6. Removing Entities
—Create a bubble of divine healing light with perfectly balanced love (yang) and gratitude (yin).
—Rather than "go to war and destroy," hold the energetic space and bubble with compassion and divine light. Though toxic, they are still part of Dao; the

clinician holding angry, aggressive thoughts might strengthen the entity rather than help its removal.

—Encapsulate the entity in the bubble of divine light and draw it away from the body (as described above).

—Create an energetic vortex from the bottom of the bubble to the center of the earth to return the toxic energy as it is stripped away.

7. Dissipating Toxic *Qi*

—Focus on removing only the yin or toxic aspect that has attached itself to the splintered *hun*.

—Use sword fingers to dissipate and "peel off" the yin energy, sending it down through the vortex.

—Consistently draw divine healing light into the bubble, thereby continually "flushing" the toxic *qi* into the vortex.

—When the dark, toxic *qi* has been cleared, seal the bubble and vortex, and overflow the bubble with divine healing light.

8. Cutting Energetic Cords

—Use the divine Sword of Truth to sever the energetic cords connected to the edge of the bubble, focusing in the following locations:

    —the internal organs and also between them;

    —each of the energetic fields from the center outward:

        essence, energy, and spirit fields of the Taiji Pole;

        Ocean of Marrow, Ocean of Blood and current of constructive *qi*;

        physical, mental, emotional, and spiritual *weiqi* fields;

    —the seven internal and six external chakras, as well as the bubble itself.

—Cut the cords from the edge of the bubble back to the patient. There are always two cords: one extends from the patient to the toxic entity; the other reaches from the toxic entity to the patient. Both most be severed in this order.

9. Releasing the Spirit Soul

—With love and gratitude, raise the now shining bubble into the divine light.

—As it dissolves into the divine light, the yang *qi* of the spirit soul will "pour out" of the bubble and flow down through the *Baihui* point and into the Taiji Pole.

10. Rooting the Spirit Soul

—Energetically purge any toxic *qi* noticed in the three elixir fields.

—Root the re-engaging splintered spirit soul into the lower field.

—Pull cords of light from each of the spirit soul's elements in the three elixir fields to the underside of the liver.

—Cleanse and prepare the appropriate place to root the previously splintered spirit soul in the liver.

—With love and gratitude, perfectly balance the previously splintered spirit soul with all other affects, present until they are completely integrated and stable.

—Close the treatment by regulating the patients' *qi* and sealing the external *weiqi* fields.

11. Spiritual Counseling

Discuss with the patient and provide tools like "Open the Door, Remove the Thief" to dissipate any remaining toxic emotions. Help them understand the importance of not allowing toxic emotions to go unchecked. Make them aware of the unintended consequences of obsessive emotional brooding and the necessity to accept responsibility for all actions and inactions. Remind them to watch their thought patterns and use proper breathing mechanics to calm the ANS. Create a daily practice of looking for and dissipating toxic thought forms.

Case Studies

M.K., female, 54

M. K. is a new patient with a master's degree in medical qigong. She had been unable to build her *qi* for over a year, and could not self-diagnose the cause.

8/15/09: Purged and dredged *weiqi* fields, and noticed a deathbringer (Peng Zhi–Maker) sitting in the field to her left front. It crouched down with an energetic cord extending from its mouth to the patient's first and second points on the lung meridian on the right shoulder. I was quite startled, as I had never seen this archetype before. I attempted to remove it using sword fingers with intention to dissipate the form. It was difficult and tedious as I worked for about ten minutes and then hoped I had enough clearing so that it would finish clearing itself.

I told M.K. that I had noticed an archetype that Livia Kohn had pointed out to me in one of her books (Kohn 2005), and I thought I had taken care of it. When I told her where it attached, M.K. said: "I bet that had to do with my Mom's illness and death." The words no more cleared her lips when the entire archetype reappeared as though nothing had been previously done!

I immediately changed my protocol, put the archetype into a bubble of divine light to contain it. I again used sword fingers, but this time I focused on only removing the toxic yin energy to separate it from the yang *qi*. The toxic *qi* quickly melted or washed away, down through a vortex in the bottom of the *qi* bubble. The only thing left was a brilliant light in the bubble, which, after closing the vortex, I attempted to raise into the divine light.

At the point where I had raised it above her head, it simply poured down through her *Baihui* point and settled in her three elixir fields.

While doing this work, I had her use Open the Door, Remove the Thief for the issues around the anger/grief with her mother. When discussing the mother issue, the archetype did not reappear, her spirits lifted greatly, and her *qi* field took and held the *qi* very well.

I then showed her the pictures of the deathbringer, and she recognized it. She said:

"From personal experience, it is apparent that these entities feed on thought energy, specifically energy from negative thoughts and beliefs. Negative thoughts may arise for anyone, but they can only grow and thicken as we give them attention. For me, I believe this deathbringer attached to me at the death of the mother and the self-recrimination I felt about her final days. I brooded about it for years. More than a decade later, I began to experience a strange sensation. I walked into my closet and felt like all my clothes belonged to a dead person. While cleaning out the house and garage, I felt like I was preparing for my own death. My vitality and energy level declined and a healer told me I was becoming more ethereal. I had the sensation that even my atoms were dissolving and dispersing. At the same time, so many things seemed wrong in my life both at home and at work. For months, I brooded about it from morning until night.

"Finally, after J. Michael pulled the deathbringer out of my energy field, my vitality began to improve. During the session, however, something interesting happened. I am naturally curious, and my first thought was, "How did this thing attach itself to me?" Immediately, I voiced both my question and my realization that it began with my mother's death. Amazingly, just that thought acted as a magnet to the entity, drawing it back to my field. I had to take my attention off the entity and the past to let it go.

"This experience shows us the power we invest in thoughts. Without our attention, thoughts and emotions ebb and flow like ocean waves. However, as we identify with them, cling to them, hold them, and feed them with our attention, they become denser and impede the free flow of energy. Worse yet, these thoughts become food for negative entities that come to live in our fields and drain away our life force. What I have learned since is to be merely present with feelings without identifying with them. Thoughts and emotions arise, but they are not who I am. If I neither hold them nor judge them nor push them away, they simply evaporate on their own. They are unable to linger and become food for other things."

H. W., female, age 77

I first treated H. W. for scar tissue removal and channel reconnection post-surgically. Her son had committed suicide approximately one year previously, and she was now ready to deal with the suppressed emotions.

7/29/09: Discussed "mother guilt" for not recognizing son was suicidal. Holding loneliness and unreal feeling that he is not here—the feeling that she could not touch him, etc. Did Open the Door, Remove the Thief on an intensity level-ten issue (scale of 0-10), and she cleared it in two passes. She said, "she felt like rain had washed her soul and totally cleansed her. She released him to God, and felt at peace finally."

8/12/09: Purged and dredged *weiqi* fields while sitting and saw deathbringer (Peng Zhi–Maker) attached at the right wrist with cords connected to the mannubrium area. Cleared it with "Demon" technique, and cut the internal cords to all affected organs and tissues. Did Open the Door, Remove the Thief technique on her daughter-in-law issue. She cleared the level-nine issue and moved from anger or grief to compassion, feeling no negative reactivity to her previous thoughts.

I mentioned before closing that I had removed a "critter" from her wrist, and she noted that she could feel the tug as I removed the cords. While sealing her qi fields after the treatment, she noted that she also "saw" an image of a "monkey gargoyle like creature, and knew that was what I had removed.

After the treatment, I showed her Livia Kohn's book (2005) with pictures of the deathbringers, and she immediately identified deathbringer Peng Zhi. She felt clearer, and she appeared to hold the *qi* tonification treatment much better than usual post treatment.

L.P., female, age 53

Previous patient who presented with thirty-two days of persistent vaginal bleeding; her physician told her that she might have endometriosis and need a hysterectomy.

8/24/09: As I purged and dredged the *weiqi* fields, I saw a deathbringer (Peng Qiao–Junior) bent over facing her abdomen with left hand deep in the liver, right hand deep in the spleen, and head buried in the lower abdomen as if engorging itself.

I dissolved the deathbringer with demon removal technique, and "heard" that it was related to her fear of impregnation (not actually being pregnant). Her body was rejecting physical/sexual relationships, and had been doing this since her abortion at age nineteen. We looked at and discussed patterns around this issue, such as fear, anger, guilt, etc. as well as bad post-surgical infection and trauma.

I had her do "Open the Door, Remove the Thief" on this issue and cleared it. She will continue to look for artifacts around this issue. I brought back three sets of splintered spirit souls: cramping started immediately. I pulled two of the sets of splintered spirit souls back out, cleaned them as well as the elixir fields once more by cutting cords to all additional anger and toxic memories. Then I resettled the two sets of souls. The cramps stopped, and the patient became calm while yet feeling tender in the abdomen.

12/14/09: She reported that she stopped bleeding the day after the treatment and had resumed normal periods. She and would not go through with the hysterectomy. I did the General Protocol and cleared her yang channels before closing.

Bibliography

Chan, Cecilia Lai Wan, and Amy Yin Man Chow, eds. 2006. *Death, Dying and Bereavement: A Hong Kong Chinese Experience*. Hong Kong: Hong Kong University Press.

DeWoskin, Kenneth J. 1983. *Doctors, Diviners, and Magicians of Ancient China*. New York: Columbia University Press.

Forke, Alfred. 1972 [1907]. *Lun-Heng: Wang Ch'ung's Essays*. 2 vols. New York: Paragon.

Hawkes, David. 1959. *Ch'u Tz'u: The Songs of the South*. Oxford: Clarendon Press.

Jarrett, Lonny. 2006. "Acupuncture and Spiritual Realization." In *Daoist Body Cultivation*, edited by Livia Kohn, 1-18. Magdalena, NM: Three Pines Press.

Johnson, Jerry Alan. 2002. *Chinese Medical Qigong Therapy: A Comprehensive Clinical Text*. Pacific Grove: International Institute of Medical Qigong.

Kaptchuk, Ted J. 2000. *The Web that Has No Weaver: Understanding Chinese Medicine*. New York: Congdon & Weed.

Kohn, Livia. 1995. "Kôshin: A Taoist Cult in Japan. Part II: Historical Development." *Japanese Religions* 20.1: 34-55.

_____. 2005. *Health and Long Life: The Chinese Way*. Cambridge, Mass.: Three Pines Press.

_____. 2007 [1991]. *Daoist Mystical Philosophy: The Scripture of Western Ascension*. Magdalena, NM: Three Pines Press.

_____. 2010. *Sitting in Oblivion: The Heart of Daoist Meditation*. Dunedin, Fla.: Three Pines Press.

Porkert, Manfred. 1974. *The Theoretical Foundations of Chinese Medicine*. Cambridge, Mass.: MIT Press.

Ware, James R. 1966. Alchemy, Medicine and Religion in the China of AD 320. Cambridge, Mass.: MIT Press.

Yü, Ying-shih. 1987. "O Soul, Come Back: A Study of the Changing Conceptions of the Soul and Afterlife in Pre-Buddhist China." *Harvard Journal of Asiatic Studies* 47: 363-95.

Health and Sexuality

Daoist Practice and Reichian Therapy

EDUARDO FREDERICO ALEXANDER AMARAL DE SOUZA

The spread of Daoist and Tantric practices in the West since the 1970s has created a new scenario of sexual culture, values, beliefs, and practices. Two main components of this world are the Daoist and the psychoanalytic model, notably Wilhelm Reich's Orgonotherapy, for cultivating a healthy sex life and a healthy life through sex. To this end, Daoists emphasize the conservation and circulation of sexual energy in both cosmological (macrocosmic) and psycho-physiological (microcosmic) aspects. Reich similarly focuses on the recovery of orgasmic potency, the ability to have genital orgasm, as a path to heal psychic and physical ailments. A comparative analysis shows the similarities and differences between the two systems and pinpoints the limitations of psychoanalytical attempts to apprehend the Daoist model.

I chose the path of a healer early, during the last years of high-school, in the early 1990s. Not satisfied with the standard medical system, I searched and experimented, working my way through many so-called complementary and alternative therapies. As a result of this quest, entered a post-graduate program called "Medical Rationalities" at Rio de Janeiro State University, where I wrote an M.A. thesis on the history of alternative therapies and the identity of the therapist.

In the meantime I also began clinical practice based on a full training course in Wilhelm Reich's orgone therapy system, combined with meditation and hypnosis. This made me a rather unorthodox therapist. I realized at the time that the body had to be included on the path to healing. During the same period I also became a dedicated Daoist, although I did not realize it. I practiced taiji quan and qigong with dedication, but did not know that these practices were connected to Daoism. Then a breakthrough occurred. I was meditating in a temple that belonged to a Western alchemical order. After the meditation the master told me he had received a "message." He had brought a book, knowing that he had to deliver to someone that night. While meditating, he had "heard" that I was that person. The book was about Daoist sexuality, extolling the possibility of a marriage between the sacred and the sexual. This was quite important to the Rio de Janeiro or Carioca life-style I was living at the time, especially in combination with my spiritual quest. Soon after, I met my first Daoist teacher of internal alchemy, and the pieces of the puzzle began to come together.

In the early 2000s, I met my current teachers of internal alchemy and Daoist sexuality. Amazed by the wonders that their teaching enhanced in both my inner and outer life, I found my early therapy training incomplete. I began to wonder how I could bring internal alchemy and this "exotic" form of sexuality into the clinic. In vain looking for relevant methods in modern Traditional Chinese Medicine schools and realizing that the potential field of "theoretically alternative sexuality" was confusing, I started to apply my scholarly training to research. This resulted in a Ph. D. dissertation on the Daoist and alchemical roots of Chinese medicine, followed by post-doctoral research on health and Daoist sexuality[1]—both of which I was able to integrate into my clinical practice. Today, after twelve years of formal training in internal alchemy, I enjoy applying internal alchemy principles in acupuncture, thereby creating opportunities to work on mental and emotional levels as well as on the physical-sexual body. The following presentation outlines some of my key findings.

Sexuality East and West

Sex: a simple word, a not so simple world. The world of sex has been a core issue to humanity for so long, and yet I ask myself whether we have made any real progress in this respect. Forty years after the countercultural "sexual revolution" we can accept that a great part of Western civilization has achieved a more liberated sexual life. Belonging to a culture where Christianity has exerted a strong influence on sexual beliefs and behavior, we have crossed many frontiers and learned to incorporate the sexual knowledge and practices of Eastern civilizations, such as Daoism and Tantra. This ancient knowledge entered a culture of "new sexual technologies" where experiments abounded—contraceptives, preservatives, Viagra, cyber-sex, to name a few—creating a new world of sex that has yet to be studied adequately.

In this paper, I would like to explore two components of this world: the Daoist and psychoanalytical models for cultivating a healthy sexual life, on the

---

1 Both research periods were supported by CNPq – Brazilian National Council for Research and Development.

one hand, and a healthy life through sex, on the other. More specifically, I will analyze Daoist literature, both contemporary and classic, and discuss Wilhelm Reich's orgone therapy system, which is a psychoanalytic-based therapy although not part of mainstream psychoanalysis.

The importance of Reich's work lies in his defense of a sexual revolution necessary to transform society and improve human mental, emotional, and physical health. His ideas, derived from the orgone therapy model, influenced the countercultural revolutionaries either directly or through bioenergetics, a lineage founded by one of his disciples. In addition, Rajneesh or Osho, the counterculture guru, supported some of these ideas, notably that sexual repression was a core problem of humanity whose solution would allow great social transformations. Although sexual life has improved in terms of overall freedom and expression, especially in the modern West, society yet does not seem to have changed in the way the revolutionaries expected. Nevertheless, Reich's works and ideas exerted a considerable influence in what sexual change there was.

The Chinese sexual arts (*fangzhong shu* 房中術; lit. "arts of the bedchamber), on the other hand, are much older than Reich's ideas. They too came to the attention of Western societies during the countercultural movement, representing one of many transformative tools used by the revolutionaries—who in addition attributed a particularly revolutionary character to them.

I use the term "arts of the bedchamber" to refer to specific knowledge and practices related to human sexuality. They are pervasive in Chinese culture and of great importance in Daoism and Chinese medicine, whose practitioners appropriated sexual techniques as a body of practical knowledge. As Douglas Wile says: "The Chinese have made an art, a yoga, a ritual, a therapy, and a meditation of sex" (1992, 72). This level of pervasion and plurality of sexuality in the culture is significantly different from its role in Western cultures and invites many different dimensions of study.

The earliest documentation of how important sexuality is to health appears in the Mawangdui 馬王堆 medical manuscripts (see Harper 1998). They outline medical knowledge and practices, including pharmacology, moxibustion, dietetics, pregnancy, childbirth, and various forms of exorcism. The texts show that in China sexual practices were therapeutic means before even the development of acupuncture. In contrast, sexuality in therapy played no role until the early 20th century, when Sigmund Freud pioneered its importance (see Freud 1977), following the construction of a rational analysis of sexuality that began in the 18th century (see Foucault 1988).[2]

---

[2] The existence of treatises on sexuality and health during late Zhou and early Han dynasties (3rd c. BCE) seems to contradict Foucault's claim that the beginning of the discursive formation and the construction of rational knowledge on sexuality goes back to the 18th century. It may be true for the West, but is certainly not so in the East.

While the bedchamber arts were also used to satisfy male lusts and energy needs as well as commercial goals (see Gulik 1961), their therapeutic dimension continued to play an active role throughout Chinese history and from an early age was connected to Daoist practice. Since they did have the potential for exploitation and sensory gratification, the use of sexual methods has always been a controversial topic among Daoists, one that frequently surfaced during debates at court and with Buddhists.

On the other hand, even eminent Daoists such as Ge Hong (283-343) have considered sexual ways of energetic transfiguration as a requirement for achieving immortality, the highest goal of Daoism. "For Ge Hong, then, without sexual practice the best elixir is useless, but without the elixir immortality is unattainable" (Wile 1992, 24). Ancient legends accordingly tell of numerous sages that achieved great longevity and transcendence with the help of sexual means: examples include the long-lived Pengzu and various female masters such as the Plain Woman (Sunü) (see Campany 2002). Early Daoist religious organizations, moreover, used sexual practices to create cosmic harmony and enhance individual attainment (see Kobayashi 1992; Raz 2008). By the Ming dynasty (1368-1644), Daoists had adopted sexual practices as part of internal alchemy. Their techniques still enhanced health and well-being, but aimed ultimately at immortality through the transformation of body and consciousness (see Liu 2009). There are still groups of Daoists and qigong practitioners today who work dominantly with sexual methods in their quest for perfection.

Sexual Cosmology

Why, then, use sexual methods for spiritual practice? Both Daoists and medical practitioners agree that it is important to conserve vital essence (*jing* 精)—usually associated with sperm and menstrual blood—in order to attain long life and prepare for the transformation toward immortality. The character for *jing* consists of three parts that reveal its deeper meanings. The radical on the left is *mi* 米 (rice), which shows the image of a grain of rice. The lower part on the right is *dan* 丹 (cinnabar), the term used for the divine, immortal elixir; the top part on the right is *sheng* 生 (life), an image of a plant birth and growth piercing the soil.

As Catherine Despeux points out in reference to *Daode jing* 21, "Vague and indistinct; but in it there is an essence," *jing* represents the life germ contained in Dao, so that *mi* is not only "rice" as a nourishing power, but as seed or germ (in Pregadio 2008, 1:562). *Dan,* similarly is not just the mineral cinnabar, but the base substance of the alchemical elixir, which has the power of rejuvenation and even immortality. The power of this elixir, moreover, comes from a perfect combination of the Three Treasures (*jing* 精, *qi* 氣, and *shen* 神) which enables the substance to hold and carry the generative power of chaos at the root of the cosmos. The third part of the character, *sheng*, then means life at the state of creation, being in the process of generation or birth. To sum up, *jing* cosmologically indicates the generative power contained in seeds that can give life to and eternally renew the myriad beings or all embodied life. On the level of the human body it points to a seed that contains the generative power to conceive a child and sustains its life after birth, sperm and menstrual blood being specific places where this power dwells

Translating *jing* as "essence" and connecting it to the material image of human sperm loses the cosmological aspects that make it present in other places in nature. As the sexual manuals *Sunü jing* 素女經 and *Sunü fang* 素女方 (Book and Prescriptions of the Plain Woman), as well as the pharmacological *Shennong bencao jing* 神農本草經 (The divine Farmer's Materia Medica) note, it can be found in turtle shells, lizard or gecko tails, deer antlers, human hair, black sesame seeds, and more—all substances used in Chinese medicine to enhance and augment *jing*.

What then do these substances have in common? Turtles are known to represent north, the phase water, and the ancestors; they live for over a hundred years, sometimes reaching even 200. Their longevity means that they have plenty of *jing*. Lizards show immense regenerative physical power: some parts of their body will regrow if severed. Their regenerative ability means that they have lots of *jing*, the vital essence the Daoist practitioner hopes to cultivate. The same applies to deer antlers, which regrow and are very strong. In the human realm, hair is seen as "excess *jing*", essence that grows outside the body: the darker it is, the more essence it has. *Jing* is thus a power that, like Dao, pervades all nature, with certain creatures or parts having it in higher concentration. Despite this concentration, however, it is ubiquitous in nature and all bodies, and can be exchanged among the myriad beings.

Within human beings, sperm and menstrual blood are most concentrated carriers of *jing*. They are essential in keeping the person vigorous and healthy and the subject of medical discourse. In the Daoist context, moreover, *jing* is one of the Three Treasures, and every adept is held to guard and enhance it. Through this cosmological connection of *jing*, all sexuality takes place in a sacred context, its core power perceived as an expression of a cosmic power acting inside the human body. What the individual does with this power, therefore, concerns all nature.

Daoist Sexual Therapy

One fundamental sexual practice in Daoism involves the cessation of ejaculation for males and of menstruation for females, poetically called "subduing the white tiger" and "decapitating the red dragon," respectively (Despeux and Kohn 2003, 20). The model is based on the idea of the economy, circulation, and transformation of *jing*. Thus the first step is economy: the avoidance of unnecessary waste such as, for example, an ejaculation that does not lead to impregnation.

Sources of both, classical Chinese medicine and Daoism, emphasize the importance of this economy. Thus the medical text *Huangdi neijing suwen* 黃帝內經素問 (Yellow Emperor's Inner Classic: Simple Questions; trl. Veith 1972; Lu 1987; Ni 1995) describes the human life cycle in terms of *jing*:

> When a girl is 7 years of age, the kidney *jing* becomes abundant. She begins to change her teeth and the hair grows longer. At 14, she begins to menstruate and is able to become pregnant. The Governing Vessel begins to flow, the menses come regularly, and the girl is able to give birth.
>
> At age 21, *jing* is steady, the last tooth has come out, and she is fully grown. When she reaches the age of 28, her tendons and bones are strong, her hair has reached its full length, and her body is flourishing and fertile. At 35, her yang brightness vessel begins to slacken, her face begins to wrinkle, and her hair starts falling out.
>
> When she reaches the age of 42, the pulse of the three yang regions deteriorates in the upper part of her body, her entire face is wrinkled, and her hair turns gray. At age 49, she can no longer become pregnant, and the Governing Vessel is empty. Her menstruation is exhausted, and the gates of blood are no longer open. Her body declines, and she is no longer able to bear children. (ch. 1; see Maciocia 1996, 54)

This passage—matched by a parallel sequence for males in eight-year intervals—describes the body parts, tissues, and functions under the direct influence of *jing*. The bones and teeth, and especially the bone marrow, the hair, are its clear expressions. So is the overall vitality of the person as well as her genital, sexual, and reproductive functions. The medical text further calls attention to signs and symptoms related to *jing* deficiency: impotence or weak sexual function, memory loss, reduced concentration, tooth decay, prematurely graying hair, back pain, and so on. The text further identifies "sexual indulgence" as an important pathogenic factor (Maciocia 1996).

The same idea is also expressed in the *Sunü jing*, especially when the Plain Woman encourages the control of male ejaculation and the limitation of its frequency as a primary method to protect *jing*. The text says:

Men differ in respect to strength and weakness, old age and youth. Each must act according to the strength of his *qi* and never force orgasm. Forcing orgasm brings about injury. Therefore, a strong lad of fifteen may ejaculate twice in one day and a weak one once a day. . . . Strong men of thirty may ejaculate once a day and weak ones once in two days. Strong men of forty may ejaculate once in three days and weak ones once in four. Strong men of fifty may ejaculate once in five days and weak ones once in ten. Strong men of sixty may ejaculate once in ten days and weak ones once in twenty. Strong men of seventy may ejaculate once in thirty days but weak ones should refrain from ejaculating altogether. (Wile 1992, 92)

The idea here is that "indulging" in an excess of ejaculations consumes large amounts of *jing*, which is given to each individual in limited quantities at birth. The scenario at first glance is thus that sexuality is inherently pathogenic and has to be controlled at all cost. On the other hand, the Plain Woman is not against sex or pleasure. She continues:

All debility in men is due to violation of the Dao of intercourse between yin and yang. Women are superior to men in the same way that water is superior to fire. This knowledge is like the ability to blend the "five flavors" in a pot to make a delicious soup. Those who know the Dao of yin and yang can fully realize the five pleasures; those who do not will die before their time without ever knowing this joy. Can you afford not to view this with utmost seriousness? (Wile,1992, 85)

This passage is quite revealing. First it claims that all human illness has a sexual base, a claim that modern psychoanalysis—and especially Reich—would partially repeat centuries later, when it attributed the cause of mental-emotional illness to sexual energy. Second it states that those who do not realize the pleasures of the five senses will suffer early death—so abstinence and celibacy are also seen as pathogenic, consuming the *jing* in their own way. Third, it implies that the resolution of these two forms of pathogenesis can be resolved by resorting to being more feminine or like water since "women are superior to men."

For Daoists the sexual realm is ruled by women. This superiority has many aspects. Most importantly women do not waste *jing* during the sexual act, because but their main carrier of essence is menstrual blood. Mysterious in its metamorphic properties, it converts into the basic matter forming the body of the embryo during pregnancy, and is released as milk during breast-feeding. Thus, menstruation, pregnancy and breast feeding are the most relevant events for the protection of female *jing*. Women lose this form of *jing* every month if untrained but they can learn to control and reverse this loss through specific internal practices. On the other hand, her sexual fluids also contain some essential energy (*jingqi* 精氣), as documented in certain kinds of traditional sources that focus on males "harvesting" women's *jing* through intercourse.[3] Since the loss of such fluids may be harmful to health, according to some contemporary medical texts (e.g., Maciocia 1996), women need to practice the same frequency restrictions as men. However , even if she loses some sexual fluids during intercourse, this is minor in comparison to menstruation and male ejaculation.[4] The *Sunü jing*, moreover, does not prescribe and frequency restrictions to women but sees them as vastly superior to men in terms of unrestrained sexual frequency.

Another aspect of female superiority is orgasm. Key to the Daoist model is the understanding that human orgasm is not uniform. Male and female bodies are expressions of the archetypal forces of yin and yang and thus have different pathways to sexual energy. Thus, Daoists distinguish yin and yang, feminine and masculine orgasms. The latter is externalizing, dispersing, expelling, and exploding, all qualities of the seminal emission process related to external nature of male genitalia. The former, on the contrary, is a form of internal pleasure and activated life force, matching the movements of the *jingqi* in the female body whose genitalia are internalized. In other words, while males tend to externalize and disperse their essence during intercourse, females internalize and store it. Their orgasm is thus ideal for guarding *jing*: it is accordingly the model that men should strive to achieve if they intend to preserve their health.

The female body and female forms of sexuality, then, are the natural place where pleasure and health meet, resolving the conflict wasting *jing* either through an excess of sex or its complete avoidance. Following this model the second stage of practice begins, which focuses on circulating and storing essence in other parts of the body. This step inaugurates Daoist sexual therapy not just as a preventive method but as an active way of healing physical and psychological conditions through the sexual act. The main idea is to make stored essence circulate through the body and direct it to certain problem areas. The time when *jing* is most accessible and this circulation is easiest, then, is during sexual intercourse itself.

---

[3] Which kinds of text speak of which dimension has to do with the specific sociological and historical background of the sources, an issue that requires further study.

[4] Examining again the term jing, we might ask ourselves if the female sexual fluids emitted during the sexual intercourse are really full of essence. Has someone seen a mixture of sperm with those fluids result in pregnancy? Do those fluids have the power to generate life? Even accepting that they have some jinq qi 精 氣, the amount is much less important than the one lost through the menses.

Healing Techniques

Circulating *jing* makes it possible to heal ailments by directing pure vital force to a problematic area. In addition, the practice can also enhance vitality, lead to longevity, and even lay the foundation for the energetic transfiguration that leads to immortality (see Souza 2008).

Certain ailments, moreover, should be treated with specific forms of sexual interaction. For example, for reproductive and digestive problems in women the following is advised (see Fig. 1):

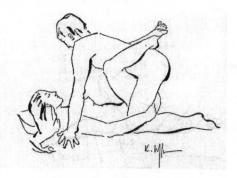

Fig. 1: Healing position for women

For the stomach, spleen, and female organs and all digestive problems, the woman lies on her back with her legs locked around the man's waist and her arms embracing him. The man is on his hands and knees and penetrates her halfway. The woman rotates her pelvis in any direction for as long as she wishes. (Chang 2001, 136)

Then there are methods by which partners mutually cultivate their *jing*, massaging the kidney area where the life force is stored. As can be seen in Fig. 2, the two partners face each other and have full body contact.

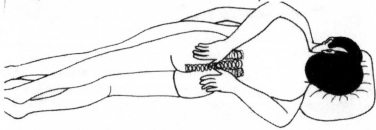

Fig. 2. Enhancing kidney *jing* for longevity.

Their genitals are joined and they use their hands to rub and knead the vital area of the kidneys. Sexual contact is slow and deliberate, focusing on the partners" internal sensations and experiences (see Wik and Wik 2005). The goal here is less the healing of a specific condition than to store and concentrate vital essence for enhanced vigor and longevity (Chia and Chia 1986, 232).

Yet another dimension of sexual practice is its application as a means to immortality. This involves the transformation of ordinary consciousness into a state of cosmic consciousness. Here the key practice is "reverting essence to nourish the brain" (*huanjing bunao* 還精補腦). A powerful depiction of this dimension of Daoist sexual practice is the *Neijing tu* 內經圖 (Chart of Internal Passageways), a 19th-century painting and stele inscription that shows the internal landscape of the human body full of allegoric representations and powerful symbols (see Fig. 3).

The river on the right of the chart, for example, represents the spine, along with the essence, shown by the waters below, is moved toward the central mountain massive, the central world mountain of Kunlun, in the head. It is activated through the impulse given by a boy and a girl working a water wheel and passes through various elixir fields, depicted as symbols of yin and yang and as spirals.

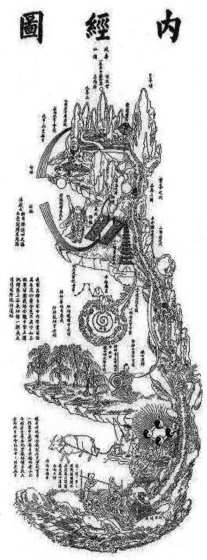

Fig. 3: The *Neijing tu*.

Various deities help the process along, which eventually results in the concentration of essence as pure spirit in a divine pearl above the head—the symbol of immortality (see Kohn 2005, 36; Despeux in Pregadio 2009, 767; Komjathy 2009a; 2009b).

This reversion and circulation of essence can be achieved through solo practice by focusing on the inner realities of the self in meditation or in partner practice during the sexual act. In the second option the partners join in the expansion of pleasure and orgasm, which allows a high level of essence circulation and a transformation of consciousness. This process is sometimes called "cultivating superior orgasm" and can be depicted as follows (see Fig. 4).

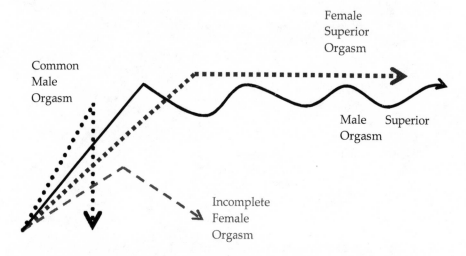

Fig. 4: Superior versus common orgasm.

Unlike in common orgasm, where the male climaxes before the female and the woman tends to experience the sexual act as an incomplete process, here the orgasm is sustained for longer periods, and the man has the opportunity to develop a female-style superior orgasm that is also more interior and pervades the entire body. If both achieve this high level of pleasure, the female is considered higher and less oscillating than the male (Chang 2001, 117).

In this setting of highly exultation, the partners can then circulate their *jing* and induce various changes in their body and consciousness. The goal is not only to find health and longevity but to experience "cosmic union": the partners merge into each other, and the couple becomes one with the cosmos.

The preferred posture to achieve this level is with the woman above the man and both partners with their heads oriented toward heaven, sitting upright and keeping the spine straight. The process of essence circulation is represented by the circular circuits inside their bodies (see Chia and Chia 1986; see Fig. 5).

Fig. 5: The posture for the dual cultivation of superior orgasm.

Deeper into the Psyche

How, then, can Daoist sexual therapy in its various levels be interpreted psychologically? How is the Chinese medical body relevant to psychological transformation? How does the spiritual experience of oneness relate to psychic events—both in preparation and in effect?

Over the last decade, certain masters of Chinese medicine have made it their goal to recover the full potential of its classical form, after its alternation under the influence of Western biomedicine and in the political climate of Chinese communism (see Fruehauf 1999). Important representatives of this effort include Jarrett (2000; 2003), Dechar (2006), Willmont (1999), and Kaatz (2005). One of their strategies involves the recovery of the Daoist roots of Chinese medicine, especially through what Fruehauf calls the "science of symbols" (2002a). This entails finding the deep hidden meaning of the names and characters used for specific areas of the body, such as key acupuncture points and energy centers, allowing a deeper appreciation of their cosmological, psychological, and spiritual aspects. A key question in this context is whether a meaning attributed to any given character or symbols is actually old in the sense of reflecting the intent of its original creators or whether it is being created by projection of the minds of contemporary Westerners. While this question also has a theoretical, hermeneutic dimension, I prefer at this time to present common interpretations of important symbols from the perspective of the therapist.

For this, I make use of the work of the medical masters listed earlier as well as my personal experience in the clinic.

Central to the practice of Chinese medicine, Daoist cultivation, and sexual therapy is the idea that vital energy and essence flow through the body along channels or meridians that connect internal organ-complexes energetically to the extremities, hands and feet, as well as the body as a whole to the environment. They are called *jingmai* 經脉. The first word, literally "passageway," shows water flowing underground on the right, while the radical on the left means "silk" and shows threads in a fabric (Wieger 1965, 41, 230). The second word, translated as "vessel" or "pulse," consists of the symbol for "flesh" or "body" on the left combined with "line" or "pattern" on the right. Combined the term is rendered "meridian" and thus denotes the flow of life's water interwoven like a fabric through underground lines in the human bodymind. The term *mai* also implies the capacity to hold in its meaning of "vessel" and the power to set a pace for this flow in its meaning of "pulse."

The flow of the life force through this potent network, moreover, organizes all life, not just in the microcosmic body of human beings but also in the greater cosmos and in the relationship between the two (see Kaatz 2005). The flow of life inside thus has a matching correspondence outside; the meridians are internal pathways of the life force that are reflected in the pathways in our outer life. The textile character of the meridians, moreover, implies the existence of nodes or areas of connection. Acupuncture points, where the life force is most concentrated and most accessible, are such nodes. Thus if we follow a thread in the fabric or the meridian, we pass through some areas that are like milestones, marking and connecting the evolving stages of that thread.

There are a number of points that are most powerfully connected to *jing* and thus essential for understanding the workings of sexual therapy. They include points on a number of different meridians, notably those associated with the organ-complex of the kidney (which rules *jing*) and with the channels running along the front and back of the torso (Conception and Governing Vessels) (see Deadman 2001, 334; Auteroche 2000, 166).

To begin, there is the first point of the kidney meridian known as Bubbling Spring (*Yongquan* 涌泉) and located centrally on the soles of the feet. Its main function is an upward movement of vital force, picking it up from the ground like a bubbling spring (Kaatz 2005, 508). Lonny Jarrett sees it as having the capability "to empower our connection to the cosmological pole of the earth" and "initiate the rising of essence through us toward heaven, thus propelling evolution" (2003, 430). In other words, the point and the energy moving through it relate to our feelings toward having a body and living an incarnated life. The deeper our connection to this stage of the life force, the more grounded we are and the better we can deal with the limitations of material life we may face. In addition, this quality of energy also represents the initial stage of our personal evolution. It connects us to the essential energy of the earth, allowing our personal sexual and productive energy to be part of something larger and more powerful. My experience as a practitioner has shown that sexual energy at this stage is related to the unconscious drive to reproduce, to engender a new human being. It is a raw force that comes from the *jing* of the earth.

Moving upward along the legs and through the kidney meridian, this energy is refined until it reaches Meeting Yin (*Huiyin* 會陰), the first point of the Conception Vessel that runs along the front of the torso. Located on the pelvic floor at the perineum, it is the point from where the *jing* spreads throughout the genitals via branches of the kidney meridian on the tendino-muscular level. Here all the yin energies meet that come from the earth. Reading the *Neijing tu*, Komjathy suggests that this point is related to the "reversal of the flow of vital essence" (2009, 74). Instead of moving outward through seminal emission or menstrual blood, the *jing* is "sealed" at this point through mental concentration and physical contraction. This allows the practitioner to guide it up along the spine to another major energy node. My interpretation is that at this stage there is a choice between using the *jingqi* to create another body through reproduction and by moving energy out through the genitals or to convert it into creative, vital energy used to enhance the evolution of one's personal and spiritual life. It is also the point where the earth's collective sexual energy meets with our personal *jingqi*.

Making the conscious choice as a practitioner of internal alchemy to use it for personal enhancement, or even subconsciously experiencing the spontaneous reversion of energy, is the starting point of major shifts in psychological reality and personal identity. One takes a step back from the common social goals of family and fortune and dedicates oneself more to internal and spiritual goals. From here, the next major point is Extended Strength (*Changjiang* 長強) at the coccyx, the first point of the Governing Vessel running along the spine. Shown in the *Neijing tu* as a gate, it is where sexual energy steams and ascends (Komjathy 2009, 74). It, too, is part of the active choice to be made: to deny the way of reproduction and set out on the way of developing personal potential. The two points Meeting Yin and Extended Strength represent the choice one makes to deny the way of reproduction (by sealing the *jing* – yin) and setting out on the way of developing one's personal potential (steaming *qi* – yang)

After this, the reverted energy reaches the Gate of Destiny (*Mingmen* 命門), the fourth point on the Governing Vessel. As *jing* passes through here, it begins to turn subtler and transform into *qi*, pure vital energy (Komjathy 2009, p.75). This has major psychological impact., signaling the activation of one's personal *ming*, which is not so much pure "life" but "destiny," the "mandate" or "order to be" one has received from heaven. A central concept in Daoism, destiny propels the individualized life of any given being on its authentic path as determined by Dao. There is a great increase in vitality when one reaches out to this level and undergoes the major change in the psyche, hence the alternative translation of this point as "Gate of Life." At this stage the transformed sexual energy manifests as the will (*zhi* 志) to live a full life of Dao while embodied on this planet. This is an essential step toward healing and fullness: it is the recovery of one's original being on an existential level. One gains the sense that life is worth living since it has an authentic purpose—given by Dao through destiny and carried hidden in the *jing*.

From here, the energy continues to move through the torso, reaching the point Pass Origin (*Guanyuan* 關元), the fourth point on the Conception Vessel located near the navel. Here the original (*yuan*) life force of the individual opens and begins to spread throughout the bodymind. The energy here is original or primordial (*yuanqi*), understood as the life force related to the individual's destiny. Once activated by the movements and transformations of sexual energy, it propels the person toward life experiences that will fulfill his or her particular *ming* in life.

From here the energy reaches three upper points on the kidney pathway that gather around the heart center. They are Spirit Seal (*Shenfeng* 神封; K-23), Numinous Hill (*Lingxu* 靈墟; K-24), and Spirit Repository (*Shencang* 神藏; K-25). They represent the alchemical stage where vital energy (*qi*) developed from the refinement of sexual essence is transformed into spirit (*shen* 神). Spirit Seal, first, "helps to reveal one's real inherent nature," to find awareness of one's authentic self and "empowering one to live according to this true identity in spite of external antagonistic forces" (Willmont 1999, 147). Numinous Hill, second, "empowers one to be an effective force in the world" (Jarrett 2003, 454), as a result of fulfilling one's inherent destiny. Taking these paths and acting in accordance with one's authentic self, thereby manifesting all one's potentials as given by Dao, the individual feels able to exert a numinous influence in the world (*de* 德). Spirit Repository, finally, is the storehouse of the generated spirit, providing enhanced lucidity, awareness of one's inherent nature, and an intuitive knowledge of the paths one has to follow in life to become a self-realized being. From here one lives a life that feels authentic, purposeful, and fulfilling. One has what Gary Zukav calls "authentic power":

> Authentic power feels good. It is doing what you are supposed to be doing. It is fulfilling. Your life is filled with meaning and purpose. You have no doubts. You have no fears. You are happy to be alive. You have a reason to be alive. Everything you do is joyful. Everything is exciting. You are not worried about doing something wrong, making a mistake, or failing. You do not compare yourself with others. You do not compare what you do with what others do. (2002, 105)

The transformations of sexual energy as proposed in the Daoist model is thus not merely the process of bringing body and mind to a level of greater health; it is the alchemical quest for the dual cultivation of inherent nature and destiny, the path to full self-realization in this and the spiritual realm through a complete transformation of the psyche.

Wilhelm Reich's Model

Psychoanalysis emerged at the end of the 19th century, creating revolutionary changes in Western beliefs and values about sexuality. In his works, Sigmund Freud proposed ideas that were shocking at the time. They include especially the notion of libido as a kind of physiological energy of a sexual nature, related to a healthy mental and emotional development while its repression can cause psychic illnesses. Claiming that this energy is present already in children, Freud moreover sexualized childhood and the relationship to the parents (see Freud 1977).

Wilhelm Reich (1897-1957), a student of Freudian psychoanalysis, came to propose even more provocative views on sexuality. Working with the classical model at first, he found that the fundamental methods of psychoanalysis, such as interpreting unconscious material emerging in therapy as well as working with the transference of the libidinal-affective charge projected by the patient and the subsequent conscious condemnation of neurotic desires ,were not sufficient to heal the neurotic symptoms on a permanent basis. As a result, he distanced himself from Freud as well as from the psychoanalytical field in general and developed certain new ideas, creating a model to explain his clinical observations (see Reich 1986).

For Reich one essential element was missing: he would came to call it the recovery of orgasmic potency. He found that it was necessary for patients to recover the capability of achieving genital orgasm during the sexual act if they wanted to heal neurotic symptoms with a lasting effect. The rationale behind this notion is that the sexual life force discharged during orgasm is the same as that which would sustain the neurotic complex if retained (see Reich 1966).

With this notion Reich placed himself in diametric opposition to the idea of a sublimation process, that is to say, the concept that repressed sexual energy could be converted into work, exercise, or creative activities such as arts or science. He believed that the free circulation of sexual energy could only be free and complete if genital orgasm was achieved. Anything else would keep the neurotic complex and its symptoms in operation, the absence of orgasm assuring the continued presence of neurotic energy.

Having come to this conclusion, his next step was to develop a model of sexual economy in terms of libidinal charge and discharge. Its first level is simple: desire and sexual excitation charge part of the body's nervous system; this charge should be released through genital orgasm, thus eliminating tension from the nervous system. His main proposition here is that the difference of energy between charge and discharge equals the amount available to sustain neurosis. Going deeper, he believed that the energetic imbalance between sexual desire and excitation and its orgasmic counterpart was at the root of the problem. In other words, orgasmic potency in Reich means the capability to achieve an orgasm that gives pleasurable sensations (discharge) equivalent to the amount of energy trapped in the nervous system building up as sexual desire and excitation (charge).

Over the years, Reich added a second level to this theory, trying to turn it into a full scientific model and thereby recovering a project that mainstream psychoanalysis had already renounced or was about to renounce. Beginning with the belief that the charge and discharge of libidinal energy could be measured, he experimented with measuring the electric charge of the human body during sexual excitation and orgasm. Based on these experiments he then put together the following graph[5] (see Reich 1986).

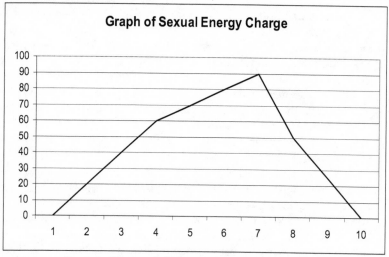

Graph 1: Charge and discharge of sexual energy.

In addition, he developed another notion, which turned his work away from science, although he was convinced to the very end that everything he did was scientific. He believed that the energy he measured was a vital force he called "orgone," a concept that has a great deal in common with *qi* in the Chinese

---

[5] Masters and Johnson followed a similar approach in the 1950s and 1960s in their studies devoted to male and female sexual responses. Their work set the stage for the modern scientific study of sexuality but they stayed strictly focused on biology and avoided all discussion of energy (1966; 1970).

system—a universal energy that may take many different forms and that we must balance to maintain health. However, at the time, this kind of "vitalism" was frowned upon by all biological and medical scientists in the West.

Reich's orgone is a physical life force responsible for the enlivenment of the body; it is also a psychological force inasmuch as it moves the psyche. It is thus almost a substitute for libido, but becomes the core of a psychosomatic model that goes far beyond the Freudian notion since it links psychological reality with biological life in a clearly outlined format. More specifically, Reich sees the expression of orgone in seven segments of the human body and life, as summarized in the table below:

Segment	Body Area	Some Psychological Functions
1-Ocular	Head, eyes, ears, nose	Perception, contact with the world and other.
2-Oral	Mouth and upper cervical spine	Request for care and nourishment.
3-Cervical	Throat and cervical spine	Expression of emotions and desires.
4 – Thoracic	Chest and arms	Emotional contact and intensity. Formation of autonomous identity.
5-Diaphragm	Diaphragm and solar plexus area	Body vitality, assertiveness.
6-Abdominal	Navel to pubic bone region	Contact with body through vegetative sensations. Security in possession of the body and its spontaneous expressions.
7 – Pelvic	Pelvis, genitals and legs	Sexual potency and expression. Autonomy, grounding.

Table 1: Summary of the seven segments and psychological functions.

These basic functions are further related to the Freudian notion of libido development through the oral, anal, and phallic stages. For example, the demands for nourishment, care, and safety a newborn child exerts upon his or her caretaker (oral stage) manifests through the second segment: mouth, jaw, teeth, and parts of the back of the head and upper neck. Psychological conflicts emerge, depending on how the person deals with these demands and their possible frustrations. What happens when you do not receive what you desire? Anger and frustration? These feelings create changes in the neuronal and muscular patterns of the second segment, affecting the ways orgone flows in the body and creating both physical and psychological symptoms.

Reichian therapy combines body work with verbal exchange as based on psychoanalytical dynamics, the unconscious transference of libido and emotions. Each segment of the body has specific exercises to move orgone with the goal of releasing tensions, recovering their source in the mind and emotions, and helping the person toward greater autonomy. The exercises relate to movements of libido development from childhood into adulthood, i.e., the time of orgasmic potency.

For example, a man may be passive and orally fixated, always looking for a good mother to feed him and supply his needs rather than developing autonomy in life. A possible therapeutic setting would have him work on exercises that mobilize the muscles around the mouth in a way that does not enhance the suction movements of breast feeding, but rather induces oral breathing. In this manner, he would learn to change his unconscious need of being fed into the ability to gather his own energy and thus autonomy through air intake, enhancing his power and autonomy.

Reich further arranged these patterns in two main categories: hypotonic and hypertonic. The first indicates the absence of orgone at the specific segment; the second describes the hindrance in expression of the energy once it is there. For Reich, they are like the registration of psychological conflicts and their unconscious solutions in the body (1972). He thus creates a system of character analysis to read and evaluate the construction of personality and the correlated patterns of orgone flow imprinted on the body. He finds that many illnesses, including cancer (see Reich 1974), come from the uneven and blocked distribution of orgone in the body, which in turn matches the personality's neurotic traits—a vision that is highly compatible with traditional Chinese ideas of qi-flow in relation to health and disease.

Comparative Considerations

Douglas Wile has emphasized just how important and rewarding it is to study sexuality in a comparative cultural context. Examining Reich's theory in comparison to the Chinese model, he finds that the notion of orgone is similar to Daoist *jingqi* or *qi* and that both systems are "sexually revolutionary" in cultural terms, meaning that they accept and sometimes even support sexual liberation and polygamous habits as a way of health. In this sense they are both opposed to a morally regulated sexuality and prefer sexual contact to sexual repression (Wile 1992, 69).

Supporting this understanding, I also find that both systems consider sexuality as a dominant power in the determination of health or illness. As the *Sunü jing* has: "All debility in men is due to a violation of the Dao of intercourse between yin and yang." This can be read as a 2000-year-old version of the psychoanalytic claim that all psychological illnesses are rooted in sexual energy or libido. Reich, moreover, had very similar ideas, seeing how psychological problems created bodily patterns of imbalance leading to all kinds of diseases (1972; 1986). For him, orgone-libido was the basis of almost all illnesses and good sexuality formed the root of health. In addition, both systems share notions of sexual economy although with considerable differences.

Differences, then, come to the fore when psychoanalysts come to interpret Chinese and Daoist sexuality, finding that the latter focuses heavily on *coitus reservatus*—the practice of intentionally stopping the excitation that leads to genital orgasm—which leads to what they call an oral or anal fixation (see Wile 1992, 67). For Westerners, then, the preferred method of the Chinese is essentially a pathogenic habit (Weakland 1956; Reich 1986). However, is this really the case?

The starting point for the understanding of the Chinese system as a form of oral fixation is the association between Chinese eating habits and oral fantasies projected on the sexual act, such as "feeding" the penis, fears of being drained and losing energy, and the role of the wife as an nurturer. All these are projections typical for an underdeveloped sexual energy, when the subject instead is fixated on the primary relationship of breast feeding, receiving pleasure and nourishment from the mother. Chinese sexual habits are thus seen as based on the failure to renounce oral sexuality and achieve true genital sexuality. In this scenario, *coitus reservatus* appears as a denial or at least avoidance of genital orgasm, which reinforces or creates fixations of sexual energy or libido in the early stages of development. As Douglas Wile says, with justification: "In Freudian terms again, could one not also make an argument for *coitus reservatus* as a sexual manifestation of anal retentiveness?" (1992,69).

However, Wile also claims that " the practices of yoga, Daoist meditation, and sexual practice are aimed at breaking down what Reich called muscular armor." From our perspective today, this is certainly the case, but for Reich who constructed his system in the 1920s and 1930s, yoga was still an exotic practice which he found based on physical and mental control, thus potentially generating obsessive behavior (i.e., anal fixation) (see Reich 1972). He claimed that any attempt to control the natural muscular contractions of breathing and the pelvic floor led only to a greater reinforcement of armoring and neurosis— including common yogic practices such as breath control (*pranayama*) and pelvic contractions (*mula bandha*). Along the same lines, the Chinese and Daoist practice of *coitus reservatus* would be a way of controlling the involuntary muscular contractions during of orgasm, leading to anal fixation and intensified armoring.

In other words, although both systems—the Chinese and Reichian— understand sexuality to lie at the root of health, they are yet considerably different on the level of application and practice. Psychoanalysts, including Reich (see 1972; 1986), summarily dismiss the value of Daoist sexuality as methods of nourishing health, while Daoists would have little patience with the extended verbal unraveling of neurosis in psychotherapy.

The fundamental graphs of the two models already show this discrepancy. In the Daoist model as outlined by Chia and Winn (1984), the act of "holding energy" is represented by a line of excitement that goes up and does not go down—this is exactly the how Reich's graph defines the genesis of neurosis. On the other hand, as Wile points out (1992, 69), the Reichian idea of a clouding of consciousness as the effect of a potent and non-neurotic orgasm facilitated by natural, involuntary muscular contractions is completely opposite the vision of *shenming* 神明, the illuminated consciousness that results from a more feminine type of orgasm to be pursued according to Daoist proposals. One way to understand this difference is with Douglas Wile's observation that "for them [the Chinese], contact and arousal are the most fundamental biological needs, not orgasm. The energy discharged during sex should not be drained from the body, but shared with the organism as a whole, specially the brain" (1992, 69) or, rather, be distributed orgastically throughout the body.

Conclusion

To conclude, I would like to present my own perspective on the two models and the way they are interpreted and compared. First of all, I consider it a mistake to think that *coitus reservatus* correctly describes what happens in a Daoist sexual context. It seems more of a Western construct than an accurate description of the sexual practice and experience, being more a term to describe the pathogenic replacement of genital with anal or oral pleasure, the denial, avoidance, or withdrawal of sexual energy and pleasure from the genitals. To me this is not what happens at all during the Daoist "refusal" to enter genital orgasm. On the contrary, pleasure here is not taken from one place and moved into another but expanded internally so that there is orgasm throughout the entire body.

In other words, the Daoist way involves a genitalization of the entire body rather than an oralization of genital energy. It is about making the body as a whole able to feel orgasmic, high intensity pleasure. The energy is not "held," as suggested by psychoanalysts. Instead, it is amplified and circulated through the pleasurable sensations of sexual act. It thereby expands consciousness rather than inhibiting or constraining it. Some may not agree that this is historically accurate, but classics such as the *Sunü jing* clearly bear it out. Thus, its reference to the "five flavors" and "five pleasures" represents an interpenetration of the five phases model within the sexual arts, connecting them with the five organs and the five senses. It can thus be understood as a reference to a practice that allows sexual energy and pleasure to expand through the five organs with the support of the five senses. It says essentially that "those who cannot achieve the pleasure of spreading their orgasm through the entire body"(represented by five organs) while protecting essence through non-ejaculation in the male are bound to suffer from various ailments and die prematurely.

Next, I would like to examine the graphic representation of the two systems. The graph of Reich's system shows a steady, steep ascent, followed by a sharp decline; that by Stephen Chang (2001)—and a similar one in Chia and Winn (1984)—also shows a steep ascent, but it is followed by an up-and-down wave that does not go into obvious decline. Assuming that the energy depicted is in fact libido, which needs to be released in order to prevent neurosis, this would indeed show that the Daoist system is prone to creating neurosis; after all, it proposes a charge without discharge.

However, looking at the graphs more closely, we understand that they do not represent the same kind of flow. Reich measured electrical charges in the nervous system and his graph is about the charge and discharge of electricity in the body, as they are associated with orgasm (see Reich 1986). The Daoist authors do not define their parameters exactly, but rather than massive electrical charges, I assume, they are measuring pleasure and a subjective feeling of high-intensity energy. Seeing the parameters of the graphs in this light, they become more coherent. Both systems hold the belief that higher pleasure enhances health, but they represent pleasure in different parameters—one more objective, the other more subjective, again reflecting a pervasive difference between Western science and Eastern spiritual practice.

My last point is that those psychoanalysts who have examined and interpreted Daoist practices never really understood their concepts nor could they fathom the experience of expanded orgasm. As a result, their interpretations were more the projection of psychoanalytical beliefs into the Daoist experience than an accurate assessment. They were closed to the potential benefits of Daoist sexual therapy because none of them, not even Reich—as is made clear in his various works (1966; 1972; 1986)—share the central belief of Daoist sex: *that male and female orgasms are qualitatively different in nature.*

Looking at Reich's model, it becomes obvious that his idea of orgasm, how he apprehends it, reflects the male experience. It is a building of tension followed by discharge, an explosion that moves outward. Reading him from a Daoist perspective, his entire model is revealed as an attempt to generalize a male (yang) orgasm as the human standard, making it universal. This, of course, is part of the curse of the modern West, and many are the critics who have pointed out just how phallo-centric psychoanalytical theory is. It is most obvious in the question of orgasm. Far be it from Western psychology to follow the *Sunüjing* when it states: "Women are superior to men in the same way that water is superior to fire." In other words, the female orgasm is superior to the male or at least leads to superior sensations of pleasure because it is of a fundamentally different nature and has a stronger and more lasting power. Essentially internal, it spontaneously brings sexual energy and pleasure to the inner parts of the body. There is no need to explode, no necessity of outside discharge. Rather, it manifests in inward nourishing, the reflection of the power of yin. The Daoist model thus postulates that the experience of the inner, superior, all-body orgasm is a secret found in the female body—making women superior to men.

In my opinion, psychoanalysts cannot fully understand the notion and the experience of what they called *coitus reservatus*, because their model is limited by a patriarchal culture from which a phallo-centric system emerges that privileges one kind of climax as "the orgasm." This limitation hinders the apperception of the internalization of pleasure and the genitalization of the body. Going far beyond the psychoanalytical model and even Reich's orgone theory, Daoist sexual therapy thus has much to offer modern psychologists. It can open people's minds and bodies toward a new and higher level of pleasure. As more people adopt it, they can let go of the need to release sexual and potentially neurotic energy, instead accepting the idea of its refinement and transformation. Thereby they can allow sexual energy to spread inward and flow through the entire body, creating an all-round pleasure-based identity that is in harmony with self, society, and the cosmos.

Bibliography

Auteroche, B., L. Mainville, and H. Solinas. 2000. *Atlas de Acupuntura Chinesa: meridianos e colaterais*. São Paulo: Ed. Andrei.

Campany, Robert F. 2002. *To Live as Long as Heaven and Earth: Traditions of the divine Transcendents*. Berkeley: University of California Press.

Chang, Stephen T. 2001. *The Tao of Sexology: The Book of Infinite Wisdom*. Reno: Tao Publishing.

Chia, Mantak, and Maneewan Chia. 1986. *Healing Love Through the Tao: Cultivating Female Sexual Energy*. Huntington, NY: Healing Tao Books.

_____ and Michael. Winn. 1984. *Taoist Secrets of Love: Cultivating Male Sexual Energy*. Santa Fe: Aurora Press.

Deadman, Peter , M. Al-Khafaji, and K. Baker. 2001. *A Manual of Acupuncture*. East Sussex: Journal of Chinese Medicine Publications.

Dechar, L. E. 2006. *Five Spirits: Alchemical Acupuncture for Psychological and Spiritual Healing*. New York: Lantern Books.

Despeux, Catherine, and Livia Kohn. 2003. *Women in Daoism*. Cambridge, Mass.: Three Pines Press.

Eberhard, Wolfram. 1967. *Guilt and Sin in Traditional China*. Berkeley: University of California Press.

Foucault, Michel 1988. *História da sexualidade: a vontade de saber.* São Paulo: Edições Graal.

Freud, Sigmund 1977. *Edição standard brasileira das Obras Psicológicas Completas de Sigmund Freud.* Rio de Janeiro: Imago.

Fruehauf, Heiner. 1999. "Science, Politics, and the Making of 'TCM': Chinese Medicine in Crisis." *Journal of Chinese Medicine* 61:6-14.

_____. 2002a. "The Science of Symbols: Exploring a Forgotten Gateway to Chinese Medicine." Part 1. *Journal of Chinese Medicine* 68:33-39.

_____. 2002b. "The Science of Symbols: Exploring a Forgotten Gateway to Chinese Medicine." Part 2. *Journal of Chinese Medicine* 69:20-26.

Gulik, Robert H. van. 1961. *Sexual Life in Ancient China.* Leiden: E. Brill.

Harper, Donald. 1998. *Early Chinese Medical Manuscripts: The Mawangdui Medical Manuscripts.* London: Wellcome Asian Medical Monographs.

Jarrett, Lonny S. 2000. *Nourishing Destiny: The Inner Tradition of Chinese Medicine.* Stockbridge, Mass.: Spirit Path Press.

Jarrett, Lonny S. 2003. *The Clinical Practice of Chinese Medicine.* Stockbridge, Mass.: Spirit Path Press.

Kaatz, D. 2005. *Characters of Wisdom: Taoist Tales of the Acupuncture Points.* Soudorgues: Petite Bergerie.

Kobayashi, Masayoshi. 1992. "The Celestial Masters Under the Eastern Jin and Liu-Song Dynasties." *Taoist Resources* 3.2: 17-45.

Kohn, Livia. 2005. *Health and Long Life: The Chinese Way.* Cambridge, Mass.:, Three Pines Press.

_____, ed. 2006. *Daoist Body Cultivation: Traditional Models and Contemporary Practices.* Magdalena, NM: Three Pines Press.

Komjathy, Louis. 2009. "Mapping the Daoist Body (2): The Text of the *Neijingtu.*" *Journal of Daoist Studies* 2:64-108.

iu, Xun. 2009. "Numinous Father and Holy Mother: Late-Ming Duo-Cultivation Practice." In *Internal Alchemy: Self, Society, and the Quest for Immortality,* edited by Livia Kohn and Robin R. Wang, 122-41. Magdalena, NM: Three Pines Press.

Lowen, A. 1982. *Bioenergética.* São Paulo: Summus.

Lu, Henry C. 1987. *The Yellow Emperor's Book of Acupuncture.* Blaine, Wash.: Academy of Oriental Heritage.

Maciocia, Giovanni. 1994. *The Practice of Chinese Medicine: The Treatment of Diseases with Acupuncture and with Herbs.* New York: Churchill Livingstone.

_____. 1996. *Os fundamentos da medicina chinesa: um texto abrangente para Acupunturistas e Fitoterapeutas.* São Paulo: Roca.

Masters, William H., and Virginia E. Johnson, V. E. 1966. *Human Sexual Response.* New York: Bantam Books.

_____. 1970. Human Sexual Inadequacy. New York: Bantam Books.

_____. 1974. The Pleasure Bond. New York: Bantam Books.

Ni, Maoshing. 1995. *The Yellow Emperor's Classic of Medicine*. Boston: Shambhala.

Pregadio, Fabrizio. , ed. 2008. *The Encyclopedia of Taoism*. London: Routledge.

Raz, Gil. 2008. "The Way of the Yellow and the Red: Re-examining the Sexual Initiation Rite of Celestial Master Daoism." *Nannü: Men, Women and Gender in China* 10:86-120.

Reich, Wilhlem. 1931. *A irrupção da moral sexual*. São Paulo: Martins Fontes.

_____. 1966. *A Revolução sexual*. São Paulo: Círculo do Livro.

_____. 1972. *Character Analysis*. New York: Farrar, Straus and Giroux

_____. 1974. *The Cancer Biopathy*. New York: Farrar, Straus and Giroux

_____. 1982. *Bioeletrical Investigation of Sexuality and Anxiety*. New York: Farrar, Straus and Giroux.

_____. 1984. Children of the Future: On the Prevention of Sexual Pathology. New York: Farrar, Straus and Giroux.

_____. 1986. The Function of the Orgasm. New York: Farrar, Straus and Giroux.

Souza, Eduardo. 2008. *Nutrindo a vitalidade: questões contemporâneas sobre a racionalidade médica chinesa e seu desenvolvimento histórico cultural*. Ph. D. Thesis. Social Medicine Institute, Rio de Janeiro State University.

Veith, Ilza. 1972. *The Yellow Emperor's Classic of Internal Medicine*. Berkeley: University of California Press.

Weakland, J. 1956. Orality in Chinese Conceptions of Male Genital Sexuality." *Psychiatry* 19:237-47.

Wieger, Leon. 1965. *Chinese Characters: Their Origin, Etymology, History, Classification and Signification*. New York: Dover Publications.

Wik, Mieke, and Stephan Wik. 2005. *Beyond Tantra: Healing through Taoist Sacred Sex*. Forres, Scotland: Findhorn Press.

Wile, Douglas. 1992. *Art of the Bedchamber: The Chinese Sexual Yoga Classics Including Women's Solo Meditation Texts*. Albany: State University of New York Press.

Willmont, Dennis. 2001. *The Twelve Spirit Points of Acupuncture*. Marshfield, Mass.: Willmountain Press.

Zukav, Gary. 2002. *Soul Stories*. New York: Simon & Schuster.

Dual Cultivation in Modern Relationships

STEPHAN WIK

Daoist sexual yoga is a form of Daoist energy work which, like many others, relies on inner softening, i.e., on relaxing, tensions while releasing obstructions that stand in the way of a free flow of life energy or qi. Daoist practices have a beneficial effect not only on intimate connection between partners but can transform the entire relationship. Divorce statistics today show that many people have trouble maintaining intimate relationships. Traditional family structures no longer provide the solution to their need for love, intimacy, and connection. Daoist practices allow them to release rigidity, develop gentleness and compassion, and open to new scenarios. They thus achieve a strong, resilient, and durable connection that can withstand the various social and personal stresses of modern life. They discover their own personal truth, begin to live authenticity, and thus create healthy, sustainable, and life-giving relationships.

My journey of discovery into the world of Daoism started, as for so many others in the West, with the Wilhelm translation of the *Yijing*. As I read it, I marveled at how such an ancient document from essentially a foreign culture to me could yet provide such timely insights into my life. Having said that, I must admit that some of the insights were not always particularly understandable or clear to me and after some time my copy of the *Yijing* became a permanent fixture on my bookshelf, rather than on the coffee table.

A few decades later, another Daoist-inspired book, Mantak and Maneewan Chia's *Healing Love: Cultivating Female Sexual Energy* (1986), suffered the same fate. I had bought the book during a period of research into sacred sexual practices and traditions but, despite my best efforts, I found that the descriptions and explanations were very hard to make sense of in any meaningful way. This book, too, ended up on my bookshelf next to the *Yijing*.

However, this particular book did not remain there. Some years later, my wife Mieke became seriously ill and I decided to look at Healing Love once again. Our doctor had determined that Mieke's illness did not come form anything immediately visible such as a growth or a tumor. Instead, it seemed that her endometriosis was most likely the result of a hormonal imbalance.

Since Mieke was not immediately interested in any of the suggested conventional treatments—such as surgery and then HRT, which has since been widely discredited—she asked me to look into what alternatives might be available. I remembered the book on "Healing Love" I had purchased many years earlier. It detailed specific practices for "increasing blood count" and "healing the sexual organs." After reading the book again, this time together, we decided that the Daoist practices were worth trying. If nothing else, they seemed gentle enough and we felt confident that they would not cause any damage.

After many months of study and practice we found that, for us at least, the practices did work, and much to our joy and relief Mieke started to recover. After a year, not only was she fully healed but her vitality was at the highest level it had been for years. She literally felt like a new woman and our family and friends noticed and commented on this. They also remarked on how our relationship seemed to be in much better condition, and that we seemed to have fallen in love with each other all over again after twenty years of marriage, four children, and all of the inevitable relationship vicissitudes that couples go through.

At that point, one of our friends, a publisher, asked us whether we would be interested in writing a book about our healing journey. This led to a long conversation. On the one hand, we felt that what we had discovered might be of great interest and use to other people who were dealing with similar issues. On the other hand, the practices we used were very intimate and not something most people speak openly about, much less write a book on. In the end, however, we decided that the opportunity to be of service was more important than our own personal discomfort, and so we started on the book.

What followed was an intense period of learning as I soon discovered that I knew what practices we had done but was not entirely clear as to why they had worked. I first spent many months in the Chinese and Japanese section of the library at the University of Leuven, Belgium, where we lived at the time, reading everything I could find that might explain how these techniques work. Original works and translations by Douglas Wile, Livia Kohn, Catherine Despeux, and Michael Winn were my primary sources of academic input during this time. I also enrolled at Shenzou University in Amsterdam and started TCM training, and both Mieke and I began to take classes in taiji quan from some excellent Chinese teachers.

After six months of study, I felt I had the beginnings of an understanding of what we had done and together we wrote the book *Beyond Tantra: Healing through Taoist Sacred Sex* (2005). It appeared in the fall of 2005 and has received numerous favorable reviews since.

Once the book was published, we settled back into our normal lives. I ran an internet hosting company and Mieke served as financial administrator for a publisher. In many ways, our lives were the same as before, with the addition of dual cultivation and qigong practices. These practices had clear physical benefits, and we both noticed that we were stronger, healthier, and less stressed. I personally noticed that I was calmer and more relaxed, although not at first, since the effect occurred very gradually. Others did notice, however, and slowly but surely I began to realize that the *qi*-guiding and energy management practices I had been doing were starting to have a profound effect not only on my physical but also on my emotional body.

Emotional Baggage

> People are born soft and supple;
> Dead, they are stiff and hard.
> Plants are born tender and pliant;
> Dead, they are brittle and dry.
> Thus, those stiff and inflexible are disciples of death.
> Those soft and yielding are disciples of life.
> The hard and stiff will be broken.
> The soft and supple will prevail.
> —Laozi, *Daode jing*

My cultural and family backgrounds both emphasize achievement, the pursuit of excellence, and dedication to self-development. These are all worthy goals, however, in my particular case these noble aspirations were delivered together with a heavy dose of guilt, blame, non-communication, and emotional denial. As one can imagine, this is not a recipe for a relaxed, open, and gentle approach to life.

This childhood indoctrination meant that as an adult I became very good at getting things done, but my achievements tended to come with an unpleasant emotional price tag. This often has had a negative effect not only for myself, but also on others around me. I never thought to question the emotional turmoil in myself, though, because I believed that the anger, fear, and resentment I often felt were simply part of who I was.

Only when I first experienced the emotional calm that the Daoist energy practices deliver did I begin a process of self-reflection and observation as to not only *what* I did, but also *how* I did it. It became clear to me that the negative emotions I was carrying and expressing were not helpful. Instead of giving myself a hard time, as a result I practiced the Inner Smile and other qigong exercises that led me to have compassion for my process and myself.

One of the first things I realized in this process of emotional awakening was that it would be helpful if I could to learn to become more yin and less yang. I saw that instead of trying to "make things happen," I could make space for things to happen. I began to cultivate patience, openness, respect and to learn skills of supportive and "agenda-less" inquiry when interacting with others.

This was in many ways in direct opposition to what my upbringing had taught me. It did not take very long for me to notice the benefits of this softer approach to life. I soon discovered that interactions based on a gentle give-and-take were far more satisfying, nourishing, and productive than the harsh "I am right and you are wrong" kinds of behavior I was used to. In addition, most surprisingly, I discovered that indeed "soft" could be much more powerful than "hard," as Laozi already indicates.

Inner Softening

Water is fluid, soft and yielding.
However, water will wear away rock,
Which is rigid and cannot yield.
As a rule, whatever is fluid, soft and yielding
Will overcome whatever is rigid and hard.
This is another paradox:
What is soft is strong.
—Laozi

In tandem with this new-found emotional self-awareness, I noticed that a curious thing was starting to happen. People, almost always in an active intimate relationship, started to contact Mieke and myself, wanting to know if we would give workshops and/or would be available for private consultations. We were very happy to speak with these couples and to answer any questions they might have about our experiences. We never tried to give advice or guidance, though, as neither of us felt we were qualified to be teachers. However, we soon discovered that by simply being available to listen and share our experiences we were providing a valuable service and have continued to receive very positive feedback after such conversations.

After a year or so of talking to couples, I began to notice something interesting. Although we had written in detail about the Daoist practices of dual cultivation in our book, the couples who were approaching us were not, for the most part, interested in speaking to us about the actual sexual techniques or practices we used. Instead, they wanted to know more about how we managed to revive our relationship, how we found a way to start communicating again, and how we rebuilt the trust between us that had been lost over the years. They also wanted to know how we learned to focus on what was working for us rather than all the problems we had. One of the most common questions from many of them was: Did you use your study and knowledge of the Daoist practices to do this all this? Our answer was, and is, a strong and clear "yes."

Mieke and I refer to this softness and suppleness as Inner Softening. By this we mean the process of releasing stagnation and obstruction, both within the individual and within the relationship. In our experience, this softening allows a fresh, energizing, and healing flow of conscious awareness and mindful interaction to provide healing and renewal.

Releasing Rigidity

One of the primary issues we hear about from couples over and over again is that people want to be together, but that at the same time they want to preserve a sense of self-identity and individuality. Many people seem to us, indeed, to want to maintain the freedom they had while they were single while enjoying all the benefits of being in a couple. Inevitably conflict arises when one or the other, or also both, of the partners find it difficult or impossible to compromise this need for individuality in a given relationship situation.

For example, Yves and Birgit are both highly educated and outgoing. They met when they were both in the early thirties. They had both developed successful careers and lives before they met five years ago. Yves is an artist and Birgit is an economic analyst and, in many ways, they are quite different from each other. Yet these differences are exactly what they find so stimulating and they have a rich and varied life together as a result. There is one issue however that they keep running into: their decision-making styles clash. When decisions are to be made, Yves tends to rely on gut-feeling and emotional input whereas Birgit likes to consider all of the information available and work through options rationally before coming to an informed conclusion. In addition, Yves likes to talk through his feelings with Birgit, while Birgit prefers to contemplate quietly and then present her conclusions to Yves when she is ready.

In the heady days at the beginning of their relationship, these different decision-making styles were usually glossed over and, in fact, Yves often gave way to Birgit's rational decision making. As time went on, however, Yves began to feel that his input was not valued and, even worse, that Birgit often discounted his views as unimportant or irrelevant. For her part, Birgit many times felt that Yves either did not trust her competence or failed to understand how she had arrived at conclusions. When he insisted on talking about how he felt about things, she often felt criticized and unheard.

In individual discussions with the two partners, I made a few suggestions. I suggested to Birgit that she try to find a way to include Yves's emotional and intuitive input into her fact gathering process. I pointed her at some research that indicates that we filter out up to 94 percent of our sensory input and asked to her consider whether Yves's input might provide some data that cannot access personally. When speaking to Yves I encouraged him to explore ways of communicating his feelings using "I" statements (rather than sweeping generalizations) and to check with Birgit if she was ready to hear what he had to say. Above all I encouraged them both to consider sharing their observations with each other, without judgment or harshness. By softening their interaction with each other their relationship would benefit as well their decisions.

In essence, I was sharing my understanding that none of us can really know the whole truth. All we can do is use the best of our (combined) abilities to navigate life based on the tools we have available. In doing so, I went back to Laozi who admonishes us to let go of all forms of rigidity, one of the primary causes of relationship difficulties that so many couples are experiencing. This includes rigid ideas as to who we are, rigid concepts of what the relationship should be, and social strictures to conform to rigid relationship roles. All these create stress and strain. It is, therefore, no wonder that so many relationships struggle and even end in divorce—as the current statistics demonstrate all too well.

The traditional family roles of the mother as carer and nurturer and the father as provider have been breaking down for several decades at this point. Yet the desire and craving for intimacy and family are as strong as ever. What we have seen is that there is a need for a different worldview or paradigm to help people find a balance between the desire to be in a relationship and the need to maintain a sense of independence and self.

This is where the Daoist concept of releasing rigidity becomes crucial. What we have seen is that happy, contented and relaxed people have less of the rigid "I should" in their lives and instead make decisions based on the informed choice of "I want." This leads, in turn, to healthy and more sustainable relationships. After all, a couple that chooses to be together is bound to be happier than one that is together out of coercion, whether religious, moral or financial.

We have also discovered that gently introducing this paradigm of gentle, subtle, and gradual development in a phased manner seems to work best and that the results can be far-reaching. Let me outline, then, the phases we often propose.

Phase One — Re-discovering Oneself

> At the center of your being you have the answer:
> You know who you are and what you want.
> — Laozi

The first thing many people say when they come in for consultation is that, after many years of being in a relationship, they have lost touch with their own center. They no longer know exactly who they are and what constitutes their core values. Many times, they say: "I know what I don't want, but I'm not sure what I do want."

So how does one know what one wants? Interestingly, many Western Daoist commentators speak of the difference between what is called "the head brain," sometimes also described as the monkey mind, and the "belly brain," sometimes referred to as intuition or gut feelings. No matter what we call it, almost everyone has experienced a strong hunch, the sense of just knowing that the belly brain provides.

Getting in touch with this belly brain is thus often a good place to start when trying to regain a sense of self. There are many Daoist practices we suggest for helping with the process of developing a greater inner awareness: meditation, taiji quan, qigong, and/or self-reflection. All these help people to reconnect to their own sense of centeredness and to learn to pay attention to what their belly brain says.

Phase Two — Practicing Self-acceptance

> When you accept yourself, the whole world accepts you.
> —Laozi

The second step of self-discovery is learning to accept who one is. We have seen that people who can simply say "I am who I am" stand a much better chance of taking the conscious steps they need to move forward and change. A positive sense of self-worth is not about ego, but about a deep sense of inner peace, a centering from which true power can emanate.

When your partner also accepts that "you are who you are," this can be a powerful support in the process of learning to respect each other. We encourage people to tell their partner whenever they realize just how much they love and appreciate him or her, to tell them that "I love you just the way you are." This attitude and behavior is, for us, a direct practical expression of the Daoist value of deep respect for self and others.

This process of self-acceptance can at times be difficult and lead to a process when parts of oneself, previously suppressed or ignored, suddenly thrust into the forefront of consciousness. This is especially true in a relationship where individual needs and desires in the realms of sexuality, self-fulfillment, and power-balance may have suffered suppression for some time to serve the so-called good of the relationship or simply to keep the peace.

Before tackling these topics with one's partner, however, it is crucial to find out who and what our needs are as individuals. Only then can we communicate with our partner from a place of authenticity and strength.

Phase Three — Developing Gentleness

> The soft overcomes the hard;
> the gentle overcomes the rigid.
> Everyone knows this is true,
> but few can put it into practice.
> —Laozi

When observing couples I am sometimes amazed at how two people who, in theory at least, profess to love each other can in their concrete interactive behavior be so harsh and unyielding. I do not believe that most people actually want to be harsh with each other. It is simply that over time we may become less sensitive to how our words and actions affect others—and especially those near and dear.

In fact, many of the couples that come to talk to us are amazed when they see a video recording of themselves. They had no idea just how rude and unfeeling they were when speaking to their partner and were shocked at how harsh they sounded. One way to learn healthy verbal interaction patterns, then, is to rephrase statements to avoid any form of blame or attack. It is best to concentrate on simply stating our own positions, gently and clearly.

We often use taiji push-hands practice as a way to demonstrate that sensitivity and awareness are just as much strength as straightforwardness and goodwill. When people learn to interact in gentle, graceful, and thoughtful ways—verbally, emotionally, and physically—there is much more room for building trust and rapport.

Phase Four — Eliminating Emotional Toxins

Almost all couples over time create unhealthy patterns of interaction that generate anger, fear, worry, and general upset. These negative emotions in turn create so-called toxins that are stored in our physical and emotional bodies. Indeed, the accumulation of these toxins often brings the relationship to a breaking point when one, or both simply can no longer stand it.

Western marriage counselors and therapists tend to focus on these negative interaction patterns, hoping to create awareness and develop strategies for change. The Daoist approach is radically different. It focuses on increasing the flow of positive *qi* or vital energy in the relationship. This roots in the understanding that, if there is enough positive *qi*, the negative, obstructed *qi* is gradually released and disappears.

In actual practice, this means helping couples to focus on what is right in their relationship and to encourage them to find ways to spend more time doing what works. Although this may sound altogether quite simple, it is actually quite hard: it requires mindfulness, clear agreement, and trust from both partners. For them it is all too easy to fall back into the bad habits of old. Learning how to give gentle, loving encouragement to move forward is often a serious challenge.

This approach to relationship healing is something Roger Jahnke states concisely in his Mind Focus Affirmation: "Purifying *qi*, I restore inner harmony by cleansing and dispelling spent, toxic, and unneeded *qi*, and by opening to the inflow of fresh, natural life force and power" (2002).

Phase Five — Making Room for Spontaneity

> Dao is unpredictable to those that live according to plans.
> Only those who have no agenda are in harmony with Dao.
> —Laozi

Possibly the most profound change we see in the couples who come to us for consultation occurs when they move out of what we call scripted relationships. By this we mean relationships that are built on preset roles, expectations, and rigidity often based on social and family traditions. When couples transform their interactions into unscripted relationships, they begin to see their partner with new eyes and wonderful, creative things happen.

Thus, when I first met Johan and Christina I was struck immediately by the way they kept finishing each other's sentences. It was as if they had said the same things so many times that they each knew what the other would say. It also seemed to me that they somehow needed to control each other to ensure that what the other person said what was "right." It was almost as if they had rehearsed a play and were using me as an audience. Above all, I found it difficult to know what each of them as an individual felt and thought. It was as if I was talking to a "couple" rather than two individuals.

The amusing thing about this was that both Johan and Christina had told me in separate, private conversations that they were feeling stuck and trapped in their relationships and were wondering if it would survive. They both felt there was no room for growth. Yet when I saw how they acted, it became clear that they created few opportunities for spontaneous, unscripted behavior with each other. I thought about trying to explain what I was observing but could not quite figure out how to do this without making them both fell either self-conscious and/or criticized. Instead, I tried an experiment. When one of them started to speak, I gave that person my full attention. When the other partner jumped in to complete a sentence I simply ignored them and kept my attention focused on the first person, waiting for them to complete their sentence.

At first, they were confused, but very quickly got the hang of it. Soon they could do it themselves and when the other person interjected something, they simply waited until he or she had finished, and then picked up at the point of interruption. Often what they then said was quite different from the completion that their partner supplied. They soon discovered that it was much better to simply listen to each other rather then try to "complete the script." As their communication skills improved, so did their individual sense of freedom and space to change and evolve.

Their experience is just one instance of how every human being is constantly growing and changing. This means that relationships also keep changing and, ideally, continue to adapt over time. I believe a healthy response to the complaint "You are not the same person I married!" is "Of course, I'm not—and neither are you!" The fact, moreover, that the only constant on the planet is change does not need to be a problem but can be an excellent opportunity to grow and develop both personally and in the relationship. In other words, when individuals begin to take responsibility for their own development, they can create new and often healthier ways of interacting with each other. These interactions, then, are based on inter-dependence instead of co-dependence.

Key tools that we introduce to people during this phase are developing awareness of their own *qi*-energy and learning how to observe the effect of their interactions with their partner on their own energetic levels. We ask them questions such as these: "How did you feel after that last conversation? Were you drained and tired or full of energy and enlivened?" This kind of query can help people to learn to observe how the choices they make in every moment can have a profound effect on the health of their relationship. This same awareness can also allow them to respond to each in the here and now rather than simply reacting based on old patterns and prehistory. Many people we speak to discover that, as they learn to become more fully present both as individuals and in their relationships, they can respond, adapt, and grow as required. They start to change their relationship from a quagmire of stagnation and blockage into an exciting venue for exploration and the free flow of energy.

Phase Six — Understanding Relationship Stress

Over the ages, Daoist practitioners and adherents have had a—sometimes no-torious—reputation of free thinking and openness to new concepts and ideas. It is therefore not surprising that Daoist practices regarding relationships and intimacy are not always conventional. For instance, the idea that sexual energy used consciously and wisely, can be a powerful source of healing is not some-thing that Western religious traditions recognize. In fact, just the opposite is true: Western traditions have tended to regard sex as dirty and evil, making it a source of shame and guilt. The increasing Western access to the rich body of Daoist knowledge in this area has proven for many (ourselves included) a pow-erful antidote to the rigid paradigm of hostility to sex.

Over the years, we have seen many couples derive great benefit from re-leasing rigidity and focusing attention on increased *qi*-flow in their relationship. But what happens when one starts to release rigidity in the relationship? After all, so much of what we think is true or right is simply what we have learned from family and society and consequently feel comfortable with. It does not follow, however, that a particular relationship form is what is best for oneself simply because "everyone does it."

Many couples we talk to are re-examining the form of their relationship, sometimes even going as far considering whether they should stay in a relation-ship at all. A very common issue they are grappling with is one of trust, and specifically broken trust. In fact one of the main causes of modern relationship breakdown is the appearance of a third party in the equation, often unknown to the other partner, and the subsequent breakdown of trust that results when the partner learns about the intrusion.

Listened to countless stories and struggles, I have come to wonder what light, if anything, the Daoist tradition can shed on this problem. Most Daoist texts on relationships and sexual practices are limited to a male-centered view and often speak of sex as a battle for high-powered essential energy (*jingqi*) and of women as the enemy. They often warn, in no uncertain terms, of the dan-gers of forming a romantic attachment with a member of the opposite sex.

I personally have found little in these materials to help in building trusting, loving communication and emotionally mature interaction between the sexes. The only glimmer of hope was a reference to the fact that women need to feel loved and respected in order to produce the best quality energy, but this felt more like the means to an end.

Having said this, are there examples of relaxed, equal, and harmonious relationships in traditional cultures? I started reading about the Na people, known as the Mosou to the Chinese, who live around the beautiful Lake Lugu in the foothills of the Himalayas. They are a matrilineal society where the mother is held in great regard. The Na favor a system of visiting marriages where the men leave their homes to visit the homes of their partner(s). Traditionally both men and women have multiple partners.

Interestingly enough, there is no word for "jealousy" (or for that matter, "rape") in the Na language. Relationships are based on mutual affection. When one or both of the partners lose interest, the relationship ends gracefully. One American scholar who recently visited the Na noted they "undeniably preserve a gentler culture than our own. Suicide is rare and murder unheard of."

I found it fascinating that a society where women (and men) are free to have multiple partners without shame or approbation turns out to sustain kindlier, gentler people and friendlier relationships. As a result, I began to wonder if jealousy and fear are not a kind of poison that makes it difficult to sustain a healthy relationship. Mieke and I had grappled with this problem ourselves and found that learning to relax and be more open and trusting when it came to having other close friends made a huge difference to the quality of our own relationship.

So what can we learn from the Na? Well, maybe that the prevailing paradigm of "the one and only person who will meet all of my needs and will love me forever" may not be sustainable or even particularly realistic. Even worse, this fairy-tale view, and the subsequent impossibility to realize it in our actual lives, becomes the source of a great deal of the unhappiness we experience in our relationships.

Phase Seven — Biology, Sociology, and Informed Choice

> The truth often sounds paradoxical.
> —Laozi

When couples are under the influence of the bio-chemical rush created by falling in love, they often feel that they have found "the One." This attraction, love, and bonding process is well known, and Daoists were well aware of this hormonally induced process and its powerful effects on mind, body, and life of the individual. The reality is of course that sooner or later, the bio-chemicals leave our system—anywhere from two to seven years after the first rush—and we often feel stuck, no longer inspired or excited by our partner. The infamous seven-year itch is a result of this perfectly normal process. Another common scenario is the empty nest syndrome, which happens when the children have moved out and one of the partners, very often a women in her forties or fifties, decides that she wants to move forward and do new things with her life.

Many people end up feeling trapped in a relationship with no easy way forward or out. On the one hand, they want to develop themselves and explore new opportunities and challenges; on the other hand, there is a strong sense of loyalty, respect, and love for the present partner. So, what are the alternatives?

There are a few options for those willing to think outside the box and challenge social norms. Traditional monogamy, as we have seen from the Na, may not be the only form a relationship can take. Many couples are now exploring consenting non-monogamy and other combinations that make room for more than one loving relationship.

However, form is not all that important when it comes to creating a successful long-term relationship. The key is informed choice. When people feel free to make choices in their life, rather than be forced or trapped in a rigid situation, creativity and *qi*-flow. Monogamy, polyamory, serial monogamy, heterosexuality, homosexuality, or any other sexual orientation and/or relationship form are not the deciding factor in successful relationships. Instead it is the willingness and courage to be open, honest and non-rigid that lays the groundwork for creative partnerships.

Life is a series of natural and spontaneous changes. Do not resist them—that only creates sorrow. Let reality be reality. Let things flow naturally forward in whatever way they like.

Phase Eight — New Relationship Forms

When Daoist sexual yoga first came to be known in the West in the late 1980s many people found them strange and even shocking. Tales of Empress Wu and her 300 male consorts, male ejaculation control practiced with multiple partners and lavishly illustrated "pillow books" all described a view of sexuality that was radically different than the repressed Judeo-Christian we have in the West. Together with a newly discovered interested in Tantra—or at the very least "neo-tantra"—the Daoist sexual practices have become part of a general exploration of alternatives to our existing sexually repressed society. Especially for women this has been an opportunity to explore ways to fully embrace their sexuality and no longer cater for a male-defined sexual ethos. The concept of sacred sexuality as practiced between two informed, consenting adults has been a powerful agent for positive change and renewal for many couples over the last two decades.

As many people, especially women, re-evaluate their sexual practices, they also begin to consider their overall relationship choices and models. They are not alone in this. The anthropologist Helen Fisher, author of *Why We Love: The Nature and Chemistry of Romantic Love*, has identified two major trends that are driving change in relationships: the increasing independence of women, and the fact that people are living much longer. More and more women, especially those in Europe and North America, are discovering that they are no longer dependent on men for their economic security. At the same time, many women are reexamining their lives. They are discovering that defining themselves purely as mother-caregiver or with a career title is far too limiting.

So what are the options available to women and men who find that their prince (or princess) has fallen off of his or her white horse and that he or she is of course all too human? Abandoning ones current partner to look for a new fairy-tale is one option. This (often expensive) option is sometimes called "serial monogamy."

However, this ultimately is a "lose-lose" scenario as increasing numbers of split families, unhappy divorces and financial nightmares bear testament to. It is also rather sad, not to say inefficient, to discard all that one has built up with someone simply because a new, exciting person has arrived on the scene.

Another option is to stop believing in fairy-tales. Although this may take some courage to admit the reality is that out of 7+ billion on the planet there is not just one soul mate for each of us. There are lots and many people with whom we can enjoy healthy, enriching, and satisfying relationships. It can be helpful when considering this to remember that marriage, as an institution, historically was not based on love, romance, or even lust.

Marriage was primarily a construction designed to ensure that families, clans and tribes could make beneficial alliances that would create strong economic ties and/or political connections. Women were not necessarily expected to love their husbands, and vice versa. How about people's sexual needs? They were satisfied elsewhere once the requisite children had been produced. Of course, men often had far greater rights than women when it came to sexual choices. The Daoist manuscripts indicate that ancient Chinese culture was no different from European in this regard.

It is only fairly recently that we have started to believe that romantic love and sexual passion should both be satisfied by the same person. The idea that intimate love should be expressed only within the confines of a monogamous relationship has become the status quo. Yet more and more people are beginning to question the validity of this received wisdom. Polyamorous (from the Greek world *poly*, meaning "many" or "several," and the Latin *amor* for "love") relationships challenge these relatively new traditions by accepting as normal the practice of both men and women seeking intellectual, emotional and sexual variety in their lives while maintaining the strong bond of love between primary partners. It is mostly used to refer to the practice of having more than one intimate relationship at a time with the full knowledge and consent of everyone involved. The relationships can be sexual or non-sexual but by definition are always based on a loving connection between the partners. Sex-only relationships are, in most people's definition, not expressions of polyamory.

In many ways, people who are practicing a polyamorous lifestyle are simply acknowledging that some of our ancestors knew more than we sometimes give them credit for when it comes to love. The difference is that the majority of modern polyamorous relationships are practicing polyamory in ways that allow women, as well as men, the freedom to enrich their lives by extending their expressions of love.

One can never be sure but I suspect that the ancient Daoists would have enjoyed the learning, growing and challenges that polyamorous relationships offer. Learning to deal constructively with jealousy, developing healthy communication skills and taking full personal responsibility for all of one's relationships are surely skills worth honing. Even those whose choose to maintain a monogamous relationship may have something to learn from these relationship anarchists as Swedish polyamory practitioners sometimes call themselves.

Conclusion

We live in challenging times of massive global change. Our relationships are not immune from the stresses and strains that we are experiencing as much as nations and the planet at large. I believe that the ancient Daoist arts and the wisdom of Dao have a profound role to play in offering tools and techniques to anyone who wishes to create more resilient, healthy, and enjoyable personal relationships.

Bibliography

Chia, Mantak, and Maneewan Chia. 1986. *Healing Love: Cultivating Female Sexual Energy.* Huntington, NY: Healing Tao Books.

Jahnke, Roger. 2002. *The Healing Promise of Qi: Creating Extraordinary Wellness Through Qigong and Tai Chi.* New York: Contemporary Books.

Linssen, Leonie, and Stephan Wik. 2010. *Love Unlimited: The Joys and Challenges of Open Relationships.* Forres, Scotland: Findhorn Press.

Wik, Mieke, and Stephan Wik. 2005. *Beyond Tantra: Healing through Taoist Sacred Sex.* Forres, Scotland: Findhorn Press.

Re-sourcive Pedagogy

Teaching and Education as Vital Energy Flow

JOHANNES GASSER

Daoist thinking and practice provide a potent source for a new, re-sourcive form of pedagogy, which works with the principle of nonaction and joins the cosmic flow, the subtle underground, the infinite stream of vitality. In practice, it encompasses courtesy and smart approaches to action, preventing interaction from becoming harsh and managing relationships and education in a harmonious and positive way. This flow has its own language: that of whispering, which enables people to influence others and their actions. This is very helpful in operational leadership, in relationships, in pedagogy and in self-formation. To show the contrast, in a model interaction the father practices the language of "hard facts" toward his son, activating a spiral of escalating opposition. The mother, on the other hand, works with subtle flow, reconnecting to the source and thus creating a beneficial spiral of mutual conduciveness.

My journey to the practice of working with energy flow in education—to "Dao whispering"—proceeded quietly, step by step. My first contact occurred during my philosophy studies at Fribourg University in Switzerland (1963-1969). There I attended a series of lectures on Eastern philosophy, based on my conviction that all thinking processes are relevant for proficient philosophical thinking. After completing my dissertation on negation in Thomas Aquinas in 1969, I started to present the *Daode jing* at a local adult education center, fascinated by its message.

In hindsight I find I had earlier contact with the secret of Dao in my life: growing up with parents who were sculptors gave me the chance from my birth in 1943 to experience the ultimate foundation for becoming a sovereign, authentic self: unconditional security. Experiencing this unreserved emotional security made it easier for me to understand what the authentic reality of life is and what the power of gentleness can do—just as Dao promises.

234

My inner path to this dimension continued over twenty-two years of intensive study of the philosophical topic "Ur und Man" (the primeval and the people) in the Heideggerian sense of "people" understood as the "average" (Heidegger 1963), that means the anonymous authority inside the person. The "Ur" describes the quintessence of that primeval so-being which makes up originality, primitiveness, authenticity, and genuineness. Using the term "primeval source" to translate this rather deep German term, I find that it lives in humans, but cannot be controlled by them. I wrote my advanced academic thesis, the basis for becoming a university lecturer, about this topic. However, it was so far from the mainstream that no second reader could be found and it did not pass. My second thesis on "Negation and Awareness" was approved in 1990. It is now clear that my intense focus on the primeval source, the "Ur," had strengthened my inner affinity to Dao.

Since I cannot read the original Chinese of the text, I found a different way to access the *Daode jing*, assuming that it reflects the author's first-hand experiences, articulated in the ancient language, the language of Dao. My observations are also based on first-hand experiences in my own life and on my interactions with others, working with softness and placidity, with force and power. The basis of these experiences I have formulated in terms of primeval potency.

My preoccupation with this notion of deep, imbued original potency also meant tracking down everything that had something to say on primitiveness, original resources, primal beginnings, being beyond being, and transcendental realities. My experiences and research accordingly deal with what earlier thinkers have described in terms of "the source of vitality," "emptiness," "creative nothingness," "creativity," "the One and the many," "evolutionary power" and *élan vital* (see Bergson 1944). The original source I also call "primeval resource" or "ex-source," terms that led me to coin the expression "re-sourcive" for my flowing, dynamic pedagogy and philosophy. A very helpful discovery was Mihalyi Csikszentmihalyi's work *Beyond Boredom and Anxiety: Experiencing flow in Work and Play* (1975). It has made the term "flow" acceptable in a psychological sense.

I was also much concerned with personal, individual identity. Who am I? Is it I who thinks and lives? Or does something else, maybe transcendent, think and live within me? The Western concept of identity is so strongly bound to subjectivity and self-control that it masks the secret of the name. Yet it is not subjectivity that constitutes the essence or deep existence of a person; rather, it is the secret hidden behind every proper name.

But how can it be argued that primeval source and flow have the same or similar meaning as Dao and virtue or inherent potency (*de*)? First, the similarity in description makes similar experiences plausible. Also, there are homologies between the two, i.e., relationships based on the same structural logic. That is to say, primeval source, flow, myself acting in relation to people, and the pair power and powerlessness relate to each other much in the same way as Dao, inherent potency, most people, and the pair activity and serenity do (see *Daode jing* 20). Third, the practice of nonaction (*wuwei*) strongly applies in pedagogy, where it is not at all like "doing nothing" or "not doing anything." Rather, it means an efficient form of passivity, which works beyond the will. Fourth, connecting Dao and flow allows the expansion or critical scrutiny of the Western practice and philosophy of the primeval flow, on which the *Daode jing* has much to contribute.

In 1987, I began teaching courses on communication in difficult situations. "Criticizing without hurting," for example, requires a unique and lively language. This in turn led me into pedagogy. In 1992, I first trained a teacher at a Swiss secondary school in my newly developed practice. In 1997, I founded the Re-sourcive Energetic School; in 2004, the Gasserschule, whose director I remained until 2010.

Doing so, I personally experienced how every tutoring or coaching activity is linked to vital powers: motivation, opposition, incomprehension, blindness, crises, and difficult family backgrounds, as well as to desire, enthusiasm, fascination, being moved, and experiencing success. The difficult part is not the general policy of teaching and education, but rather coping with a multitude of details in teaching and learning, in supervising and practicing, in memorizing as well as discipline, cooperation and in actions for effective assimilation.

The problem is not the principle but the detail of daily routine and triviality. Therefore, the central question is always: "How can I bring the momentum of the primal vitality into the ten thousand little things of everyday life?" (*Daode jing* 1). It is particularly difficult for a child or adolescent whose first 77,777 hours or nine years of life at home gave him a deficient or lacking "sense of security" or even the experience of being excluded.

In cohesion with courses for parents in flow communication and within the framework of various coaching activities, I gradually and over many years developed a coherent system of theories, methods, and practices. This made it possible to make the potential of the Dao and its inherent potency applicable in the concrete everyday routine of education, leadership and communication. This is the center piece of re-sourcive pedagogy.

The re-sourcive unification of the Dao and everyday triviality, of Eastern wisdom and Western practice, are a step toward breaking into the new age of vastness. Here consciousness and heart create life in a way that is more essential than feasibility oriented toward material possessions and goods. The potential of nonaction as well as the flow of canny powerlessness bring about a stronger evolution than force and power.

What is Pedagogy?

Pedagogy happens when one person influences another to make the latter do what the former thinks he should do. Pedagogy means that a leader (teacher, parent, conductor) makes a learner (child, pupil, student, citizen, musician) follow his beat and act in the way he wants him to. In other words, the basic question in pedagogy is: "How can I make someone do what I want him to do?"

In this broad sense, all public speeches, laws, and regulations are pedagogic interventions. Even wars are a form of military pedagogy: someone uses means of destruction or punishment to make someone else, an opponent, do what he wants. In a more narrow sense, pedagogy is the way people are influencing other people's behavior, their formal education, the way they fit into a social network, the manner in which they actively build their social context as well as their inner world. It always intends to make someone adapt to or reproduce a certain behavior—called educating him for the right and good.

All forms of pedagogy have "military intelligence" (see Virilio 1997) in common. This appears as punishment, relentless demands, enforced conditions, or strict order. It does not work, as the commonality of delinquency and educative failure in modern societies documents. Just giving freedom without managing energy is not acceptable either as has been shown in the various experiments with the anti-authoritarian approach. Instead, re-sourcive pedagogy shows that it is essential to refrain from violent and belligerent forms of leadership as much as from complete openness and freedom. Matching Daoist principles of nonaction, flow, and softness, the key is to practice a re-sourcing, supportive and efficient gentleness that brings vital energy and consciousness together. We call this re-sourcive intelligence.

Traditional pedagogy educates. Education—from the Latin *e-ducere*, which means "to bring out," "lead to"—means to bring the learning person to a point the teacher has pre-defined. In that way education builds on something that lies in the past. The learner is meant to define himself by taking in existing knowledge, by learning from and about other people's experiences.

In re-sourcive pedagogy this is not enough any more. The future lies not in merely adapting to society, learning existing methods or defining oneself in preset patterns. There is much more to do. What education should really be about is to get the full effect of the vitality inherent in everything, whether it is at the outset defined, undefined, or to be defined. Repressive energy resting in power and forced constraints has to be replaced by original and supportive forms of flowing zest for live—realization of individual *qi* in perfect adaptation to the world. The task is to change power into flow, dependency into transforming tasks, and limitations into playful boundaries. The re-sourcive intent is to create more liveliness and evolution in the form of personal development, unfolding, and innovation. It also leads to sustainability beyond education, to control beyond right and wrong. The basic question in re-sourcive pedagogy is "How can I make someone want and do what is appropriate for both him and myself?"

In the old days, the end of childhood meant the end of pedagogic influence. Today innovative forms of life and personality management have led to life-long learning, continuous training, and constant adaptation to an ever changing society. This is why in the future it will not be enough to talk of pedagogy, literally educating a child—from the Greek *pais*, "child," and *agein*, "to lead"—but of andragogy, the coaching of humans—using the Greek *aner*, "man" or "human being." In other words, we are dealing with the guided development of human beings in general.

Traditional or classical pedagogy is about setting clear objectives. It focuses on content and aims at changing behavior. The teacher is the key authority and the leading expert; he or she defines a proven path for students to take. The source issue is for them to obey under various concrete conditions ("You can't always do what you want—that's life!"), to reproduce knowledge, values, and behaviors. The forms of energy involved are: firmness, constraint, and adaptation. Independence is defined as the independent reproduction of knowledge, thinking, and doing.

This pedagogy makes sense in closed systems with clearly defined ethical values and under authoritarian, hierarchically structured leadership. It worked in the past when societies were homogeneous and had shared value systems. In modern societies, with their multifaceted cultures and complex social patterns, it does not work any longer.

There have been various similar approaches to resolve the dilemma of education in the modern world. For example, humanistic pedagogy changed the focus from the learning material and goal performance to the person. Thus Maria Montessori places the child's individuality in the center of her approach. She never compares children, but believes that a child develops best when given space and offered attractive learning material that matches his or her developmental stage and can be handled with ease (Montessori 1912).

Also, Rudolph Steiner's "Waldorf Education" builds on the principle of human harmony. He uses the fine arts for their integrating and balancing effects, to better synchronize emotional impulses. Because music, colors, and poetry affect the child in a holistic way, all other areas benefit from this focus (Steiner 1992; Carlgren 2005). Alexander S. Neill is another pioneer in this field. Reinforcing humanistic thinking, he requests his students not only to develop independently but also to create their own forms of living as well as their social environment. Skipping all pre-designed systems, he asks them to invent or define rules and forms of social existence (Neill and Lamb 1995; Summerhill 1970; Weidle 1982).

Humanistic pedagogy makes sense in open systems, in individualistic societies and biospheres, where people act with conscience. It works in the modern world, enlightening and liberating the spirit from its preset limits. On the other hand, re-sourcive pedagogy does not define and establish what is right. Rather, it causes constant flow and vitality. This is its major difference as compared to traditional pedagogy where fixed values such as respect, authority, necessities are fundamental and learning the right behaviors and reproducing the learning subjects in a correct way are the major objectives.

Adaptation is not the ultimate goal but a helpful side effect. The ultimate goal is to develop the genius evolution that lies in everybody. This includes to adapt to material, behavior and social bounds in a playful way. On the other hand, "ex-aptation" is of the same importance. This is the development—as described in the evolutionary theory of skills not yet used at this point. Nature provided brain structure over half a million years ago, long before humans first used them to speak or build tools. It is also ex-aptation when a skill or personality trait produces an unexpected, unplanned result: instead of having the essay written on it, the sheet of paper transforms into a paper plane.

Developed learning tries to exploit the unlimited opportunities that material and facilities are holding. Instead of prohibiting certain behaviors ("the chair is for sitting, the school is for learning"), re-sourcive pedagogy encourages to try other functions (the chair can transform in multiple ways, school is an ideal place for testing protest, its possibilities and limits). Writing, for instance, is not only there for writing but also for hiding (secret writing), to invent new forms of language and to prove the cultural achievement that humans made when developing word from thought and writing from word. Writing in this sense is able to invent itself and be rediscovered (see Brügelmann 1998).

The Source Concept: Vitality

To calculate the cost of vitality, we are taking the amount and quality of its energy into account, of pleasure and courage that can be disturbed, destroyed, or increased as profit. Re-sourcive pedagogy explicitly considers vitality, human energies, and the cost of vitality as central questions. How so? Classically it is the student who pays the vital costs of adaptation and self-development. He "must," he has to make every effort, facing sanctions and punishment. The burden of development and the fueling energy ("Go and do it! Be strong! Pull yourself together!") as well as all related costs (anxiety, shame, and blockage) are centrally placed on the learning person.

Like other traditions, re-sourcive pedagogy requests the learner to develop in self and learning, but "vitality" is available as a re-source to deliver the necessary energy. Through that, effort will be replaced by the lightness of swing or flow. To start this is the job of the teacher. Because vitality—a lavish prime resource—is not scarce, there are no costs. There will be unlimited energy available and even additional profits to be found: awareness, courtesy, and innovation. This approach keeps pleasure alive: pleasure to learn (for the student) and pleasure to teach (for the teacher).

Two advantages are obvious: first, there is no burn-out, a vital energetic phenomenon. Second, there is no need for motivation. Eduard Sprenger's *Mythos of Motivation* (2010) stated this in the context of managing companies: motivating people is necessary only where the pleasure to work has gone.

Re-sourcive pedagogy suggests that humans finally free themselves from vital immaturity. Humanism released reason; it is now asked to release itself from dominance. Re-sourcive pedagogy states that eliminating authority, power, and pressure are helpful preliminary stages to avoid creativity being blocked. When the individual follows the call of her needs ("I want . . . !"), her limitations ("I don't like this now! I don't need this! I don't want this!"), her traumas ("I don't like math, the teacher is so mean to me!"), or her revealing of life's deceptions ("What I loved before is getting nasty now!"), she is deliberated from external dominance but not free from being dominated by her own wishes and personality. She is free but only in the limits of her own history and personal will. Free toward the outside world, she is still stuck inside in her personal drama. Instead, she should profit from this vital intensity. In other words, she is free to live as herself and within her limitations, but not free to feed on the vitality she houses in her depth.

It is time to activate and make use of those forms of human energy, which are nourished by the stream of vitality. These energies are constantly circulating in the child, in his genes, his thinking, his soul, and his desires: longing for authenticity, loyalty, and imagination, and tenderness, interaction of body, soul, and mind. Re-sourcive pedagogy makes sense in global works of flow beyond fixed systems, in societies where people are considered to be a part of nature, of life, and of cybernetic systems—integrating resources, goods, and consumption.

This is perfect for individuals and groups who want to go beyond themselves who are no longer satisfied with themselves but want to fulfill their ingenuity and fully experience their vitality. It is the right approach for people who want to break free from their exclusive ego-identity, longing to become more than themselves: people who want to support their (w)holy evolution actively.

Re-sourcive Support Beyond Strength

Every child has his own personality and will. If we leave his will with him, it will find his way. That is enough to master the present; it is not enough to master the future. The goal is not only to find his own way but also to find the way to his hidden, internal, sleeping ingenuity. Re-sourciveness means to make a stand, so that the vital genius can make a stand. A person who wants to learn facts and behaviors follows an objective logic. One who wants to follow her or his own path follows a personal, subjective logic. Those who want to open the path of vital ingenuity in an adequate way follow the logic of vitality—a logic fundamentally different from that of objectivity or subjectivity.

That is to say, first, vitality has its own laws, different from those of the psyche or personality, a courtesy that lies beyond emotion or objectivity. Second, the will and the inherent developmental drive of the psyche are forms of vitality. There are other forms that the child should have the right to explore: security, self-evidence, dedication, and exchange on all levels.

Third, it is not the person who is thinking, but the mind. Emotion may say: "I thought I will do homework this afternoon." But ingenuity and vitality say: "It is not the person who thinks, but the ingenious mind." One of the ways in which the teacher can actively support this ingenious, vital something—and not just let it do what it does anyway—is by forming an alliance with its ingenuity. It is not enough to be "just" a specialist, it is not enough to be "just" a good, satisfied, and capable person. In addition, teacher and learner have to actively connect and hold the circle of their respective ingenuities. This installs a sense of humble genuineness beyond will and imagination.

Fourth, mechanisms are needed that make flow possible. Internal states of mind and external situations (material, environment) can be helpful (see Csikszentmihalyi 1975). The key to this, however, are not the concrete facts but first of all the state of vitality and, second, the person's fluidity. Is the person able to refrain from prejudice and expectations? Is he or she able to give up control and reach a state of mind beyond indifference and distance, a state of dedication and presence?

As children of the new age (crystalline, highly sensitive children) come to enter our school system, it is not the children that have to change but the adults. "Goodwill" should result in demanding less obedience or adaptation while giving more support. Not only what we do has an effect on others, but also what we are—beyond talk, action, and body language. The way in which the teacher opens the door to the classroom changes the vital field of all the students. If he takes a firm and solid stance in the room and has no fear, the field of exchange and naturalness changes. But if he is afraid of something or someone, this results in a provocation of that particular something or someone.

Even before we send out any stimulus, we affect our environment by sending out fields of vitality and energy. Martha Rogers first introduced the principle of human energy in nursing (1970). She considered the human being as unitary. Other explanations of human energy fields appear in Sheldrake's essays on morphogenetic fields and in John Ocean's Hawai'ian studies on paranormal exchange between humans and dolphins.

Helping students to unfold is not enough. We should win them over beyond praise and personal intention by talking "the language of the heart." Monty Roberts (1996) does this when taming horses in thirty minutes instead of three weeks. This is the horse whisperer's art. In the same way, Martin Gray (2006) had been winning Warsaw crooks over to help him against the Nazis in the Warsaw ghetto—not by violence, control, or ordering them about, but by cunning courtesy: affection and two bottles of single-malt in place of fear.

Wolfgang Hehring, the elephant whisperer of the zoo in the German town of Krefeld, too, practices winning over. He points out that his art results from hard work and great respect of the mighty animals. To break the elephants' will, he notes, the traditional way of elephant trainers or mahouts, not only shows a lack of dignity but is in fact dangerous. "These oppressed animals are turning into ticking bombs that may explode at any time" (Gasser 2005, 71).

The People Whisperer

A re-sourcive pedagogue is a people whisperer. His authority is not one of directivity or like that of a pack leader, but a sort of naturalness that does not place oneself above others. The horse or elephant whisperer learns the animal's language—*equus* according to Monty Roberts.

The people whisperer has to be able to whisper in a dozen of languages: words, thoughts, emotions, humor, playing with boundaries, and most of all ingenuity and flowing energy. Following this languages are mottos such as "turning threats into invitations," "stop having to," or "say a lot with few words." The language of truth is very simple: not what you think or intend matters, but what your heart favors: "Just say what is favorable." Whoever doesn't speak the language of vital energy, or insists on his will and values, can never work as an educational whisperer: his attitude and will are going to stand in his way. Even if he is using the right words—"I like you, I am on your side, tell me what you need"—they lack sincerity and block the flow of vital energy.

There are three major perspectives of the world: functionality, humanity, and vitality. The functional perspective judges the learning person according to his actions and his or her behavior: "You are a good person when you are doing a good job." The humanistic perspective deals with activating the learner's emotions, supporting his development and his strength, and enabling him to enter exchanges in a mature way: "Accept who and what you are. Show empathy. Let the other be what he is."

The re-sourcive perspective does not aim at doing or having anything nor does it want to be or have anything (see Fromm 1996). Rather it focuses on what is dormant in all of us, what wants to grow taller and reach beyond ourselves. In popular terms, it is all about waking the vital ingenuity of the heart, to bring to life all that we are not, all that takes us beyond ourselves. It may be called the "sense of transcendence" or the "eternal secret." However, the language is always the one of the origin of vitality, i.e., pure energy. "You must not" is a ban, expressed in the language of force. "I want" is technically speaking a form of military thinking. "No!" and other forms of banning are police-type energy forms. "You've been good/bad" reflect the judicial approach. Only words that give meaning are re-sourcive: the speech of gentleness supports the longing!

Foolishness cannot be healed with foolishness, but only with cleverness, even though—or rather because—foolishness and cleverness are irreconcilable. "The most foolish woman is capable of twisting a man around her little finger. But in order to deal with a fool correctly, you need a very clever woman" (Maurois in Ronner 1974, 85). Analogous to this, re-sourcive thinking says: Death cannot be healed with death or the repression of death, but only with life. It sounds paradoxical, but death, far from being the end of life, finds strength in the center of life, in the fullness of life itself. Vice versa, life draws its dynamic from the essence of death. Therefore, the tension generated by this death paradox creates a high dynamic in our existence everywhere.

This tension is experienced when playing, when it is all about being able to win while at the same time being threatened to lose. This tension is also relevant in the basic feeling of our existence. If our existence is threatened, we want to conquer death. But if we live without threat, we are in the certainty that we will die and in the uncertainty of when. He who does not contemplate this loses the tension; to him who does contemplate this, the tension results in the great, vital intensity of every single moment.

Thus, "in television crime series, it is a source principle that the dead enliven the show" (Vock in Ronner 1974, 285). More serious but also much harder to understand is the fact that living and dying, death and life, are one and that together they make up the fullness of being. For the Daoist thinker, however, this is self-evident.

Daode jing 50 speaks about this topic: "Men of life, yet moving to death . . . Well, for what reason? Because they live in life's abundance" (Alquiros 2011b, 50.4-7). The opposite also holds true: only he who lives out of the fullness of vitality and is infused with it, can actually use the vital power of death. "One goes out into life and returns to death," the text says (Alquiros 2011a, 50.1). Thus death is not the end of life but has life as its resource, is its essence. Lin

Yutang translates: "Out of life, death sets in" (1955, 166). The simultaneous existence of death and life leads to a fullness of life whose origin is the heart. "Death is the best invention of life. When you know that you can die tomorrow, there is no reason left to not listen to your heart" (Jobs in Gasser 2010, 26).[1]

This simultaneous existence of life in death and death in life brings invulnerability. *Daode jing* 50 says: "Three out of ten are people who move from life into the area of death. What is the reason for this? It is because they live their lives in a wasteful way. Hence, it is said: if you know well how to preserve life, you travel through the country without fearing buffaloes and tigers . . . Buffaloes do not find any place to bore their horn . . . What is the reason for this? It is because you have no mortal point!" (Alquiros 2011a, 50.1-15).

In concrete, everyday life we connect this invulnerability ("no deadly places;" Alquiros 2011a, 50.15) with two basic attributes of flow. First, flow is capable of pulling a person and his relationships forward, letting him strive upward in every situation. This is reflected in the "flow-up principle." Second, flow provides the possibility in every situation not just to live, but to realize the full life. Even if man suffers adversity he has access to the invulnerable power of the vital flow; he has access to Dao and inherent potency. With the condition that he does it smartly and wisely. The fact that the original flow is accessible at any time, we will explain with the procept "striking the holy nerve."

The Flow-up Principle

Flow is what makes life full. The full life always pulls further upward and forward. That is the *anarheontic* attribute of flow,[2] also known as the flow-up-principle.

For people in leadership positions this means: provide room for activity with your leadership, fill it with atmosphere, clear instructions and open space, in which each individual can realize his or her assignment in their particular way. The work will be perfect, the loyalty great, and the development of the business or family reliable. In his autobiography *Myself and Other More Important Matters*, Charles Handy describes how he took on a leadership role in the Shell oil company in Southeast Asia in 1959 (2007, 54-69). Although not really trained for the job, he became responsible for oil sales in Sarawak and Brunei. "In those

---

[1] Steve Jobs (b. 1955) is co-founder and CEO of Apple Inc., an American multinational computer corporation. He has charisma, a strong interest in Buddhism, and known to be very arbitrary.

[2] The term comes from the Greek *ana* (upward), *rhein* (flow), and *ontos* (belonging to the being); it means the tendency to strife forward and upward.

days Shell used the method of 'immersion' with their manager training—throw them into the water and see if they will learn to swim " (2007, 55). This atmosphere of generous trust was the fastest way for him to grow in his role and to act for the good of the company. It made him so strong that he even corrected his own mistakes in full commitment, not out of fear of a transfer or punishment but because of his pride to complete every assignment professionally and competently—even his errors.

For example, Handy had 5,000-gallon tanks set up all along the banks of the Rajang river, thinking that in this way he would be able to meet the fuel demand of many local ships in a single supply trip. However, during the dry season, the water level sank and the tanks were as far as thirty meters inland: the hoses were not long enough, and the tanks started tilting. While the tanks were beyond reach in the dry season, they would have been flooded in the rainy season had they been placed further into the river. Why did he fail in his assessment? He did not ask experienced residents for advice and instead acted willfully (acting, instead of letting think). He learned his Dao-lesson: the goal is to succeed in action by not acting (but listening instead). As a result, Handy had the tanks brought back to their home port of Sibu and scrapped. The Singapore head office remained ignorant of the incident.

The *Daode jing* expresses the conducive power and inherent potency of flow (*de*)[3] as the "mystery of the Three Treasures": "Truly, I (Dao) possess Three Treasures to hold and protect: the first is called "charity;" the second, "frugality;" the third, "no daredevil acts for all world ahead" ["humility"]" (Alquiros 2011v, 67.8-12). These Three Treasures can also be called sympathy, frugality, and not wanting to be ahead (Reichel 1995, 105). Hilmar Klaus calls them charity, frugality, and humility.

The text says, "With charity you can be brave" (Alquiros 2011v, 67.13). Sympathy or charity in our context is "understanding," which generates dedication for effective work (courage, boldness, exertion).

"With frugality you can be generous" (Alquiros 2011v, 67.14). Frugalities in the context of leadership means giving the coworkers enough space and not take all space up as leader. The coworkers, on their part, fill the space not with hardness but with an atmosphere of cooperation. In other words, authoritarian

---

[3] As regards the title *Daode jing, jing* means "book;" *dao* is original source, creative emptiness, often just called Dao, which I equate with the "Ur" and Wilhelm relates to "meaning" (1976). *De* can be translated as "inner power" (Alquiros 2011a, 55), "energy," or "life" (Wilhelm 1976). The term often is rendered "virtue" (Lao Tseu 1978); some leave it untranslated (Lin 1955). I find a good rendition in "swing" or "zest."

leadership is replaced by humility,[4] which is smart generosity that activates generosity on the side of the co-worker.

"No daredevil acts ahead of everybody—thus you can successfully let your potential mature" (Alquiros 2011v, 67.15). This humility is defined by not being the boss, but re-sourcing the co-workers and providing a surrounding in which they can develop.

Daode jing 67 says about the flow: "Heaven will save you, using love to protect you" (Alquiros 2011v, 67.22-23). In re-sourcive thinking this means: the successful, conducive (saving) direction is a continuous gift (from heaven) provided free and without payment. The drive to fullness [using love] is our protection, our never ceasing resource. Laozi adds that "this is called non-competitive inner power" (Alquiros 2011v, 68.5). The idea of non-competitiveness applies easily to the three practical main areas of the full life: education, leadership, and communication.

Education, Leadership, Communication

As regards education, "power is the straight line kept up in education and that is done in a way which is very precise and clear whilst not being hard or using pressure." This precision is not based on authority or strict norms, even less on authoritarian, authoritative, or careless demeanor, but on the subtle yet highly efficient sovereignty of the full life.

Traditionally authority is a necessary attribute among all educating and care giving staff that exercises a pedagogical role. It comes in three forms: 1. an authoritarian manner that is condescending, hard, and not considerate; 2. an anti-authoritarian manner that wants to treat the children and adolescents without a condescending demeanor and rebels against hierarchical, commanding, and absolute authority—this is the principle Summerhill applies, but it quickly becomes laissez-faire because it does not have specific leadership; 3. an authoritative manner that uses a middle way between authoritarian and anti-authoritarian: as much authority as needed, as little "top-down" structure as possible—if effortless, it is called "natural authority."

Sovereignty lies beyond the position of authority, authoritativeness, and *laissez-faire*. It has to do with a flow attribute that has no position in itself but uses position as a tool. Re-sourcive sovereignty results from the inner line of the assignment and is carried by the self-evident and present action of flow.

---

[4] By humility, we do not mean nodding your head and making yourself insignificant, but the practice of achieving fewer words and purposeful doing than by submitting to someone who is a boaster.

Sovereignty does not use authority as a justification for its own position, or as a way to assert itself. Authority is its tool, generated, so to speak, as an outward phenomenon in the course of flow for that particular moment when flow needs a tool. Sovereignty does not need power but is generated by a gentle yet highly effective impact that comes with inner strength and originates from emptiness or Dao. It supplies sovereignty with its penetrating power, its impact, and thus makes it more effective than pressure and longer lasting than power.

In leadership, this quality is "strength that is neither dominant nor hard but sovereign." The German *Duden* dictionary defines sovereignty as "1. highest force, suzerainty of the state, independence (from the influence of other states); 2. superiority, security (1994, 1279). With regard to flow and Dao, sovereignty means that no influence of any other power is capable of affecting the suzerainty and mightiness of the Dao and its flow. In other words, vital sovereignty is stronger than any form of authority or power. It makes no difference whether this power wants to impose itself from the outside or the inside. In modern management, this inner strength is called "leadership."[5] This refers to the real sovereignty that helps a person in leadership to waken and maintain drive and commitment in the co-workers for their work.

In communication this power is "the authenticity of the speaker, which makes listening possible—beyond all ifs and buts and beyond all battles and conflicts." Listening means observing silence. And the power of silence (also a book title by Carlos Castaneda; 1987) stimulates more development than making a hundred points. To implement sovereign leadership in flow communication, moreover, I have developed certain specific methods, such as the art of "talking with the ears of the listener" or the encounter-principle: "resistance is not refusal, but a proposal."

---

[5] Leadership is different from "manager" or "boss" in that the personal radiance, the How of leadership and the respect for other people, is just as important as organising, planning, leading and control. Apart from personal integrity leadership also presents open consciousness and calm sovereignty. The Lasalle-Institute, situated in Bad Schoenbrunn, Switzerland, has a comprehensive and challenging perception of "Leadership." The institute writes: "The course ®mind & leadership" is understood to be a holistic training in addition to professional training. Insights of the modern teachings of management, ethics, psychology and "consciousness" combine with traditional Asian wisdom. . . . The course is based on the "Lasalle-Institut-Modell," developed by Pia Gyger and Niklaus Brantschen" (Lasalle 2011). Translated by J.Gasser. Fredmund Malik also insists that the use of the word "leadership" alone does not lead to leadership. In his book "Richtig denken, richtig managen" (think right, manage right) (Malik 2010) he points out that terms like "leadership", "vision" or "personnel-decision" cause a lot of confusion in management because of their incorrect usage.

Escalating Conflict

The following example using a 12-year old child illustrates the concrete practical application of the key principles of re-sourcive pedagogy in everyday educational life and shows two alternatives. The first is geared towards fighting: it is used by the father, Polem; the second works with the flow-cycle and is inspired by nonaction and the Dao: it is used by the mother, Deva.

The flow-cycle and the associated whispering become apparent as a consistent opening and enhancement of thinking, speaking, and doing. The methods, however, are not specific recipes or explicit techniques but guidelines or procepts: instructions that have a precise effect as long as the specific situation is incorporated in a smart way. Procepts are similar to recipes in that they suggest instructions; yet they are also different in that they can never be applied according to the book.

In all cases, consider the *kairos*: right time, right place, right circumstances, right address, weighing of benefit and damage, incorporation of innumerable details and be very conscious of the appropriate conducive tone and specific lack of intention. A recipe (being re-ceptive) takes what was good before and repeats it. A procept (being pro-ceptive) goes beyond the repetition and also incorporates the unknown and all auspicious factors. [6] The procept "striking the holy nerve" emanates from the following conviction: in every anxious or "unnerved" person lies something healthful and holy that is merely waiting to seep through the channels of the "nerves." The irritation that circulates in such a person is accordingly a quest for letting flow, rather than irritation, circulate in the "nerves."

1a. Situation: Mike is Polem's son. (Mike could also be the girl Diana.) Mike is unnerved, because he was treated unfairly by his fellow students.

1b. Mike's behavior is rebellious, impolite, and scurrilous. He is unsocial and acts contrary to the family's communal culture.

2a. Polem's reaction is to admonish, punish, and exhort: "Don't act so dumb! I don't want to see this in our family." His so-called traditional reaction is based on the correctness versus falsehood of the son's behavior.

2b. Mike's traditional reaction: He gets angry, rants, bangs the door, and barricades himself in his room.

3a. Polem: "Don't act that way! Come out immediately and apologize!"

---

[6] "Recipe" goes back to the Latin *re* (again) and *capere* (capture), this term means "to repeat the established or captured". The neologism "procept," on the other hand, uses the Latin *pro* (for, in support of) and *capere* (capture); it means "to bring something to a conducive fit," and is interpreted in analogy to pro-cedere, i.e., "proceed" or "move forward."

3b. We all know the outcome: a bad atmosphere, Mike feels bad and mis-understood. The father is snubbed and discontent because his son acts in-appropriately and is not listening to him.

In terms of energy, these three points show actions and reactions of the af-fected people based on a logic of rivalry and conflict. They are the interactions of opponents. Mike's behavior contradicts the family order: it is impolite, in-sulting, defiant. Polem reacts to this cheekiness and rebukes his son for defying the family order. He objects to the son's objection. In reaction 2b (walking off, banging the door), Mike does not make his own behavior the subject of the matter but his father's antagonism and reprimand. All this is an escalation of Mike's initial irritation, which was a reaction to the injustice of a third party against him (1a).

Mike here does not experience the support and security he is looking for, but learns that his father resents him for his antagonism and defiance in terms of his position in the family system. He sees that his father does not understand the cause and original content of his original antagonism. At the same time, Mike feels that his father implicitly wants to argue him out of the antagonistic behavior of his fellow students—the root cause of his suffering. The wrong Mike experienced makes no difference, and his initial irritation and anger inten-sify.

Focusing on the antagonism against the family culture, Polem shows his son that he does not approve of him nor of his attitude. Thus Mike reacts, fol-lowing the logic of conflict, correctly toward his father and takes on the basic route of the "fighting-cycle" (2a). The logic of antagonism is cemented by both opponents who unconsciously feed their vital energy into the escalation of con-flict instead of enhancing cooperative vitality.

In the language of the "art of war", "fighting and winning is good." In the language of the "smart art of war," Sunzi says: "Winning without fighting is better" (Cleary 2007). This correlates directly with the Daoist wisdom that one should "achieve a lot with little."[7] As the *Daode jing* says: "Letting go again and again: thus, you will start to act without interfering. Acting without interfering leaves nothing undone" (Alquiros, 2011v, 48.3-5). Militant fighting is thus the opposite of nonaction and a great drain of inner vitality.

Upon closer inspection it becomes clear that the events in the fighting cycle are even more dramatic. Not only do we do much, but our efforts are continuously increasing, so that the cycle of mutual antagonism is intensified more and more with every step. The fighting cycle means that, despite all the

---

[7] The Daoistic principle of "achieving something with nonaction" re-sourcively phrased means "less (work) is more (result)." This is the effort-oriented version of nonaction in *Daode jing* 48. See also 27.1-10; 68.1-8; 69.6-9; 73.7-10. The Chinese practice of feint calls this "generating something from nothingness" (Senger 1992, 112).

great efforts, less and less is ultimately achieved. The more one does in reaction to antagonism, the less of the desired success will come about. There is less trust, less security, and thus less enhancement of life and vitality. In the end the reaction cycle of antagonism leads to a full-blown war, in which everyone does everything in order to win everything—yet no one achieves anything. This is because, as the fronts harden, the vital energy is destroyed and its flow obstructed.

Re-sourcing and Resonance

The flow alternative is how Deva, the mother, deals with the situation. She does not examine the initial situation and her son Mike's behavior in terms of order and disorder but looks at how the vital energy is modulated in a specific energy moment and what is at the root of Mike's behavior in the re-sourcive moment. She appears accordingly as a flow whisperer.

> 1a. Situation: Mike is Deva's son. (Mike could also be the girl Diana.) Mike is unnerved, because he felt treated unfairly by his fellow students.
> 1b. Mike's behavior is rebellious, impolite, and scurrilous. He is unsocial and acts contrary to the family's communal culture.
> 4a. Deva: "You experienced something very hard again."
> 4b. Mike: "Yes, these stupid sissies!"
> 5a. Deva: "You don't deserve that." Even if Mike had in fact started the as yet undefined conflict that led to his frustration, he still did not deserve this burden of unfairness and antagonism because in his developmental stage as a 12-year-old he cannot quite cope with it.
> 5b. Mike: "Next time I see them, I will show them!"
> 6a. Mother: "You got this drive for justice from me. I know what you feel like."
> 6b. Mike: "I don't want to have anything more to do with them."
> 7a. Mother: "How did it start?"
> 7b. Mike: "It was after school yesterday. It . . ."
> 8ff. The dialogue continues according to the flow attributes.

The mother's offer to flow along with the son is not a reaction to the frustration in the cycle of conflict and antagonism that Mike is stuck in. By offering flow, by giving the gift of understanding, Deva answers Mike's inner quest. Her statement that Mike experienced something hard is an assumption and therefore risky—it is quite possible that the reason for Mike's bad mood is something other than the bad treatment by his fellow students. But because Deva knows her son well, she realizes from experience that something has happened which really affects Mike.

Instead of reacting against the mother, Mike accordingly responds with an answer to her offer of flow (4b)—not just giving a reaction but allowing it to lead to something additional that develops within him. This happens because the flow component in Deva's first offer ("You experienced something hard") had an effect on him. Mike did not just hear the call for flow, but a sense of flow was activated within him. A cycle of resonance started—the answer matches the question.

The language of Dao describes a flow-cycle that can be paraphrased as "achieving everything by doing nothing." Deva does not act in opposition to her son, nor does she act in favor of "correct" behavior. She does not praise, nor does she reprimand. She just perceives the subtle call and confirms that in Mike's experience and behavior there is this call for flow. When she says, "you experienced something very hard again," she practices active "leaving-alone." She leaves the aggression that emanates from Mike alone as much as the injustice that the evildoers did to her son. Yet she leaves room for flow and its call. That is all she does, nothing more. Yet she gives something. Neither fighting against, nor fighting for, she does not demand anything "correct" or exclude anything "bad." She makes space.

The fact that Mike responds in this specific, cooperative way (4b) to his mother's offer (4a) has an inner, logical reason. Every individual, whether affected emotionally in a given situation or not, does not just want to live, but to live at full intensity. At the same time, she wants to be good and look good in front of others. Above all she wants the flow to be there for her and take effect in her. As a general rule, in every form of communication flow offers have priority over antagonistic reactions—they have more potential and open up greater space for controversy.

Flow offers, moreover, should not be treated like recipes but more like procepts. This means that they need to be presented with a high dose of smartness and vigilance. There is a strong suggestive power in the proposals of flow. For this reason Mike says yes already in his very first reaction (4b) to his mother's offer. He says yes to the offer of flow, and thus to flow. The clever thing here is the fact that Mike also says yes to the content, to the statement Deva makes about him having "experienced something hard." He also says yes to his relationship with his mother. In this dynamic, Mike naturally answers yes to most statements and says: "Yes, these stupid sissies." This indirectly but openly shows that he is very interested in this kind of dialogue with his mother. As all these various obvious and hidden yeses begin circulating, Mike experiences that he is taken seriously. Were he asked whether he feels that he is heard and taken seriously, he immediately would say "Yes!."

Mother Deva continues in the flow logic (5a): "You don't deserve that." This sentence is powerfully supportive, so that Mike has no choice but to accept the offer it manifests. This becomes obvious when he says: "I will show them." With this, he joins his mother against the evildoers, and a resonant alliance of flow is established between mother and son. Deva follows this up with an explanation why Mike's strong behavior makes sense (6a). She points to their connection, bringing their historical-genealogical link: "You got this drive for justice from me." Mike next shows that he is starting to detach himself from his close connection to the evildoers: "I don't want to have anything more to do with them" (6b). With this he abandons his rage and reduces his enmity to a greater or lesser dissociation. The flow whisperer continues to bank on this trend of reducing enmity and promptly ensures that a new alliance is formed between Mike and the evildoers.

With her renewed flow offer (7a), Deva prompts Mike to tell her the whole story: "How did it start?" She does not ask: "Why did you react that way?." Mike would most likely take that as an accusation, reading the implication that he did something wrong or that he should have reacted differently. Deva prepares the ground (=re-sources) for his story. Mike accepts her invitation to flow, opens up, and says: "It was after school yesterday. . . ." He can now tell the story in great detail. Flowing along with his mother energetically, the power of narration is displayed: in recounting your story, you put what really counts into words. The interactive cycle is moving in the right direction, the connection between mother and son grows stronger. Above all, Mike's experience and practice of flow expands, becoming stronger with every incident treated in this manner.

Later sequences (8ff) will turn the conversation to the evildoers and their motives, as well as to the question how their behavior could be interpreted and how the Mike's relationship to them could be reformed. Out of the wrongdoing an existential re-source arises for a new alliance between Mike and his fellow students.

Conclusion

To sum up, the mechanism contained in the procept of "striking the holy nerve" means that in every irritation, frustration, or conflict as illustrated here by Mike, there is a deep hidden call: "At the moment I am irritated and react accordingly. Actually I do not want to be irritated. I yearn to experience flow, which will carry my experience and my action, will not burden me and not bother me." The secret appeal to the parents or other educators is accordingly: "Do not take your charge's irritation as an aggressive phenomenon, but as a plea to show him the way that leads away from being unnerved towards the flow."

If the flow whisperer takes up this elementary call and responds to it, the irritated, frustrated, or conflicted child will always respond to the offer of flow. By liberating people from antagonism without fighting, using gentle whispering instead and working with the nonaction of the flow, by providing a new cycle of connected interaction, the flow practitioner becomes truly a people whisperer.

Bibliography

Alquiros, Hilmar. 2011a. *Tao Te Ching.* www. tao-te-king. org. analogous translation

_____. 2011b. *Tao Te Ching.* www. tao-te-king. org. verbatim translation

Bergson Henri. 1944 [1907]. *Creative Evolution.* New York: Modern Library.

Brügelmann, Hans and Erika Brügelmann. 1998. *Die Schrift erfinden.* Lengwil: Libelle.

Carlgren, Frans. 2005. *Erziehung zur Freiheit. Die Pädagogik Rudolf Steiners.* Stuttgart: Verlag Freies Geistesleben

Castaneda, Carlos. 1987. *The Power of Silence: Further Lessons of Don Juan.* New York: Simon and Schuster

Cleary, Thomas. 2007. *Wahrhaft siegt, wer nicht kämpft. Die Kunst des Krieges. Sunzi.* Munich: Piper.

Csikszentmihalyi, Mihaly. 1975. *Beyond Boredom and Anxiety: Experiencing Flow in Work and Play.* San Francisco: Jossey-Bass

Duden. 1994. *Das Grosse Fremdwörterbuch. Herkunft und Bedeutung der Fremdwörter.* Mannheim: Dudenverlag

Fromm, Erich. 1996. *To Have or to Be.* London: Continuum International Publishing.

Gasser, Johannes, trl. 2005. "PM. Biographie: Questions and Answers." 12/2005. Munich: Gruner + Jahr.

_____, trl. 2010. "PM. Biographie. „4/2010. Munich: Gruner + Jahr.

Gray, Martin. 2006. *For Those I Loved.* Newburyport: Hampton Roads Publishing.

Handy, Charles. 2006. *Myself and Other More Important Matters.* London: William Heinemann.

_____. 2007. *Ich und andere Nebensächlichkeiten.* Munich: Econ-Verlag.

Heidegger, Martin. 1962. *Being and Time.* New York: Harper.

_____. 1963 [1927]. *Sein und Zeit.* Tübingen: Niemeyer.

Klaus, Hilmar. 2008. *Das Tao der Weisheit. Laozi - Daodejing.* Aachen: Druck & Verlagshaus Mainz.

Lao Tseu. 1978. *Tao Te King. Le livre du Tao et de sa Vertu.* Paris: Dervy-Livres.

Lasalle. 2011. http://www. lassalle-institut. org/angebote/lehrgang-geist-leadership/

Lin, Yutang, ed. 1955. *Die Weisheit des Laotse.* Frankfurt am Main: Fischer.

Malik, Fredmund. 2010. *Richtig denken, richtig managen. Mit klarer Sprache besser führen.* Frankfurt am Main: Campus.

Montessori, Maria. 1912. *Il metodo della pedagogia scientifica applicato all'educazione infantile nelle case dei Bambini.* http://www. montessori-material. de/'source=webgains &siteid=59322

Neill, Alexander S., and Albert Lamb. 1995. *Summerhill School: A New View of Childhood.* New York: St. Martin's Griffin.

Reichel, Gerhard. 1995. *Zitate, Pointen, Geistesblitze—von Aristoteles bis Zuckmayer.* Forchheim: Brigitte Reichel.

Roberts, Monty. 1996. *The Man Who Listens to Horses.* New York: Random House.

Rogers, Martha E. 1970. *An Introduction to the Theoretical Basis of Nursing.* Philaldelphia: Davis.

Ronner, Markus M. 1974. *Die treffende Pointe.* Thun: Ott.

Senger, Harro von. 1992. *Strategeme. Lebens- und Überlebenslisten aus drei Jahrtausenden.* Vol. 1. Bern: Scherz.

———. 1999. *Strategeme. Lebens- und Überlebenslisten aus drei Jahrtausenden.* Vol. 2. Bern: Scherz.

Sprenger, Eduard. 2010. *Mythos Motivation. Wege aus einer Sackgasse.* Frankfurt am Main: Campus.

Steiner, Rudolf. 1992. *Allgemeine Menschenkunde als Grundlage der Pädagogik.* Dornach: Goetheanum. http://www. paedagogik-goetheanum. ch/

Summerhill. 1970. *Summerhill: For and Against.* New York: Hart Publishing.

Virilio, Paul. 1989. *War and Cinema: The Logistics of Perception.* London: Verso.

———. 1997. *Pure War.* New York: Semiotext(e).

Weidle, Günther Ekkehard. 1982. *Summerhill: Pro und Contra. 15 Ansichten zu A. S. Neills Theorie und Praxis.* Reinbek: Rowohlt.

Wilhelm, Richard. 1976 [1957]. *Laotse. Tao te king. Das Buch des Alten vom Sinn und Leben.* Zürich: Ex Libris.

Contributors

Elliot Cohen, Ph. D., specializes in transpersonal psychology and comparative theology. He serves as chartered psychologist and senior lecturer in psychology at Leeds Metropolitan University (UK) and is the director of the Manchester Academy for Transpersonal Studies and the general secretary of the Northern Institute for Daoist Studies. E-Mail: e.cohen@leedsmet.ac.uk

Christopher Cott specializes in the study of the links between Daoism and contemporary psychology at Deakin University in Melbourne, Australia. He is also a practitioner of Daoist meditation and martial arts. E-mail: ccc@deakin.edu.au

Donald D. Davis, Ph.D., is professor of psychology and Asian Studies at Old Dominion University, Norfolk, VA. He specializes in personal and organizational transformation. A long-term practitioner and teacher of Daoist arts such as taiji quan, qigong, and meditation, he is also director of the Tidewater Tai Chi Center. E-mail: dondavis@verizon.net

Elisabeth Friedrichs, M.D., Ph.D., is a family doctor in Augsburg, Germany. Among her specialties are acupuncture and qigong, which she studied with Jiao Guorui. Besides her busy practice, she also serves on the board of the Medizinische Gesellschaft für Qigong Yangsheng. E-mail: elfriedaug@aol.com

Johannes Gasser completed his Ph.D. in philosophy in 1969 and in clinical psychology in 1995. A lecturer at Fribourg University, he works as therapist and educator and is founder of the Gasser Schule. His major areas of research and public dedication are flow-pedagogy and flow-communication as practices of Dao and its virtue. See www.gasserschule.ch. E-mail: gasser@flow-akademie.ch

Stephen Jackowicz received his Ph. D. from Boston University in 2003 and is now both a practicing acupuncturist and adjunct faculty at Adelphi University, Garden City, NY. He is currently involved in a translation project of the *Zhenjiu dacheng* with the Chinese Medicine Database Project. E-mail: stevejackowicz @gmail.com

Livia Kohn, Ph. D., is Professor Emerita of religion and East Asian studies at Boston University. The author and editor of thirty books on Daoism, she now lives in Florida, edits the *Journal of Daoist Studies*, and runs workshops and international conferences. E-mail: liviakohn@gmail.com

Xichen Lu is the director of the Center for Ethics and Religious Studies at Central South University, Hunan, China. Her research and teaching interests concern Daoism and psychology. E-mail: lxc501@126.com

Reggie Pawle, Ph. D. teaches cross-cultural psychology at Kansai Gaidai University, Hirakata, Japan, and is in private practice as a Marriage and Family Therapist in Kyoto and Osaka. His research focuses on integrating Daoism and Buddhism into psychotherapy. See www.reggiepawle.net. E-mail: reggiepawle @yahoo. com

Adam Rock is Head of Research and Development at Phoenix Institute of Australia. His research interests include shamanism, altered states, and psi. E-mail: adam.rock@phoenixinstitute.com.au

Robert G. Santee, Ph. D., is Dean and Professor of Psychology in the Behavioral Sciences Division at Chaminade University in Honolulu, Hawai'i. He is senior instructor for the Xia Xing Martial Art Association, in Honolulu, where he teaches taiji quan and qigong. E-mail: rsantee@chaminade.edu

Eduardo Alexander Amaral de Souza is the founder of Great Triad Project—a school for education in Daoist alchemy—and also works as a clinical acupuncturist. He earned his Ph.D. (2009) from Rio de Janeiro State University, Medical Rationalities Research Group (CNPq), researching "Health Promotion and Sexuality in Daoism and Chinese Medicine." E-mail: edu.alexander@gmail.com

Stephan Wik is an author, musician, and practitioner of Daoist cultivation. He is currently directing the development of Greenstones, an ecological course and retreat center in Sweden based on Daoist principles. E-mail: stephan@wiks.net

J. Michael Wood has a master's degree in Medical Qigong (MMQ), and is a professional breath and movement coach and specialist for Optimal Breathing Development. He teaches Chinese Medical Qigong and has a private clinical practice in Nashville, Tenn. See www.5virtuesqigong.com. E-mail: jmichaelwood@comcast.net.

Index

adaptation: problems of, 39, 4, 1, 44, 52; solution of, 39-40, 46, 52, 54-55, 241

alchemy, 108, 112-113, 194

Alquiros, Hilmar, 245

animals: directional, 76; instincts, 87; vs. humans, 60; red dragon, 199; turtles, 198; white tiger, 199

Apuleius, Lucius, 105

archetypes, 112, 114, 122, 131, 173, 186, 191

Aristotle, 106

attention, 130, 136-137, 162, 166

aura, 9-10

authentic: Chinese for, 3; dialogue, 101-02, 104, 109, 119; living, 21, 25-37, 226, 240; master, 159; path, 207; person, 44-46, 49. 208, 234; power, 208, 210, 247; practice, 167; spirit, 20

Baopuzi, 183, 183-184.

Baosheng jing: 67-69, 180-181; and deathbringers, 184

Batchelor, Stephen, 101

Beck, Aaron, 37

bedchamber arts, 196-197

behavior: aberrant, 6, 47, 48, 60, 70, 74, 213, 248-250; attitude to, 47-48; change of, 46-52, 55, 71-73, 237-238; Chinese, 103; forgetting of, 52; good, 75, 132, 162, 239, 251; human, 183, 226; interactive, 226; and kinesiology, 2, 14-17; science of, 102, 161, 241; sexual, 195

Bergson, Henri, 234

biomagnetism, 9

Blackmore, Susan, 118

Bloch, Ernst, 149

blood, 10, 14, 15, 68; in East Asia, 75; menstrual, 12, 133, 200; Ocean of, 193; pressure, 42, 71, 168; and qi, 13, 158

body: comparison of, 135; Daoist, 12-13, 124-125; energy, 9; -form, 1-2, 6-8, 18, 20; and meditation, 51-55; and mind, 1-2, 4, 6-8, 26, 32, 34, 63, 74, 127, 136, 153, 160, 162, 167-168, 209; parts of, 199, 210; as physical being, 39-44, 46, 48, 54-55; reality of, 118; -self, 1-2. 6-8. 18, 29-30,

84-86, 94; in Zhuangzi, 39-44; see also meridians

bodymind, 1, 2, 4, 8-9, 11-12, 12, 15, 19, 26-27, 34, 61, 77, 106, 118

Bohm, David, 5

brain: 15, 60; function of, 106, 168; head vs. gut, 225; scan, 104; waves, 32

Braud, W., 118

breath: control, 18, 68, 213; harmonizing of, 83, 90-92, 96, 124, 136, 178; and mind, 136; and qi, 4, 35, 62, 108, 130, 150; returning to, 105-107; true, 91; works of, 113

breathing: for health, 65, 150; and nervous system, 190; practices, 5-6, 15, 31, 65-70, 113, 117, 129-130, 154-155, 166-167, 178-179, 187, 190; and stress, 41, 44-45; in treatment 187

Brügelmann, Hans, 239

Buber, Martin, 115

Buddhism: 60, 79, 97, 101, 103, 104, 126, 132, 135, 197

Cai Yuanpei, 103

Carlgren, Frans, 238

Carlson, Ed, 20-21

Castaneda, Carlos, 247

causality, 110, 123, 128, 131

chakras, 9-10

Chia, Mantak, 219

Christianity, 97, 105, 114, 124

Clarke, J. J., 112

Cleary, Thomas, 249

cognition: 61, 72-73, 162-164; restructuring of, 39-40, 42, 46-48, 52, 55

communication, 60, 114, 155, 221, 228, 230, 233, 236, 246, 251

competition, 26, 28, 34, 107, 246

conflict, 247-248

Confucianism, 25, 60, 74, 91

consciousness: 31, 70, 73; altered states of, 114, 117; definition of, 60; embodiment of, 118; illumination of, 83, 89; of levels, 125; lower, 182; pure, 88-89, 214; in relationships, 225; and senses, 60; transformation of, 87-90, 96, 118

Core Health, 2, 19-20